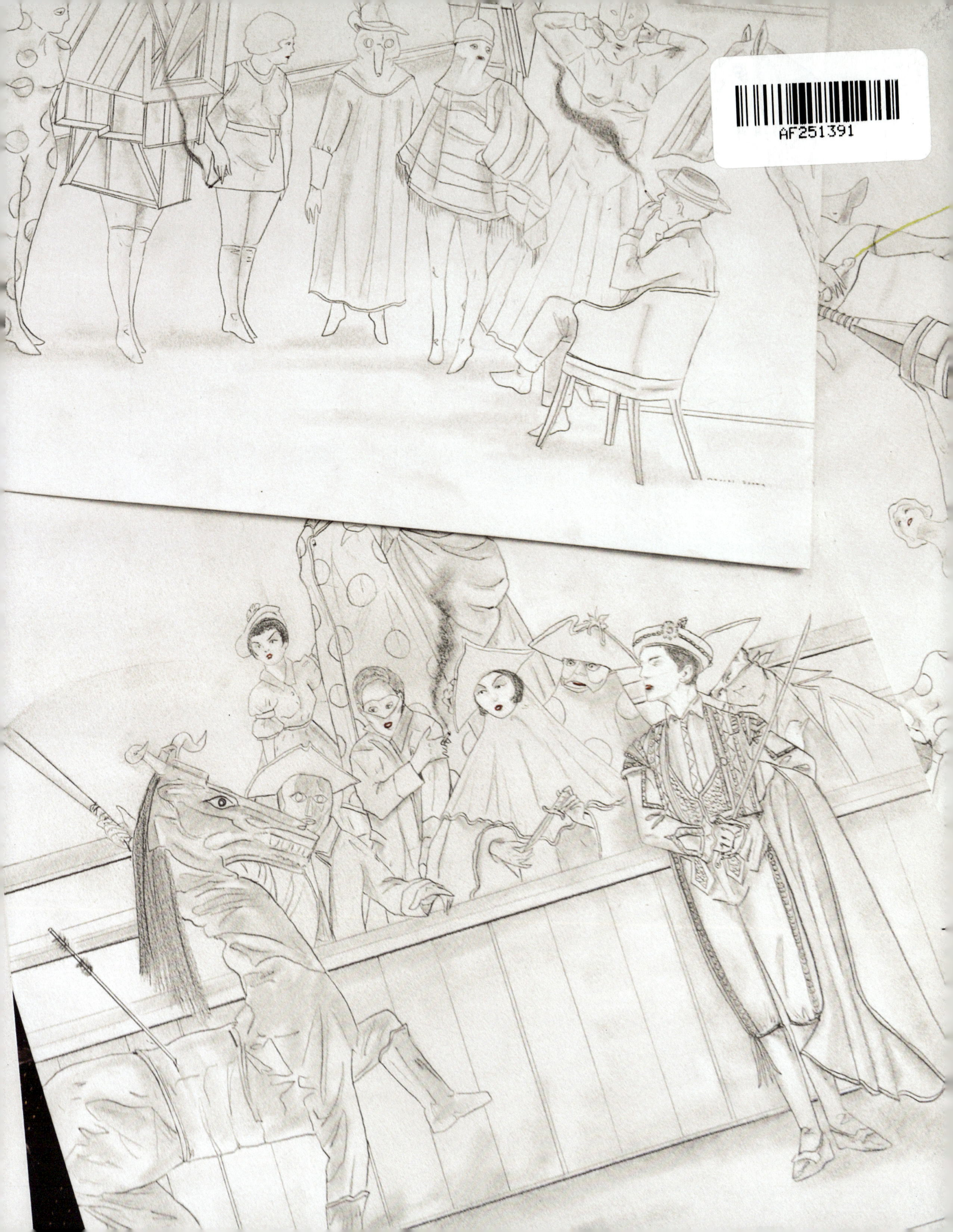

Marcel Dzama

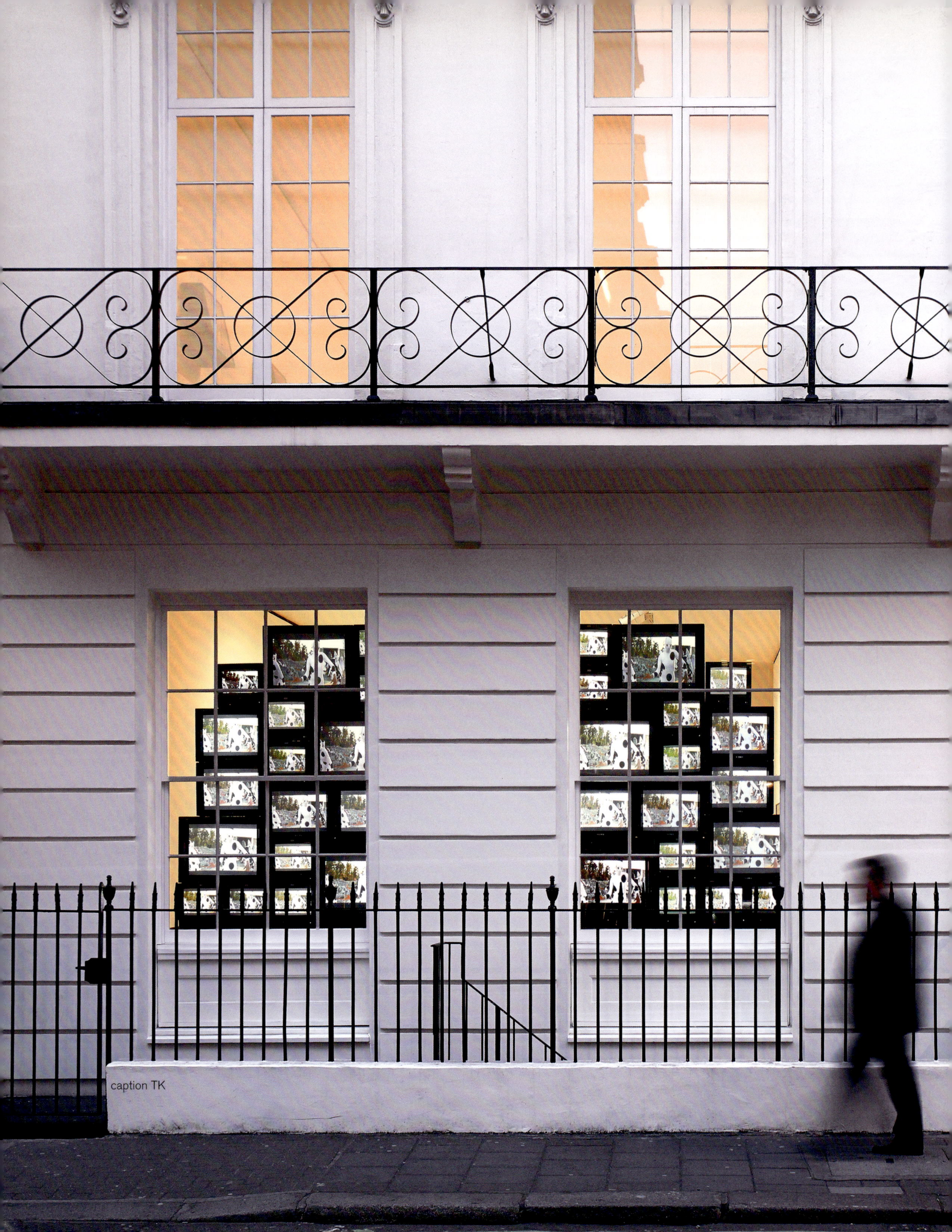

caption TK

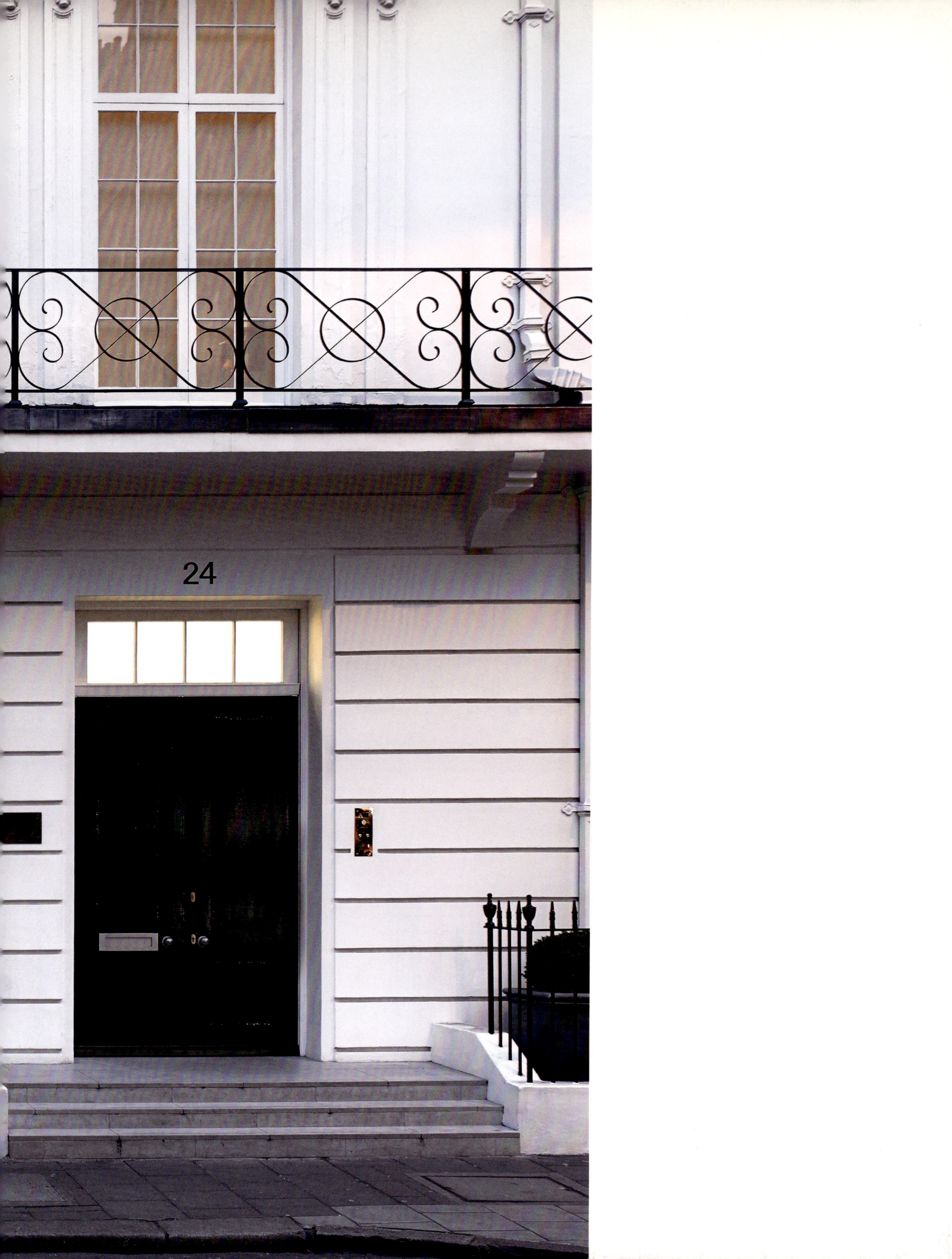

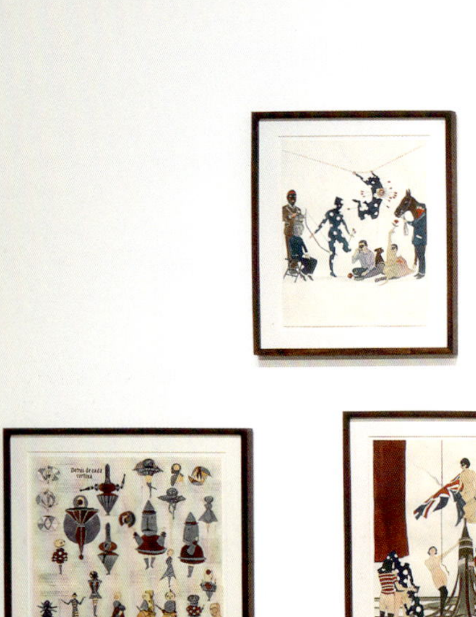
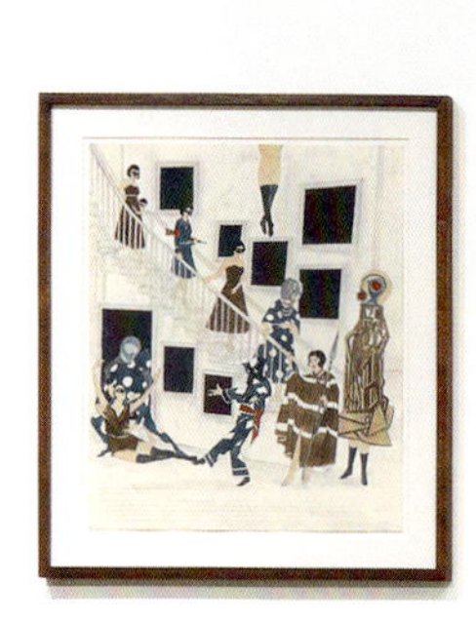
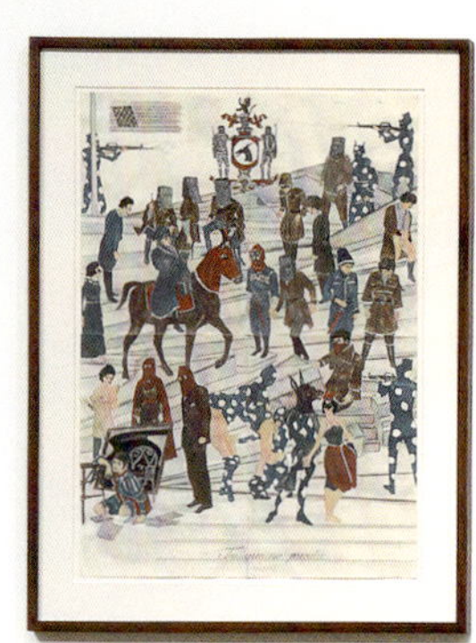
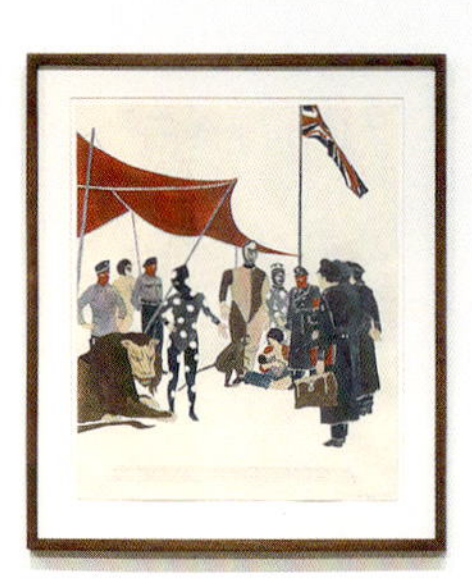
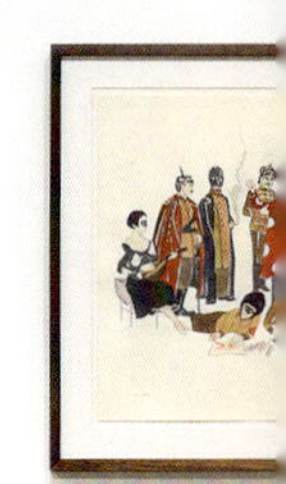
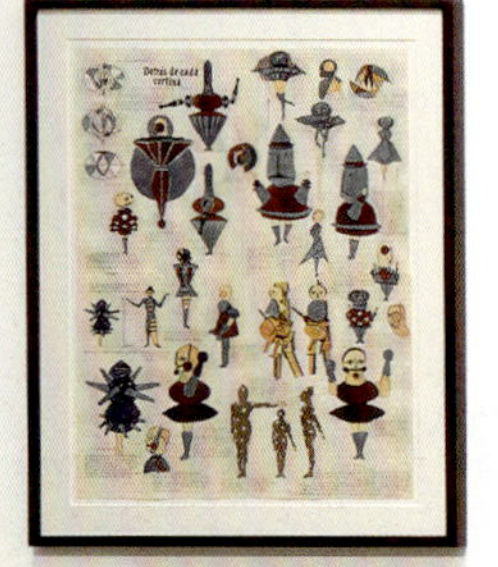
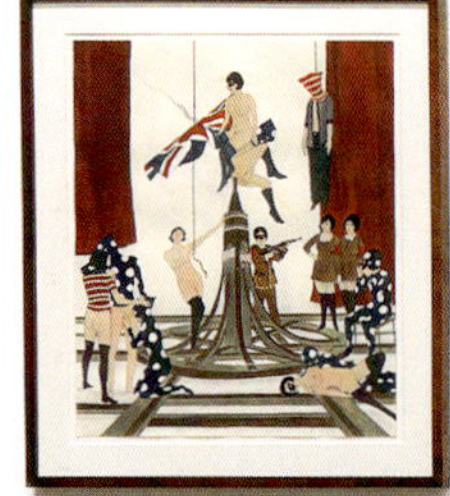
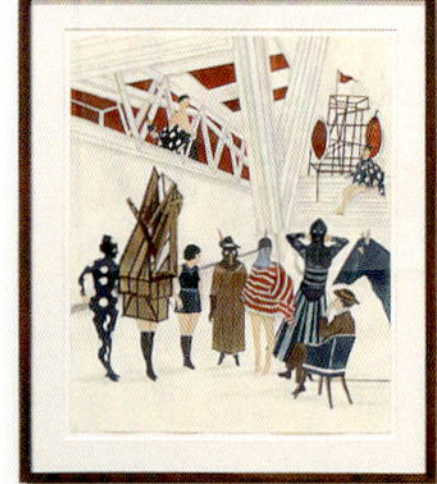
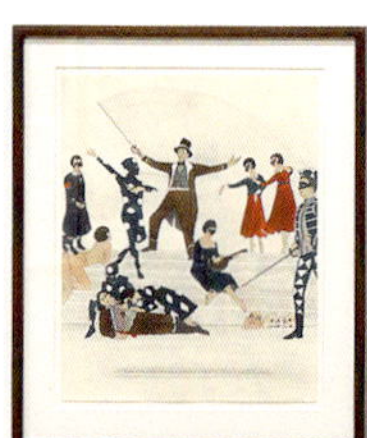
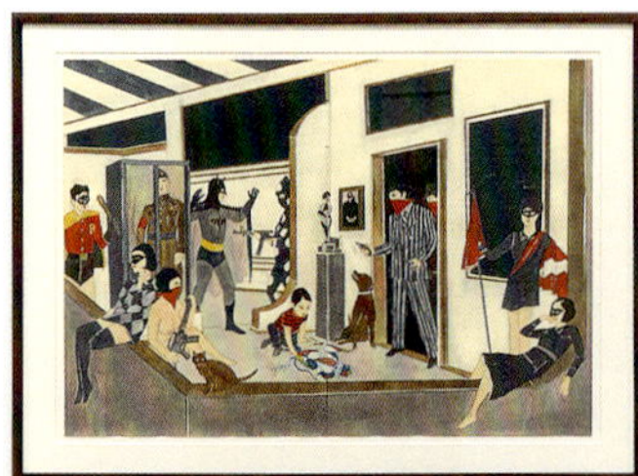
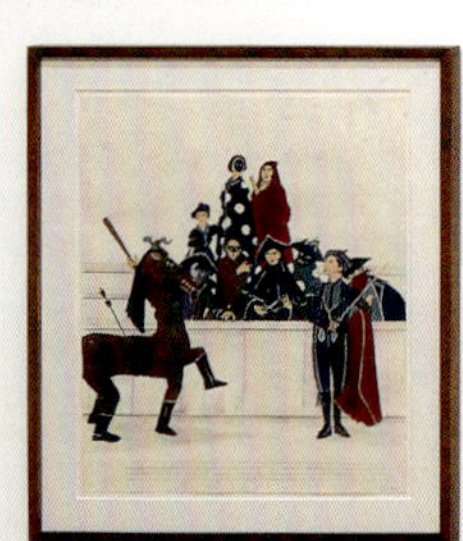
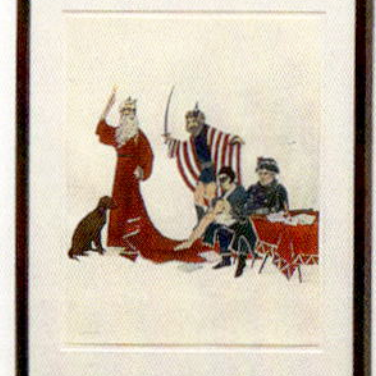
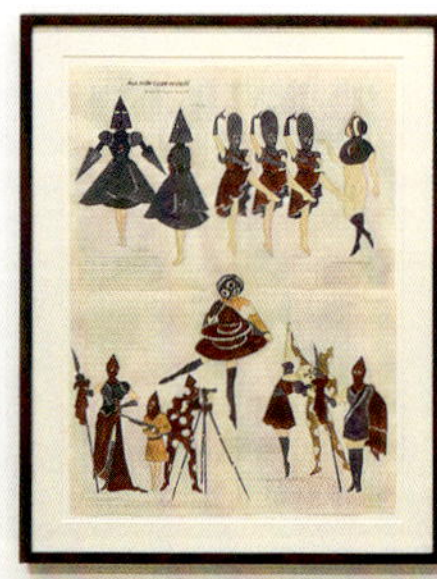
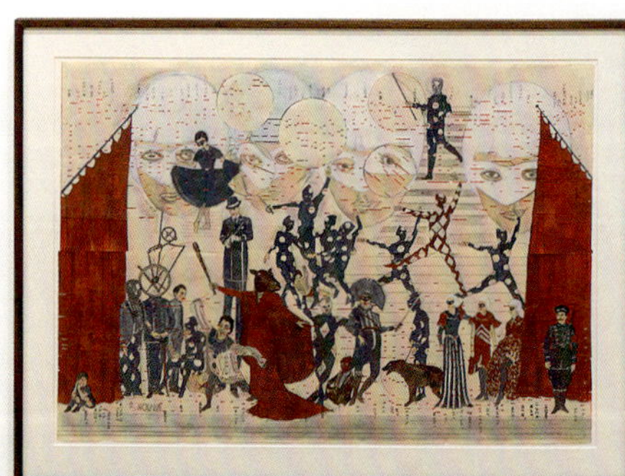

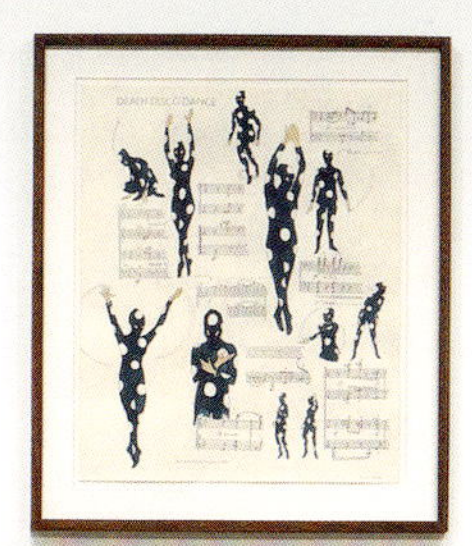
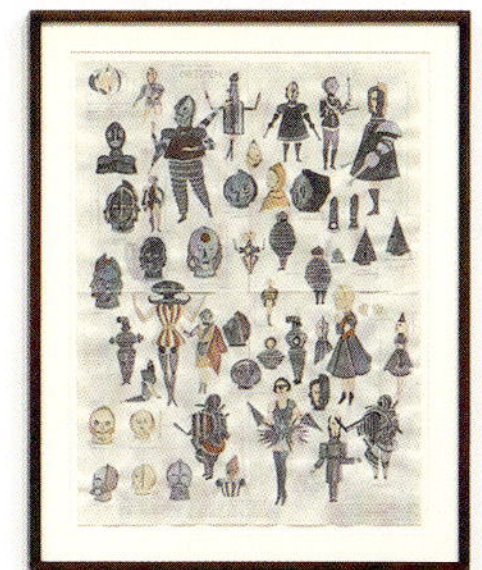
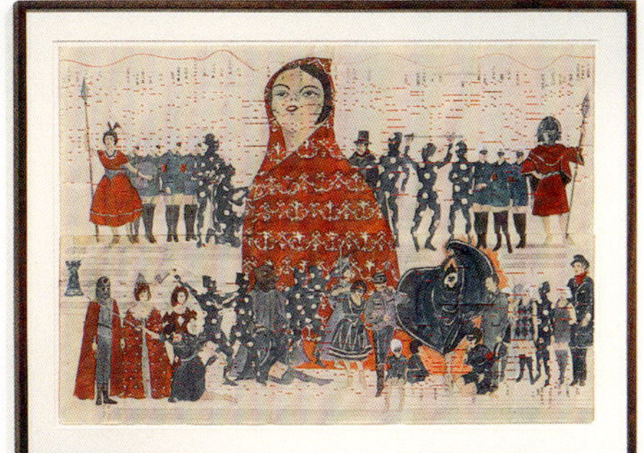
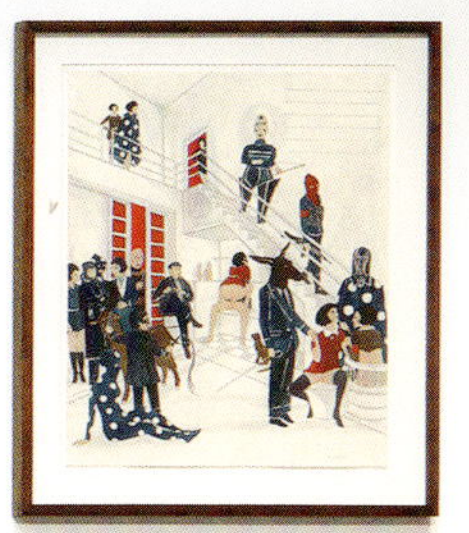
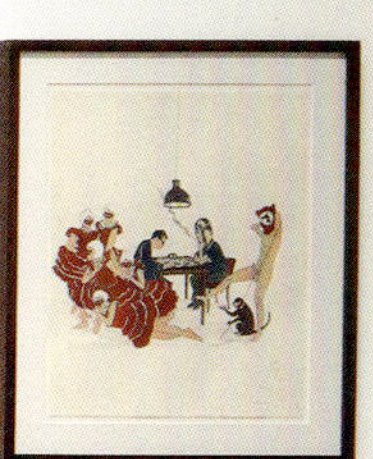
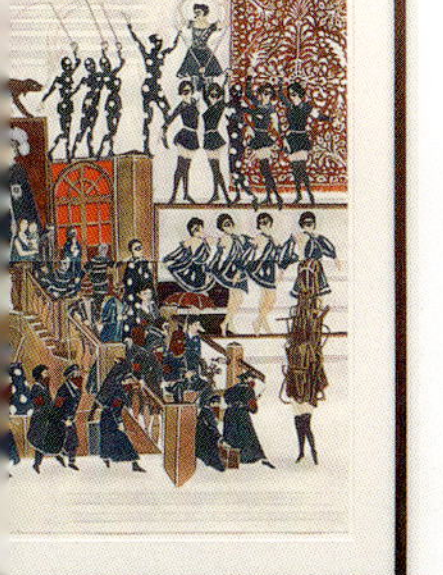
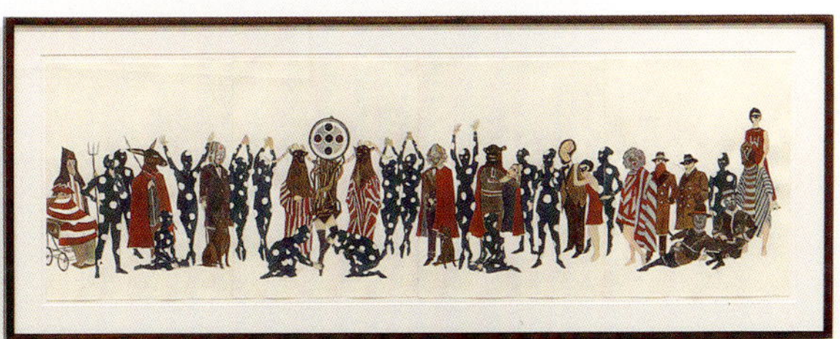
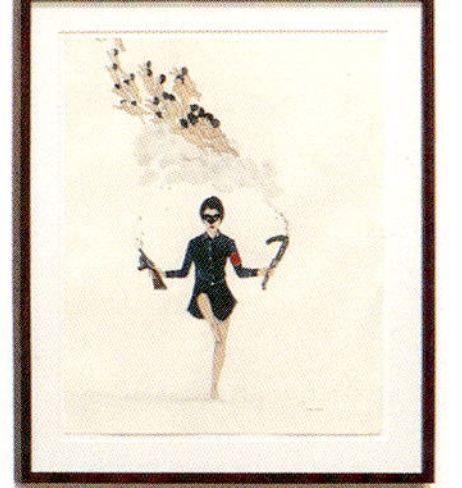
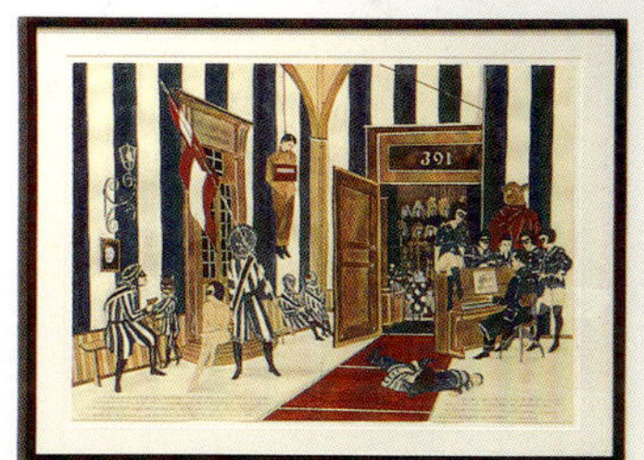
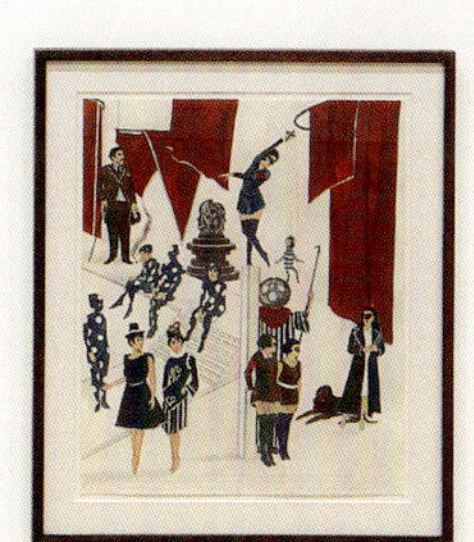
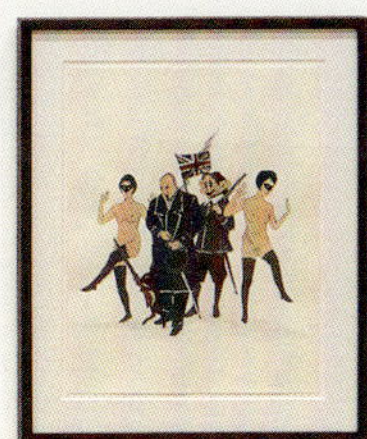
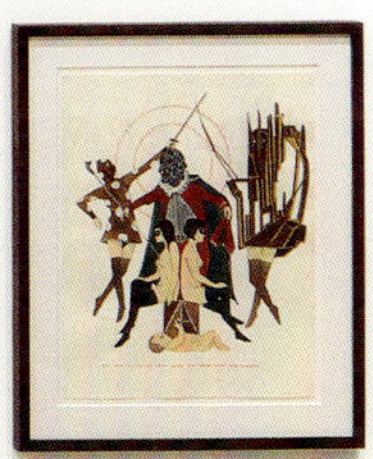
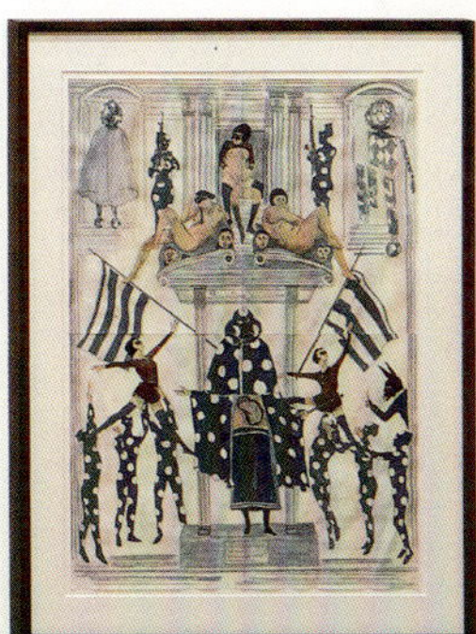

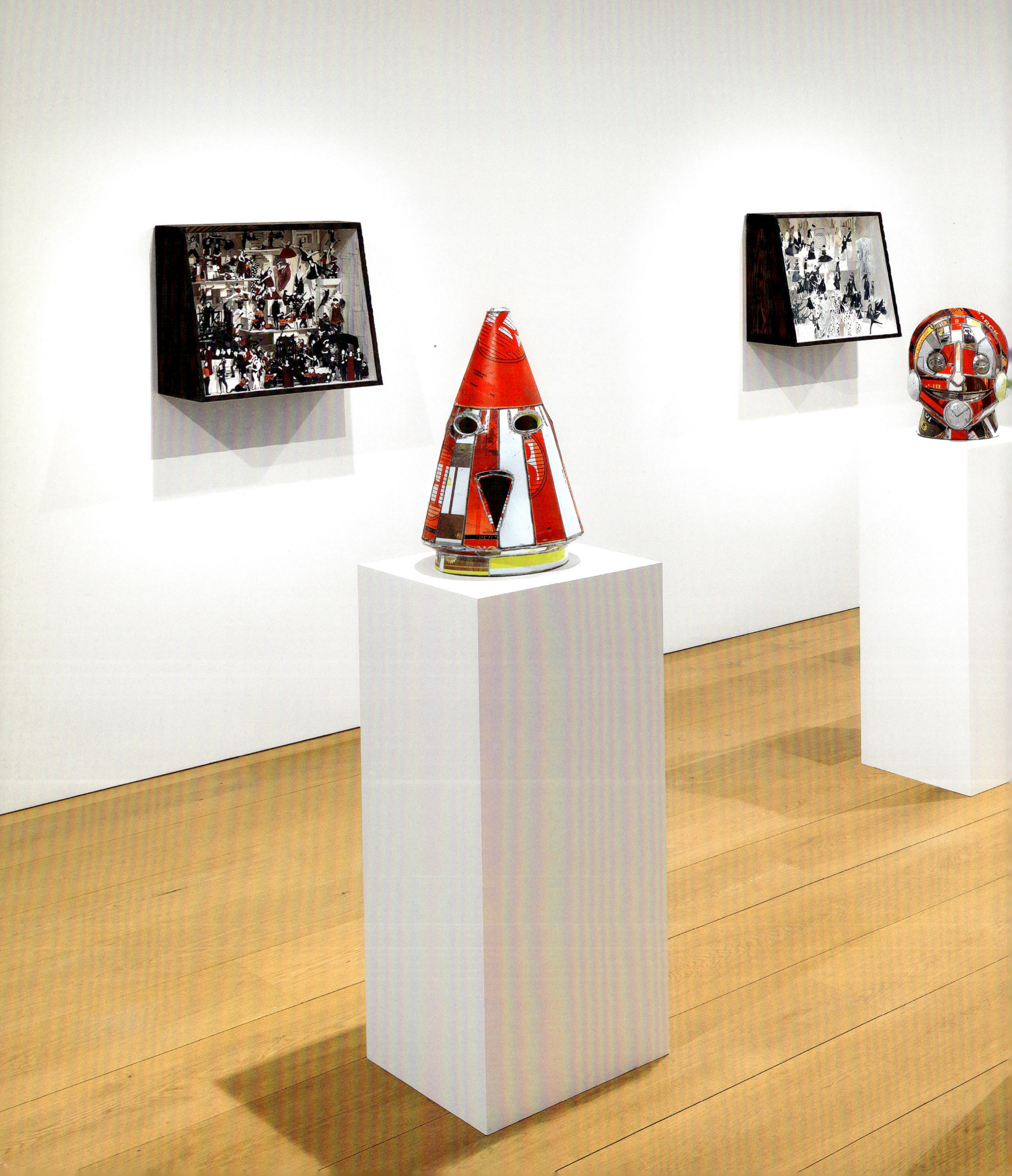

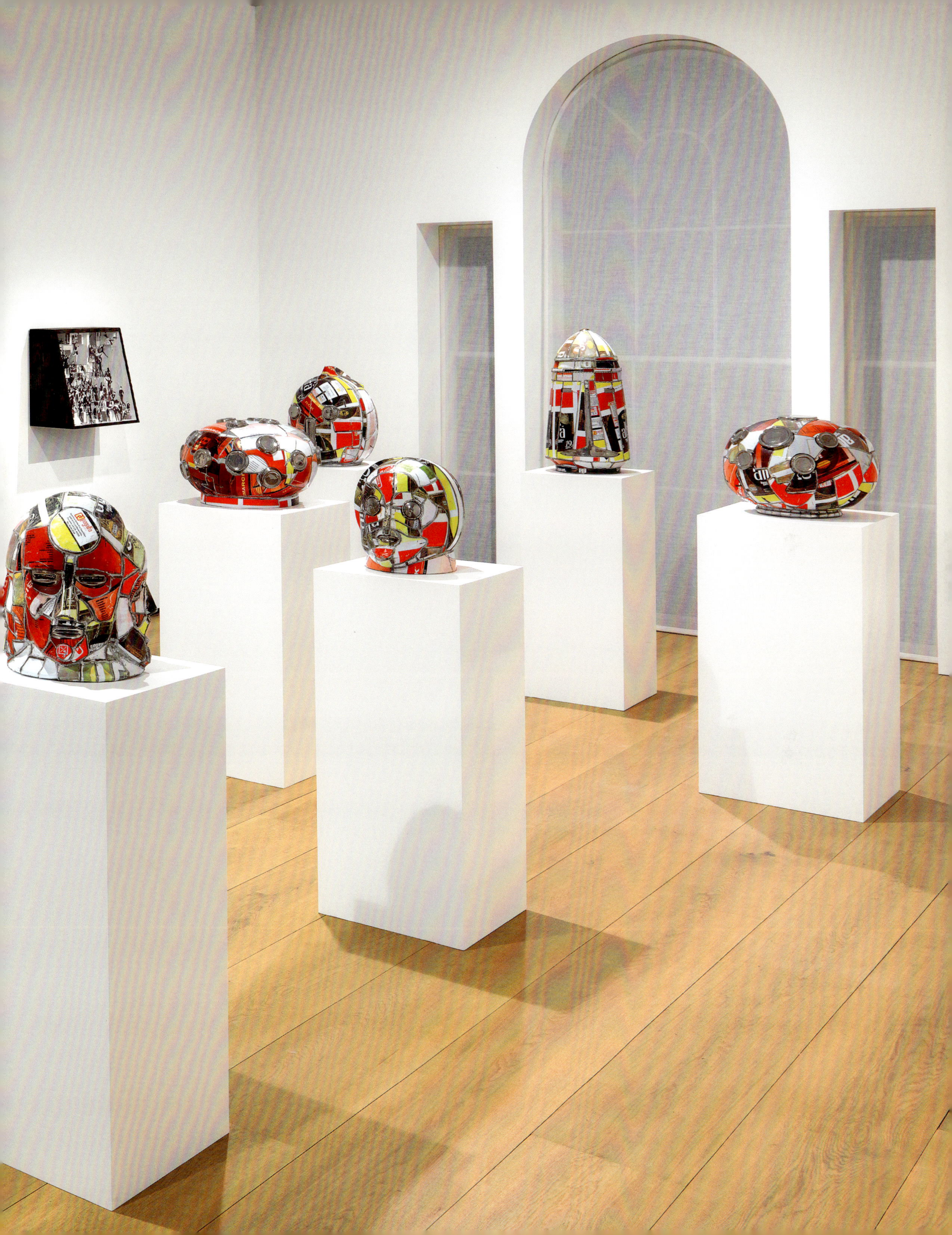

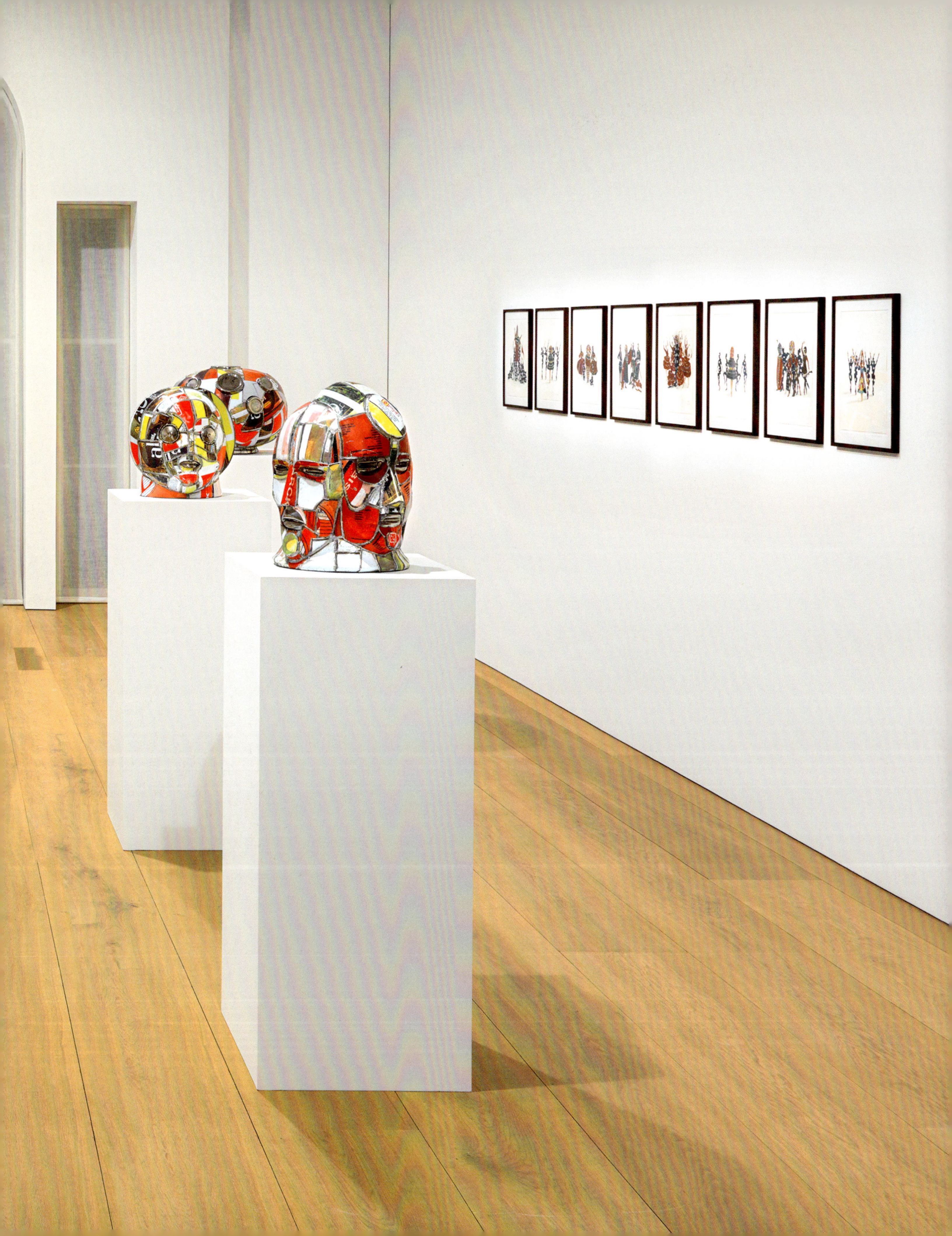

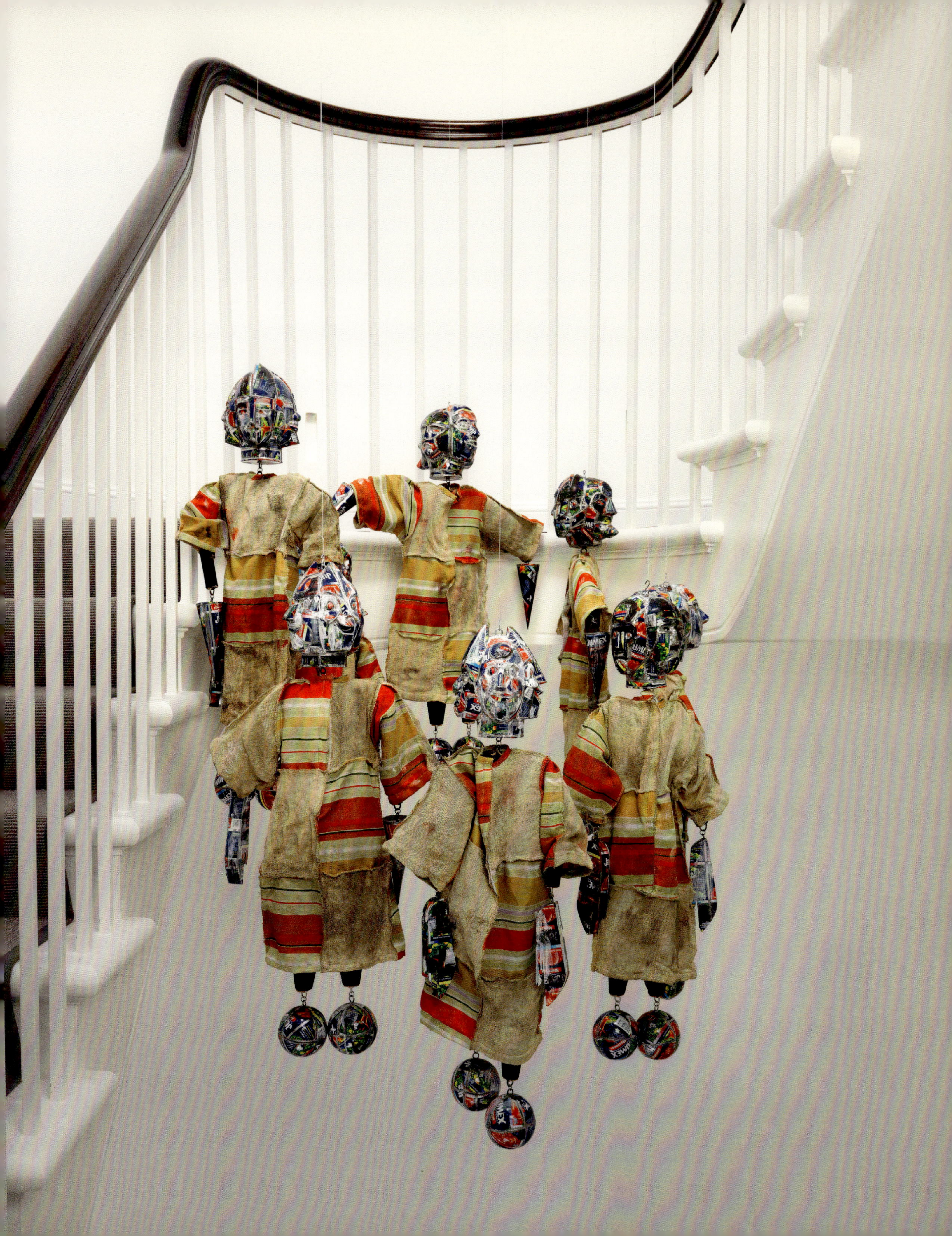

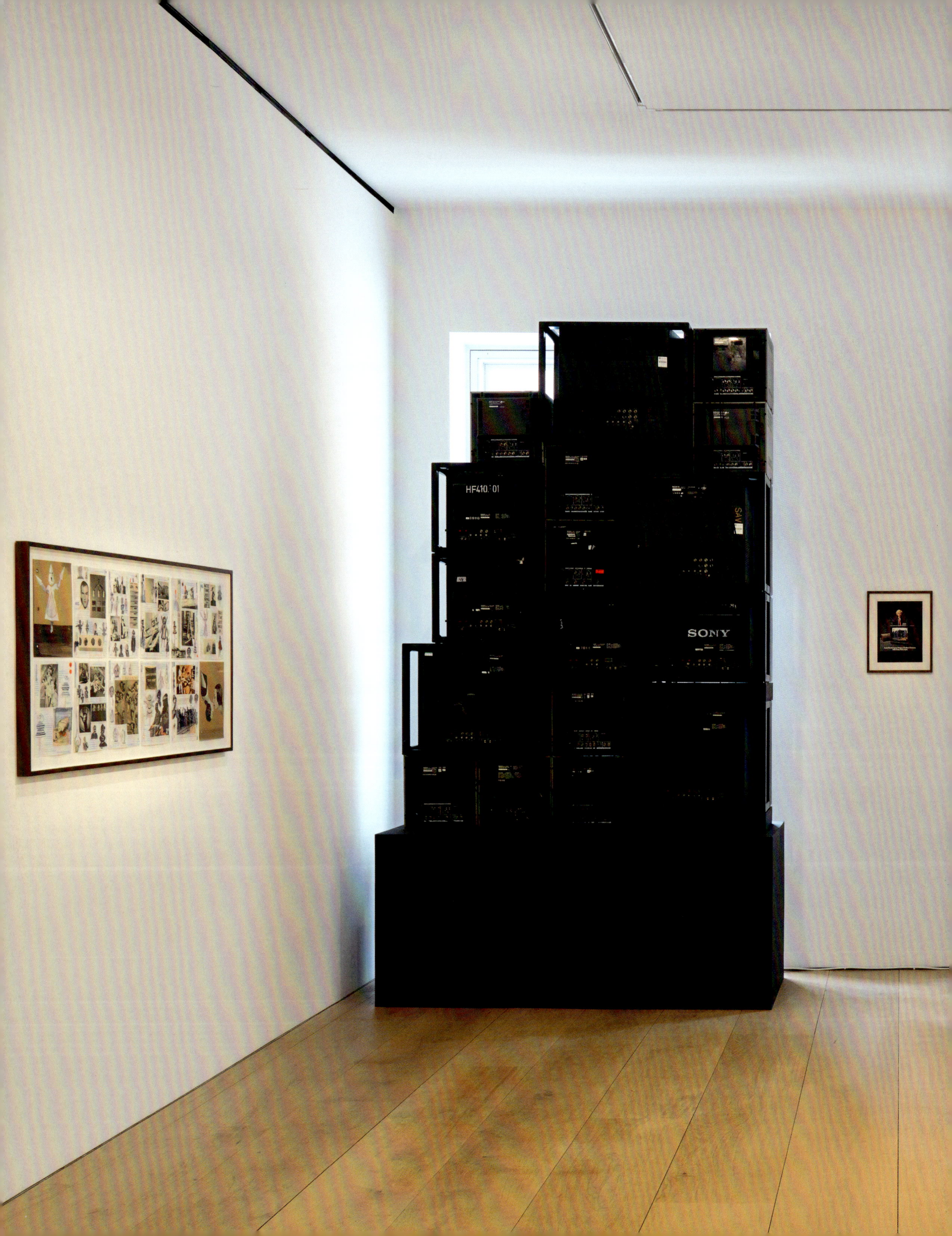

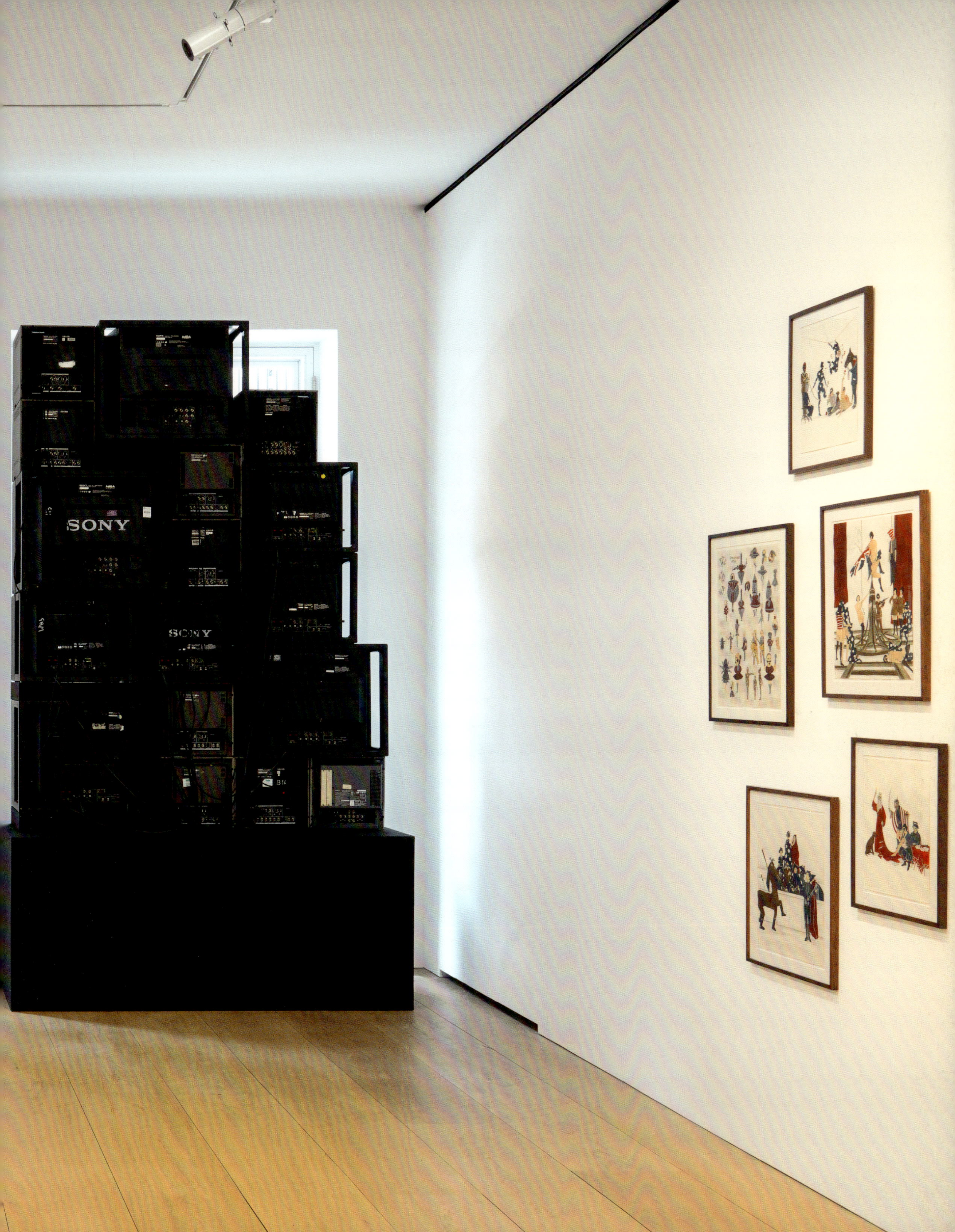

Marcel Dzama

Puppets, Pawns, and Prophets

David Zwirner

**HATJE
CANTZ**

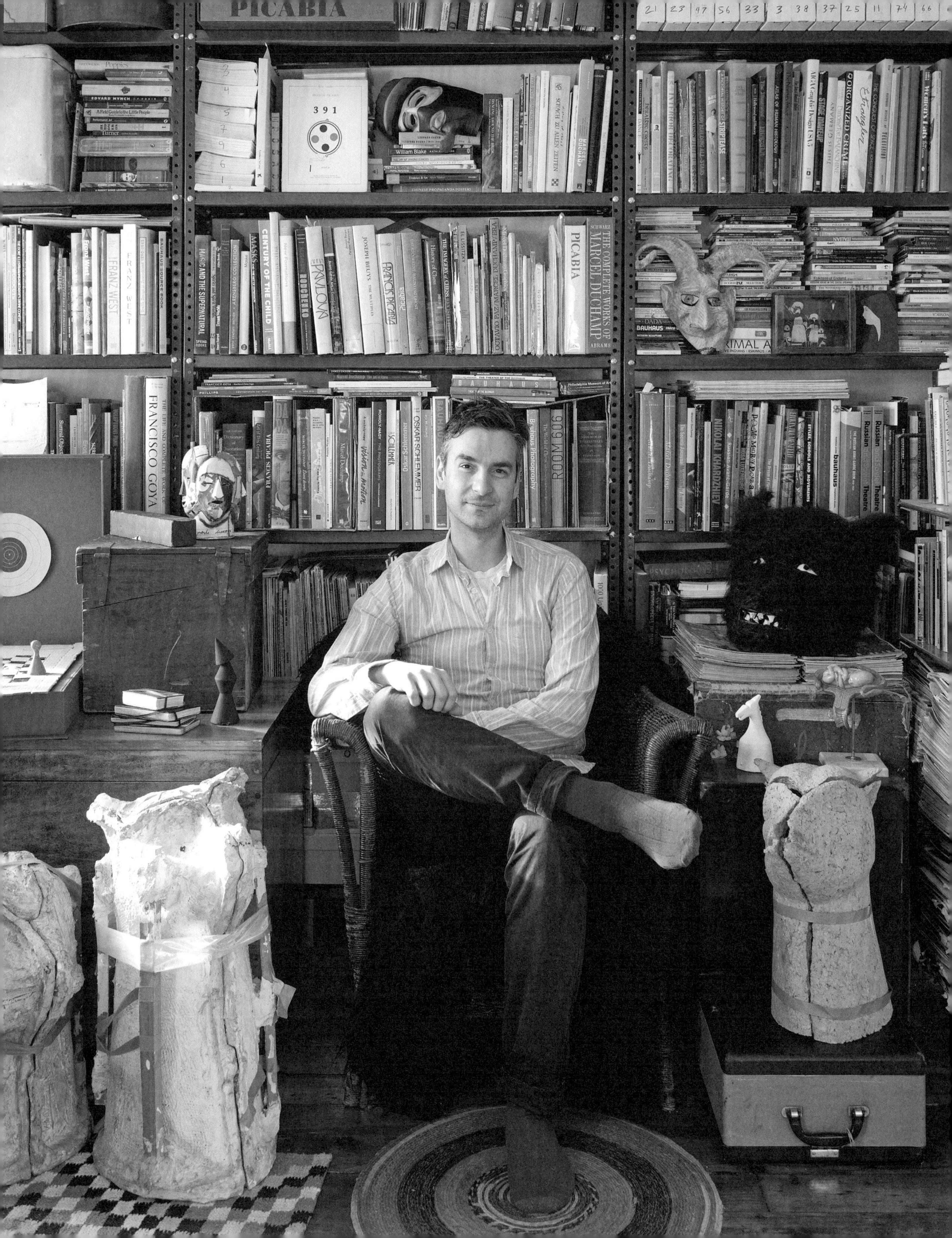

Contents

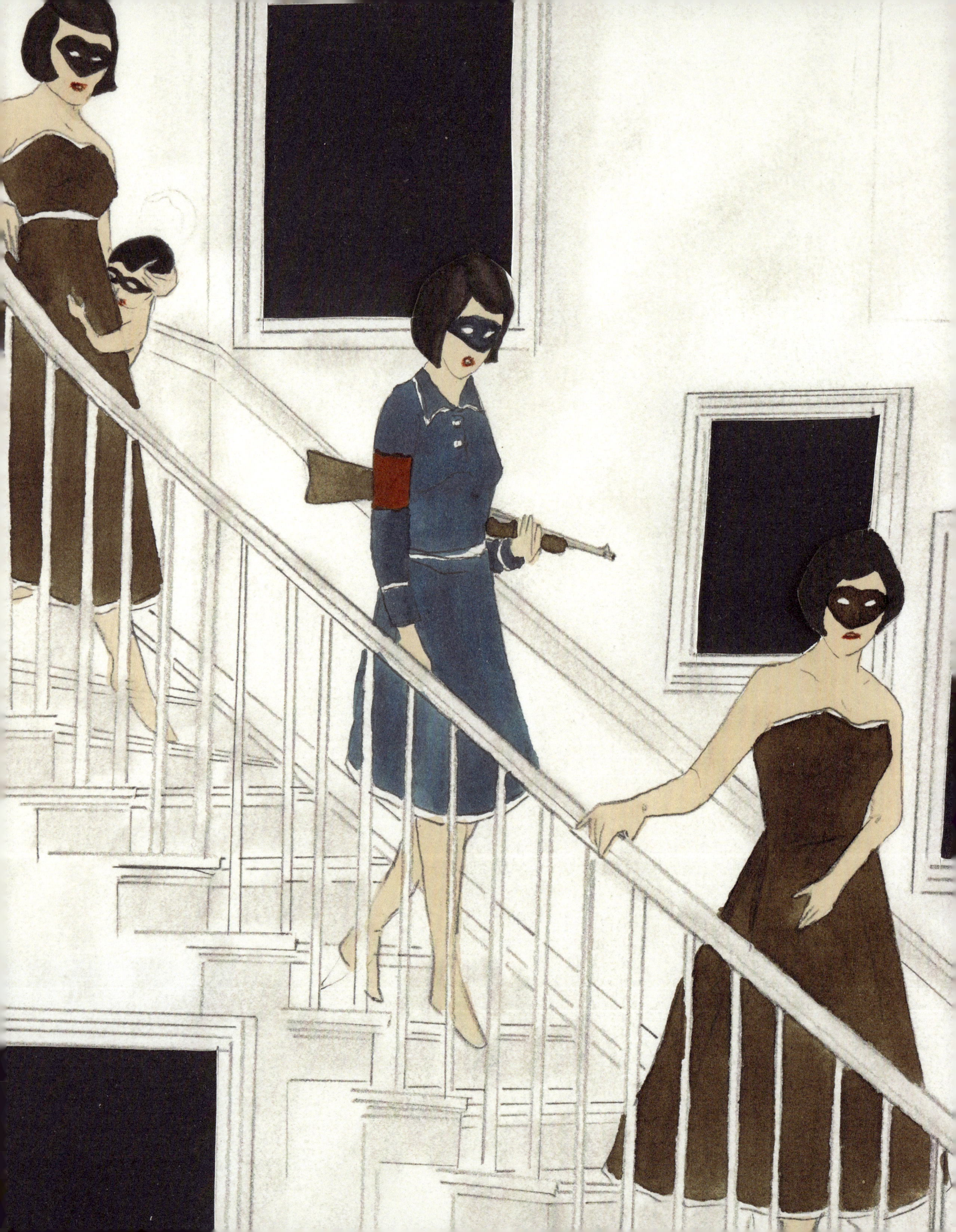

Greetings from the Dzama Conclave

Deborah Solomon

It is a rainy Tuesday in New York, and when I turn on the television news, I happen to catch the pageantry surrounding the papal conclave at the Vatican. Because I have been thinking about Marcel Dzama and looking at his recent work, I am surprised by the images on the screen. Surprised because I have seen them before. Men in red robes, oddly shaped hats, cavernous rooms with marble staircases, a plume of white smoke — so much about the scene at the Vatican echoes the costumed figures and pageantry in Dzama's recent work.

Dzama, it might be said, has always been a poet of conclaves, of invented worlds governed by their own rules and codes of behavior. He is best known for ink-and-wash drawings that have the chaste, innocent aura of storybook illustrations but attest to the sad and abusive undersides of societies and institutions. In his alternate universes, individuals are often made to endure the bruising authority of an unnamed state. His early work, with its profusion of khaki greens, beiges, and browns, deployed what might be called a military palette — the muted, muddy colors of uniforms and boots. It was a fitting camouflage for a world that at times resembled nothing so much as an internment camp.

The startling fact is that Dzama's new work, to judge from his recent show at David Zwirner, has shed some of its former menace and taken a turn for the cheerful. The mood is festive and carnivalesque and his palette has grown lush with luxuriant reds and blues. There are fewer flying bats. (I counted only three.) So too, there are fewer rifle-toting thugs, perhaps because gun violence in America has escalated to unbearable proportions and become a subject better tackled by the U.S. Congress and new legislation than by the reverie of art. It is certainly relevant that Dzama — he is thirty-nine years old and lives in Brooklyn, New York — became a father last year, making it impossible for him to sustain his early sense that the world is doomed. Moreover, the change in his work owes something to the hoopla in New York surrounding the 100th anniversary of The Armory Show; that radical event itself marked a birth — the birth of modernism in America.

Of this one feels certain: Dzama's work would not have been the same had he been a Charles or a Bob. At birth he was given a name that provided him with an instant, ineradicable link to the European avant garde. As children we are unconsciously aware of things that remind us of ourselves and of people who happen to share our name. Scientists have coined a phrase to describe it: nominative determinism, which posits that your name can have a significant role in determining key aspects of your profession or even your character.

This seems as good an explanation as any of how Marcel Dzama came to embrace the obsessions of Marcel Duchamp, not least of all the game of chess. In Dzama's recent work, rooks and pawns and other chessboard personalities appear and disappear on improvised stages, mingling with a cast that includes Winston Churchill, Dopey of the Seven Dwarfs, and a dog resembling a brown Labrador. Many contemporary artists, of course, look to Duchamp as an inspiration, perhaps because he took the hand out of art and made the brain preeminent. As everyone knows, Duchamp, an integral part of the Dada movement, announced in 1923 that he was giving up art for chess. This was not quite true, but it was not completely false, either.

*   *   *

Dzama, unlike his fellow artistic Marcels (Duchamp, Marceau, Proust), is not French, but Canadian and traces his ancestry to eastern Europe. The son of a baker who worked at a chain supermarket, he was born and reared in Winnipeg, a city known for its long, frigid winters and disproportionately large population of artists and film-makers. He attended the University of Manitoba and became semi-famous in his senior year when he founded the Royal Art Lodge, an ironically named collective whose members sat around late into the night with colored pencils and paper, completing one another's drawings.

Moving to New York in the fall of 2004, Dzama quickly became known in art and music circles as an incessant draftsman of daunting originality. His early shows in New York consisted of figurative work — drawings that had the size and scale of book illustrations and brought together an affecting cast of snowmen, talking trees, and other fantastical characters. They were done at a time when drawing was becoming hot again among contemporary artists, in part because it seemed to offer freedom from the auction house clamor surrounding painting. Drawings allow creativity to flourish away from the canvas and the market machinery that converts paintings into glinting trophies. A drawing can be slipped between the pages of a book or folded into an envelope. It seldom has what collectors now refer to as "wall power" — meaning, presumably, the ability to dominate a large living room. It is, by definition, an intimate medium, and no living American artist uses it more expressively than Dzama. He is a neo-Dadaist who deploys drawing to mine taboo worlds, with all that implies about a profusion of erotic and violent imagery.

At the same time, he is constantly doing a kind of bunny hop between mediums. His recent show at David Zwirner included collages, sculptures, and three chess-related videos. *Death Disco Dance*, a four-minute loop filmed in color in Guadalajara, Mexico, is both catchy in the way of a good song and bone-chilling. It shows a troupe of dancers in black-and-white leotards that cover their heads performing on a quiet street, amid mounds of rubble. None of them notice that one of the dancers in the troupe has been wounded and is oozing blood from his or her abdomen. Help! With their funny spotted costumes, the dancers can put you in mind of Damien Hirst's ubiquitous dot paintings but offer, in the place of anesthetized coolness, living, moving, inhabited forms. Dzama makes art that bleeds.

A longer and more complex film, the fourteen-minute *Sister Squares* takes its title from a chess book Duchamp co-authored in 1932, *Opposition and Sister Squares Are Reconciled*. It consists of a costume ballet played out on a stage with a black-and-white checkerboard floor. In describing the video, I can only say that if you have ever wondered what chess pieces do when you go to sleep and leave them unattended in the next room, here is the answer. They have a life of their own and it extends well beyond clubbing. Be sure to note the funny-creepy male viewers lined up like a row of judges, with identical pumpkin-shaped heads.

Sometimes figures spill out of the videos and assume new life as sculptures sharing gallery space with you—as for example, a group of gargantuan welded-metal heads intended to represent kings and queens and other chess people. Made from discarded tin cans—the kind with painted-on labels—they combine the tinsel brightness of commercial products with the eloquent gravity of primitive totems. Dzama made the works in Mexico, and the words and brand names scattered sideways and upside-down on their surface include references to Maxima and "recubrimientos para madera"—which I cannot translate, except as a reminder of the grievous mistake I made by taking French instead of Spanish in high school.

*   *   *

What does it all mean? The foreign words seem as good a metaphor as any for the essential foreignness of Dzama's content. His work can be hermetic, and when you stand in front of it, you inevitably puzzle over what it means. Naturally, you could make it easy on yourself and simply conclude that a work of art whose meaning remains elusive, enigmatic, and possibly impenetrable is not any less expressive. But you could also choose to enter Dzama's cosmos the same way you enter any work of art—that is, by taking it apart with your eyes, piece by lovely piece, and then standing back a bit and allowing it to coalesce into a breathing, beating whole. Or not. You will notice in this catalogue that several elements reappear, such as:

The pawns

The pawns are the easiest characters to recognize. They are dressed in uniform: white spots against grayish-blue fabric. Sometimes in the place of dots, there are diamond shapes, a sign of status. Most of the pawns look slim and fit, as if they do a prescribed number of sit-ups a day. Or perhaps it's just all that kneeling and supplicating—all that bowing to their chessboard superiors—that keeps them limber. They're on the pawn diet. As their name implies, they are lackeys whose fate is not their own.

The walking Tatlin

Among the more art-historical figures is an abstract sculpture resting atop a pair of black-stockinged legs that can belong to either a man or a woman. The sculpture is an emblem of modernism that resembles Vladimir Tatlin's *Monument to the Third International*, a constructivist tower that remains the most famous building that was never built.

The staircase

One is struck by the prevalence of staircases running through these latest drawings, some of them grand palatial affairs, some short and squat and unprotected by a balustrade or railing. Usually, the human figures are positioned at the top of the stairs, or

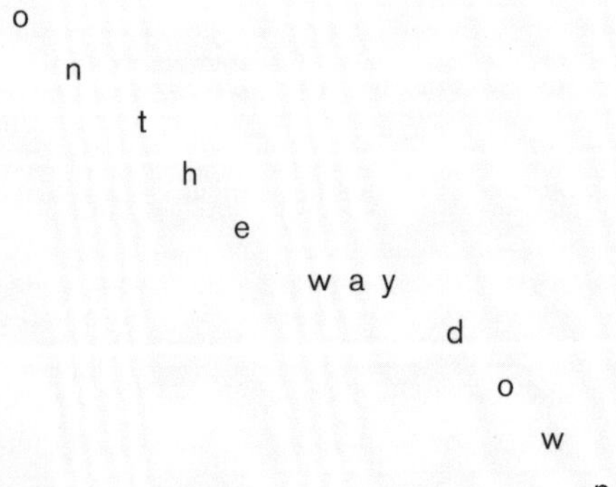

No one is going up.

There is a reason for this. As long as there have been castles, there have been jewel-laden queens making entrances on staircases. Duchamp no doubt was thinking of this when he conceived his radical *Nude Descending a Staircase (No. 2),* which not only smashed the human form but the long tradition in which women came down staircases fully dressed.

Duchamp exhibited his *Nude Descending* at The Armory Show of 1913 and it
became the defining image of the show. Newspaper cartoonists poked endless fun
at it because no one could locate the female nude tucked amid the welter of tilting
brown planes. You suspect the painting would have passed practically unnoticed had
it been titled, simply, *Composition No. 2*.

*   *   *

Dzama's drawings tend to be similar in color, size, and tone, and sometimes they
have the feeling of interconnected short stories. So probably every viewer will come
away with his or her own favorites. One of my own favorites is a humorous and
cryptic ink-and-wash drawing titled *Shall we venture outside*. It takes you into a
hallway where a king and queen lead a procession of women down a staircase that
stretches diagonally across the composition. At the bottom of the stairs, the queen
stumbles upon a little ballet-in-progress that involves a woman doing what looks like
a Pilates stretch on the floor as two or three pawns flutter solicitously around her.

Instead of being intrigued by this display, the queen, who is wearing a brown cape
and holding a medieval-style spear, appears somewhat annoyed. The title of the work
refers to her comment to the king that they "venture outside"—perhaps she wants
fresh air because she is not accustomed to seeing performers in her home and feels
a bit cramped. It's as if she is thinking, "Oh, no, not those loopy dance people again."
Behind her, the palace walls are hung with empty picture frames, a hint of a world
emptied of sensual beauty. In the end, you can read the work as a fable about the
indifference of the ruling class to expressions of artistic daring and whimsy.

Perhaps the world can be divided into people who desire beauty and people who
get in the way of it.

Or perhaps Dzama thinks no such thing. Naturally, it is a futile endeavor to try and
extract anything as compact as a moral or a single storyline from the twisty symbolism
of his art. But you can say, at the very least, that his latest work is suffused with a
sense of nostalgia for the European avant garde in its heyday—it invites you to enter
a world filled with costumes and masks and erotic play, with chessboard personalities dancing their heads off, with the sort of brazen gestures in which the Dadaists
and the Surrealists specialized. To be sure, the old avant garde is long gone. It isn't
coming back. What Dzama offers us in its place is a fairy tale about a world where art
once tried to be pathbreaking and revolutionary, and which lives on today as a story
we tell and re-tell about a lost civilization.

Shall we venture outside, 2013

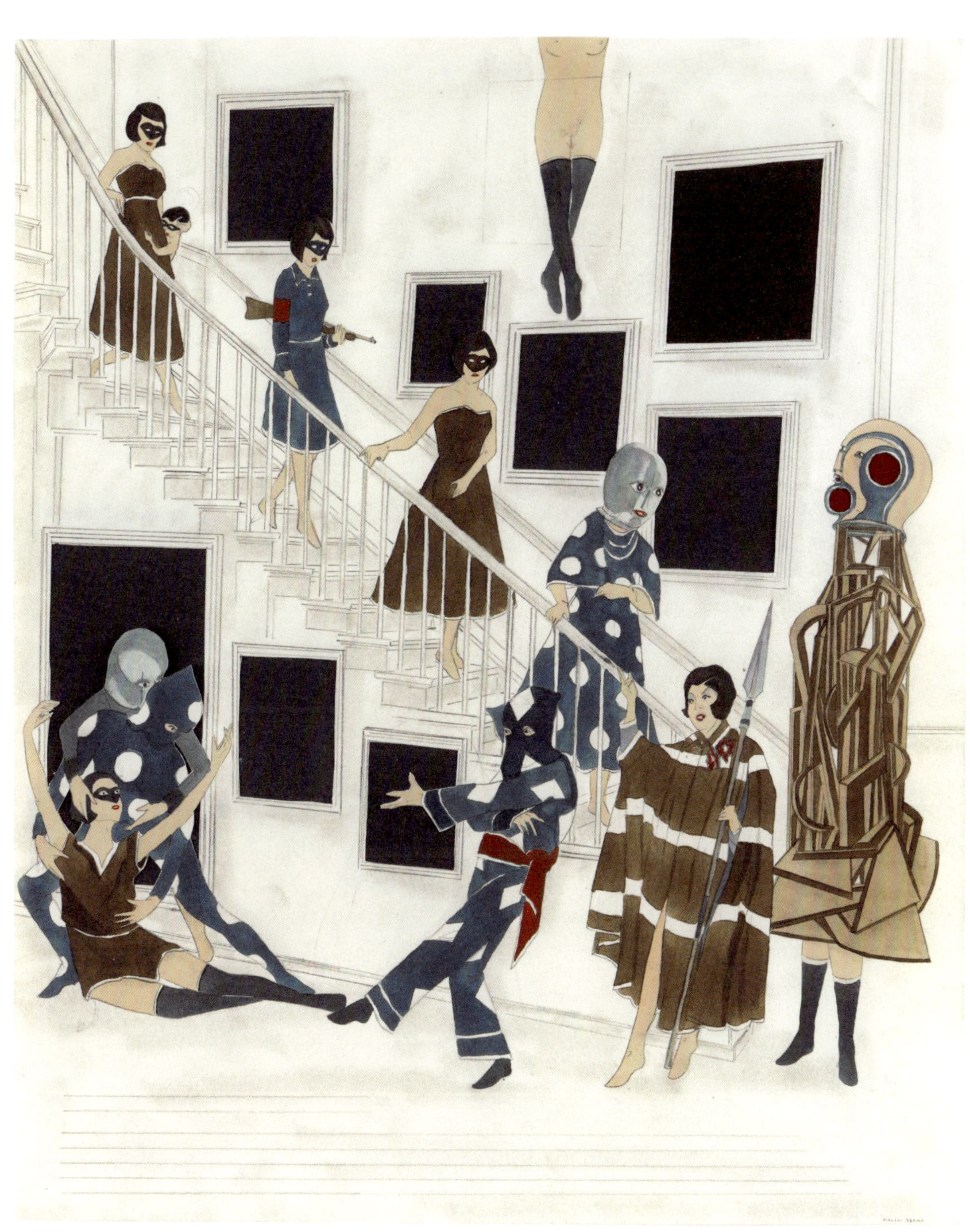

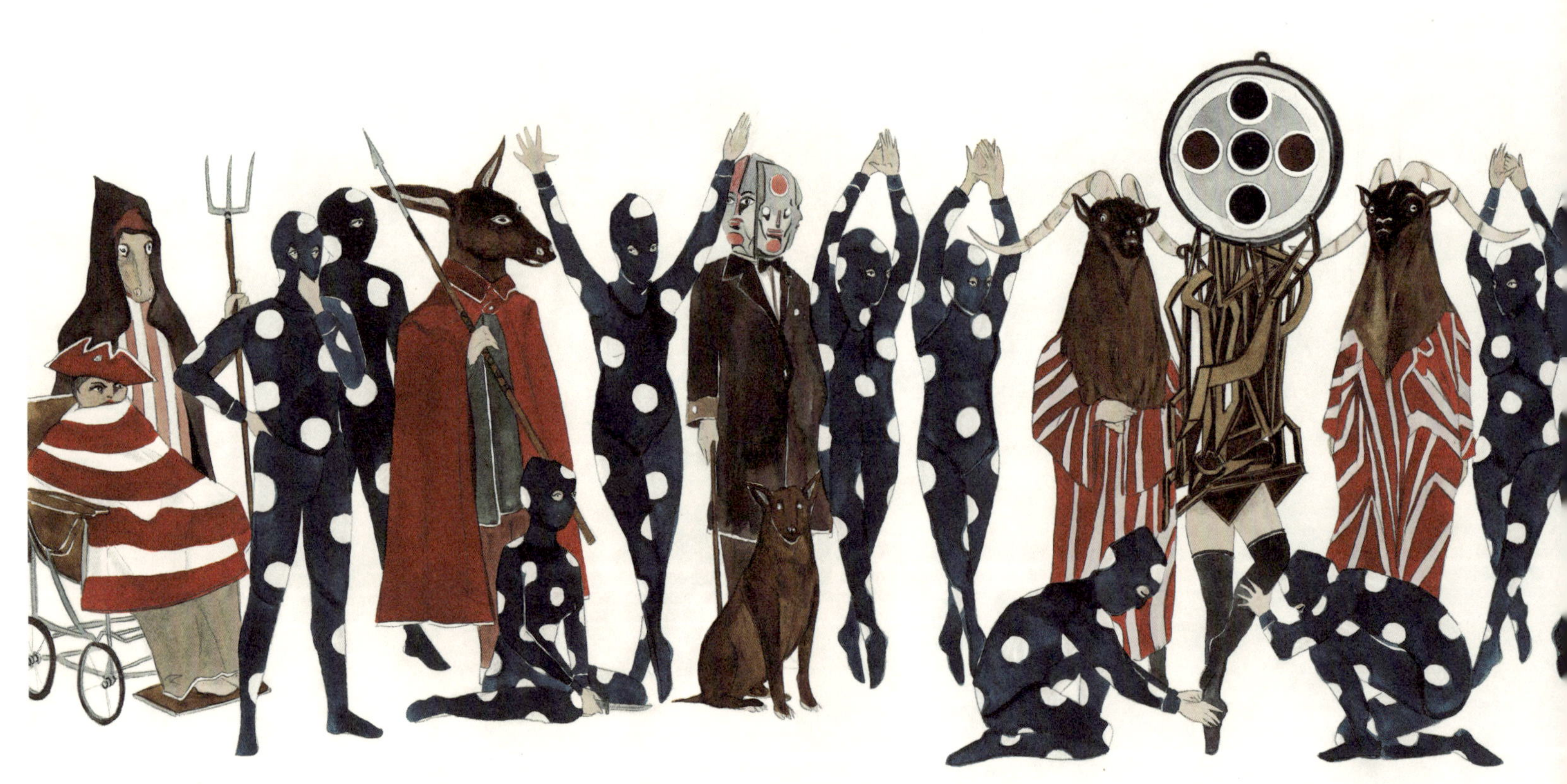

Myth, manifestos, and monsters, 2013

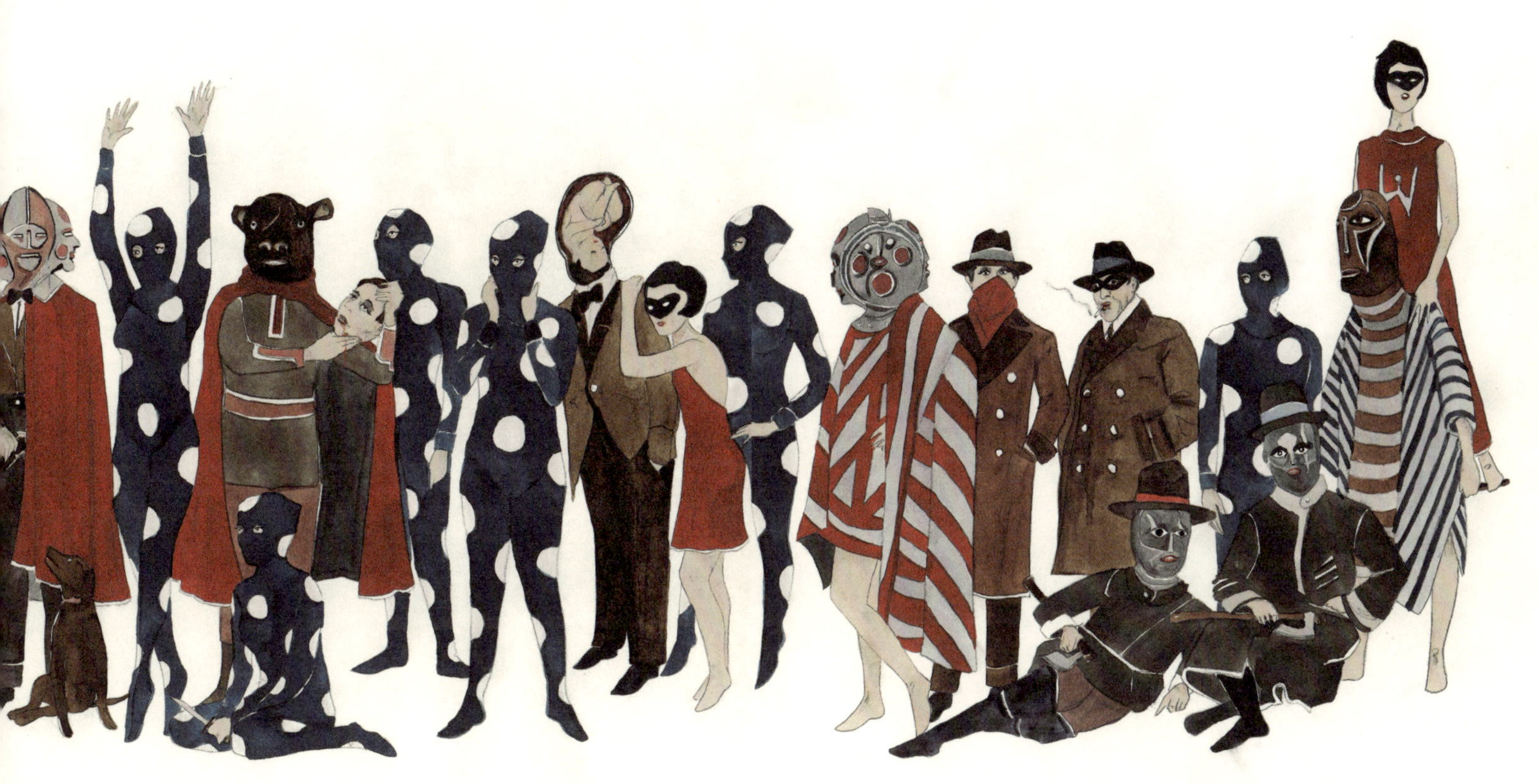

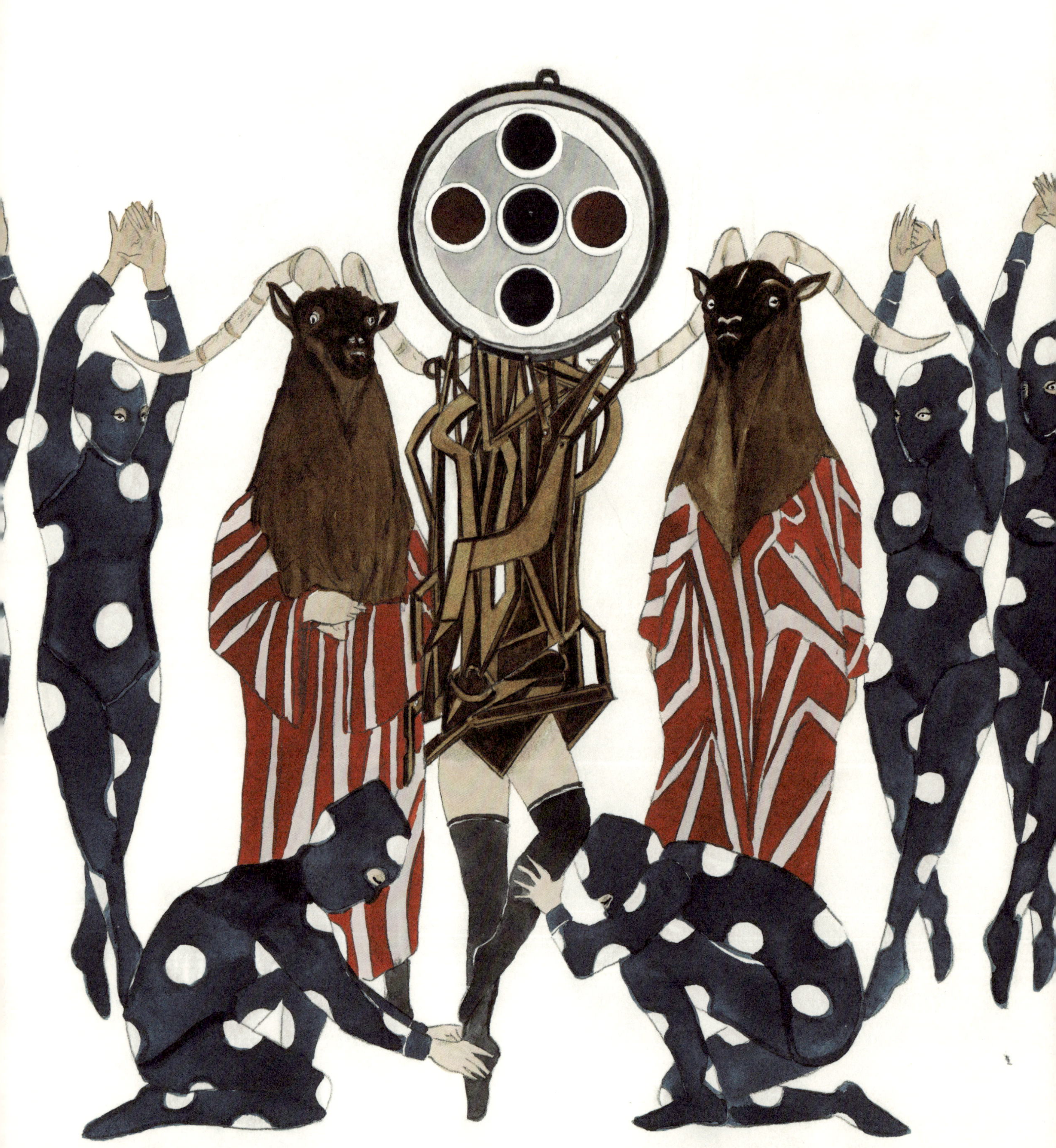

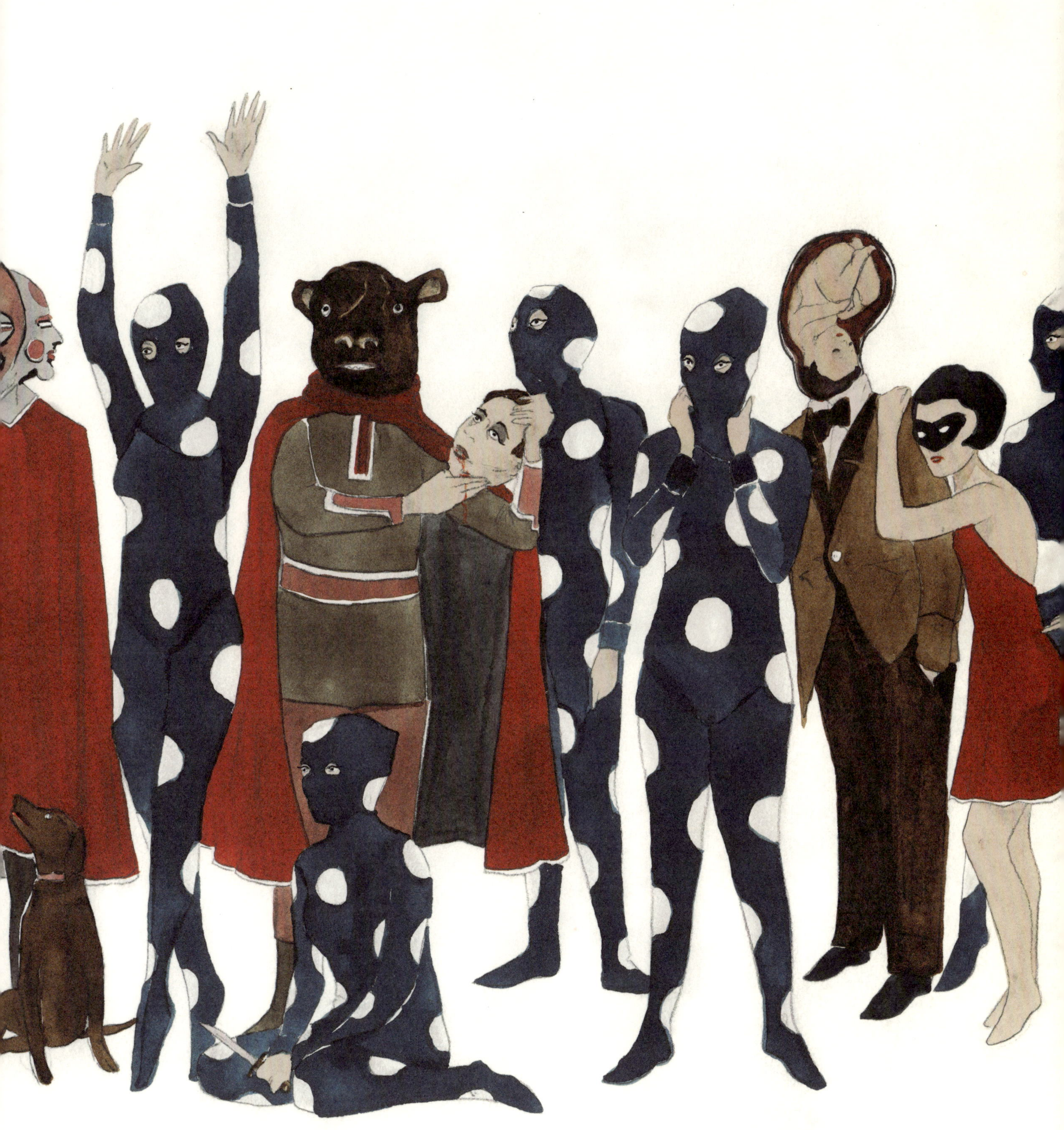

The Death Disco Dance steps, 2013

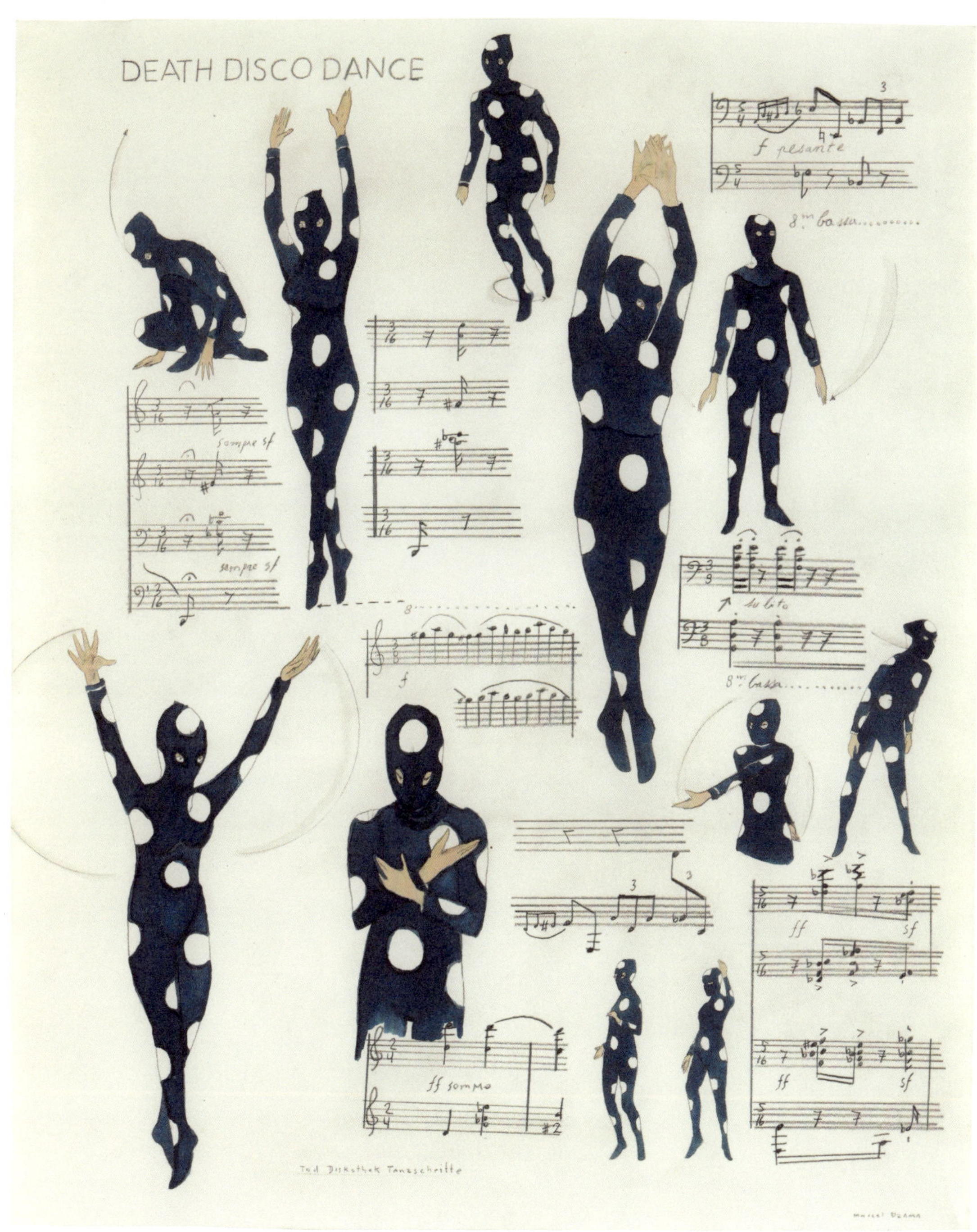
DEATH DISCO DANCE

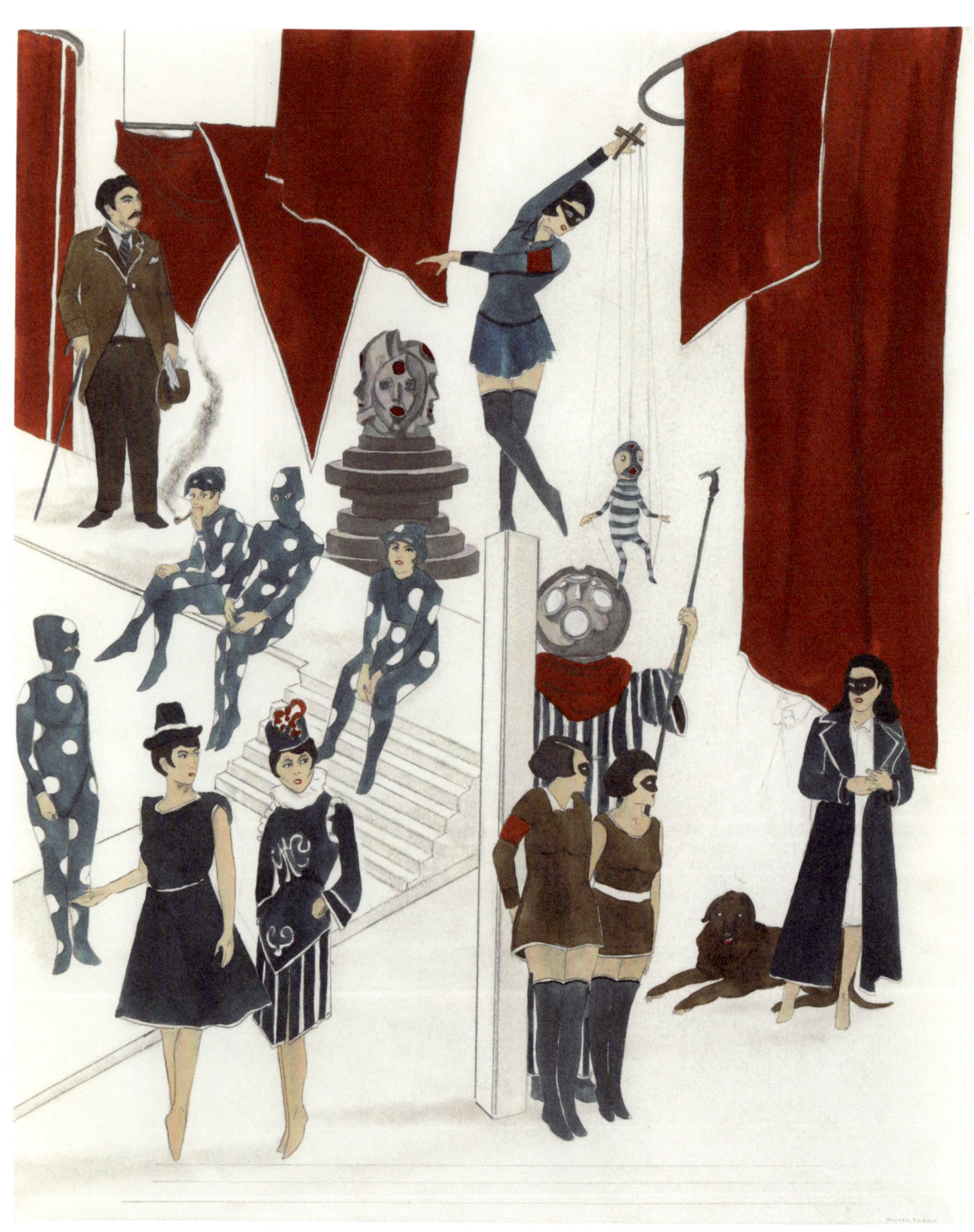

A play for puppets and people, 2013

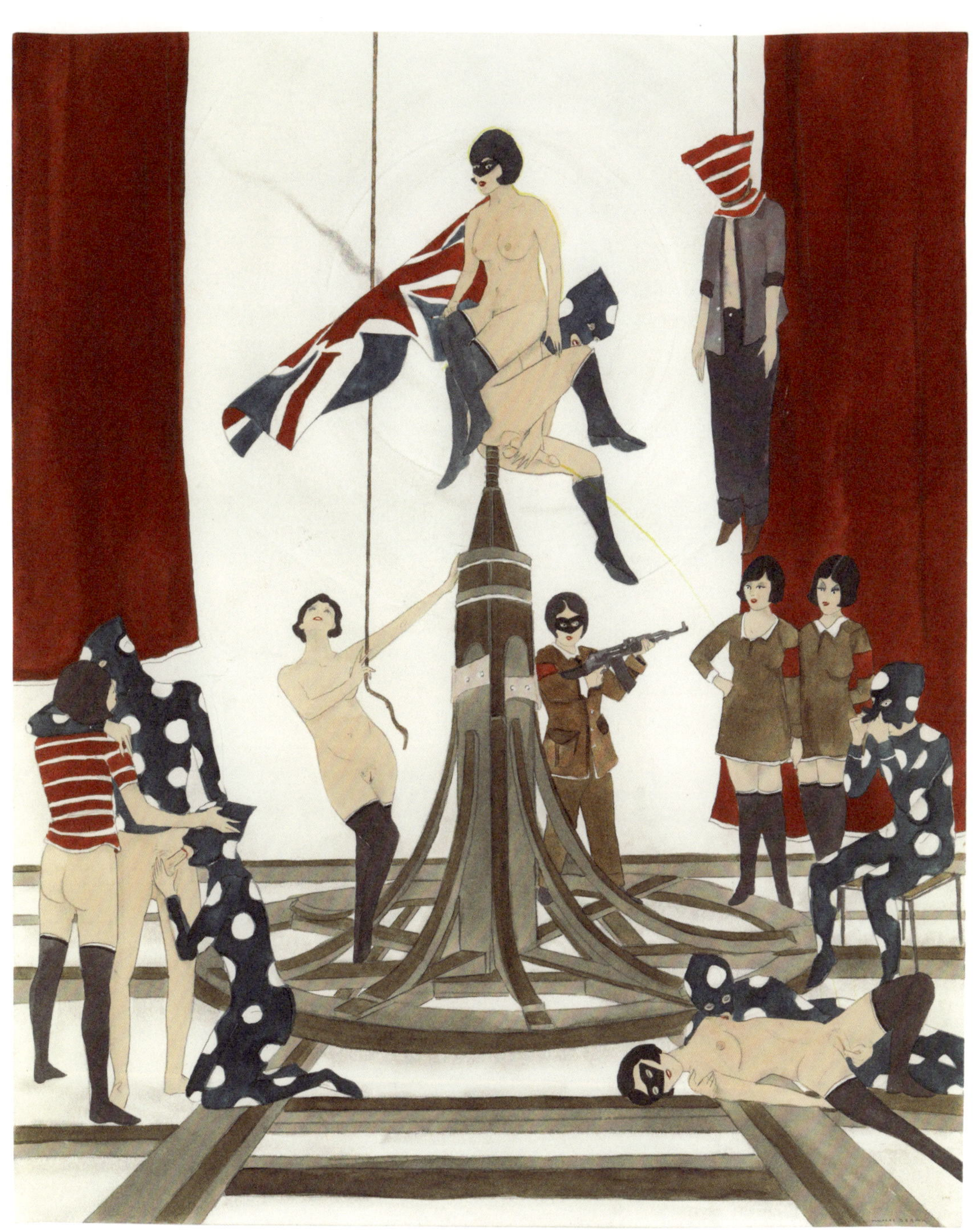

The renowned Union Jack off, 2013

The tension around which history is built, 2013

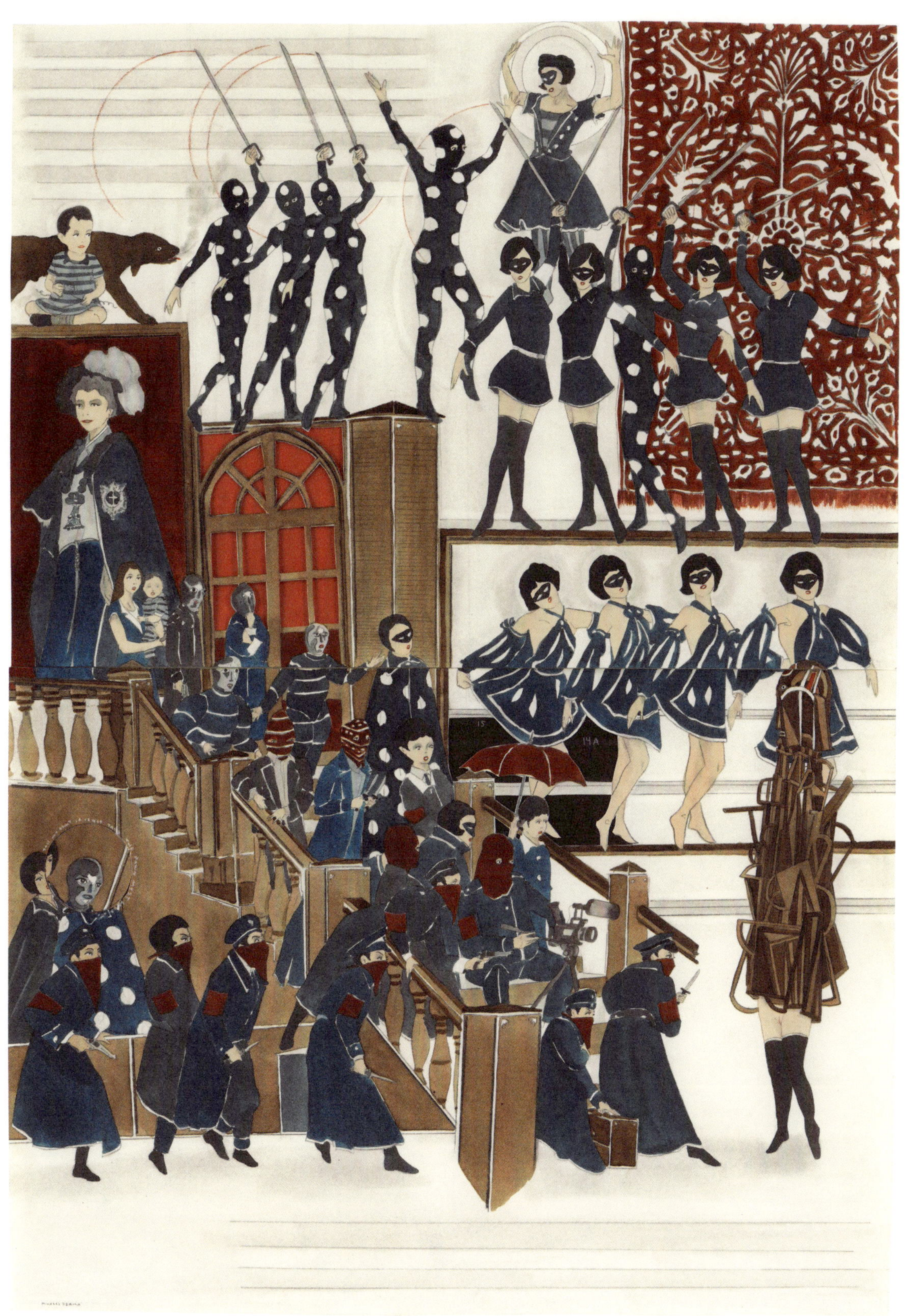

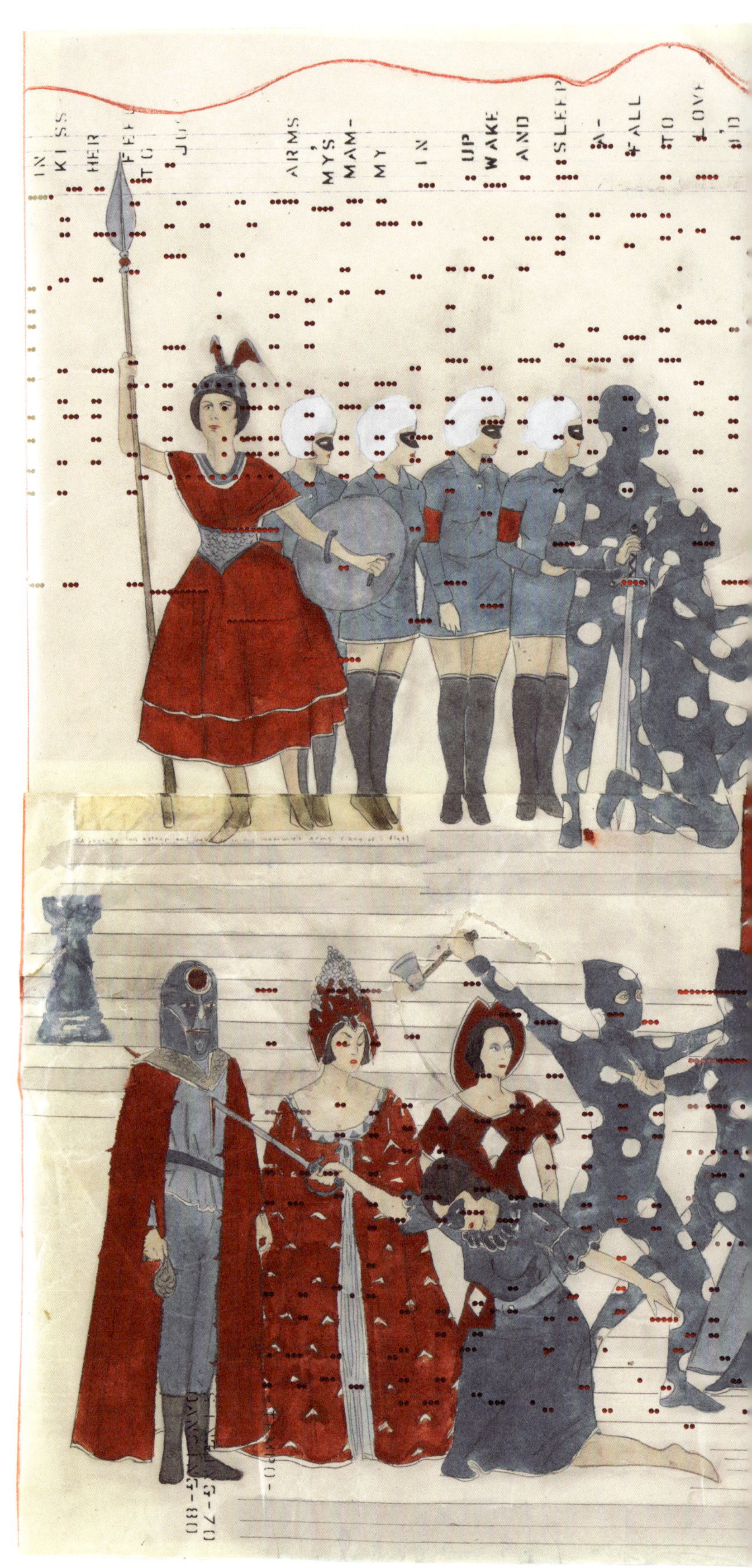

Malala will have her revenge, 2013

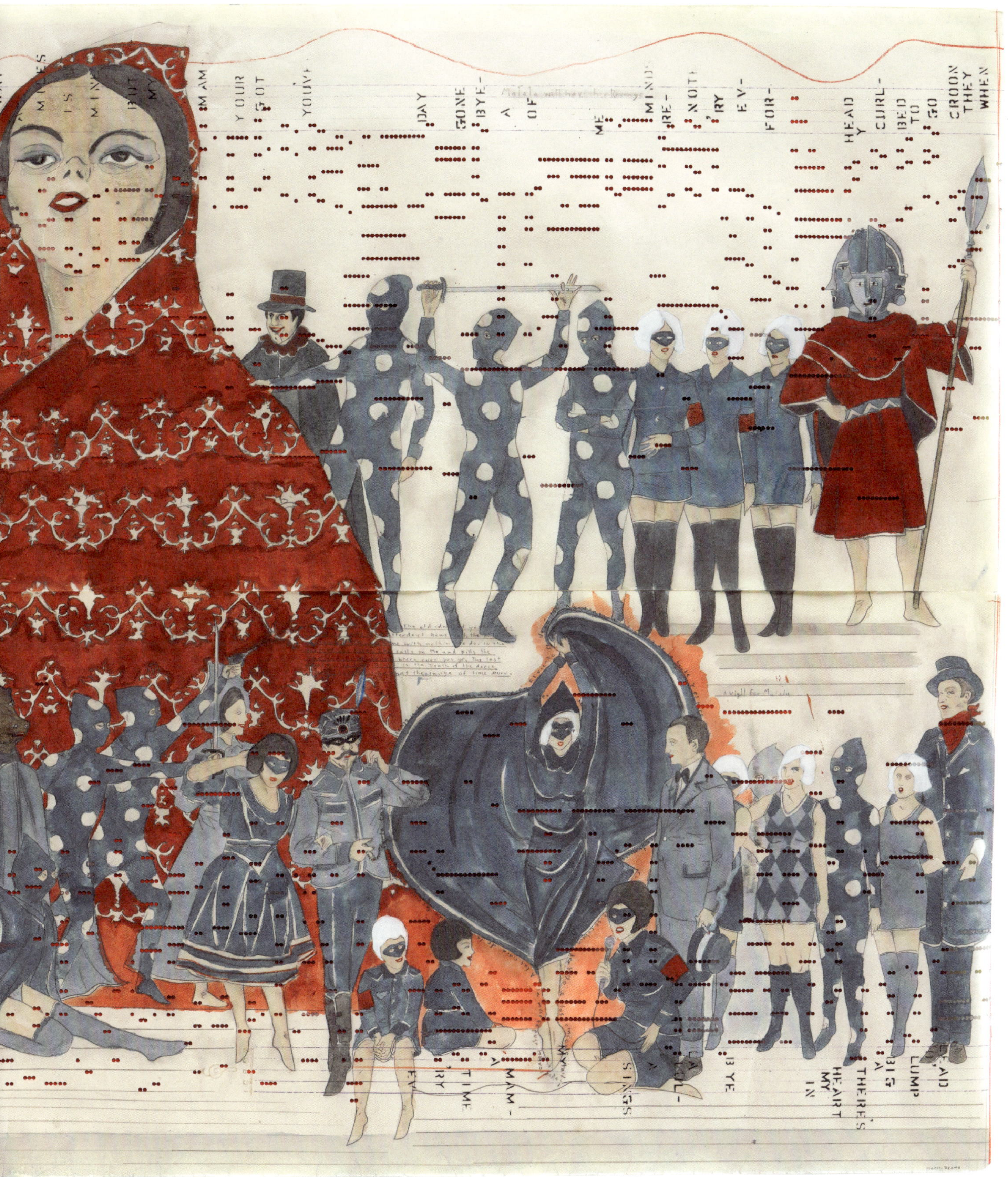

MILES IS MINE BUT MY MAM
YOUR GOT YOUVE
DAY GONE BYE- A OF
ME RE- NOTH RY EV- FOR-
HEAD Y CURL- BED TO GO CROON THEY WHEN
Malala will have her revenge
a wish for Malala
BE-AID LUMP BIG A THERE'S HEART MY IN
13 YE LA- COL- SINGS A MAM- A TIME RY EV

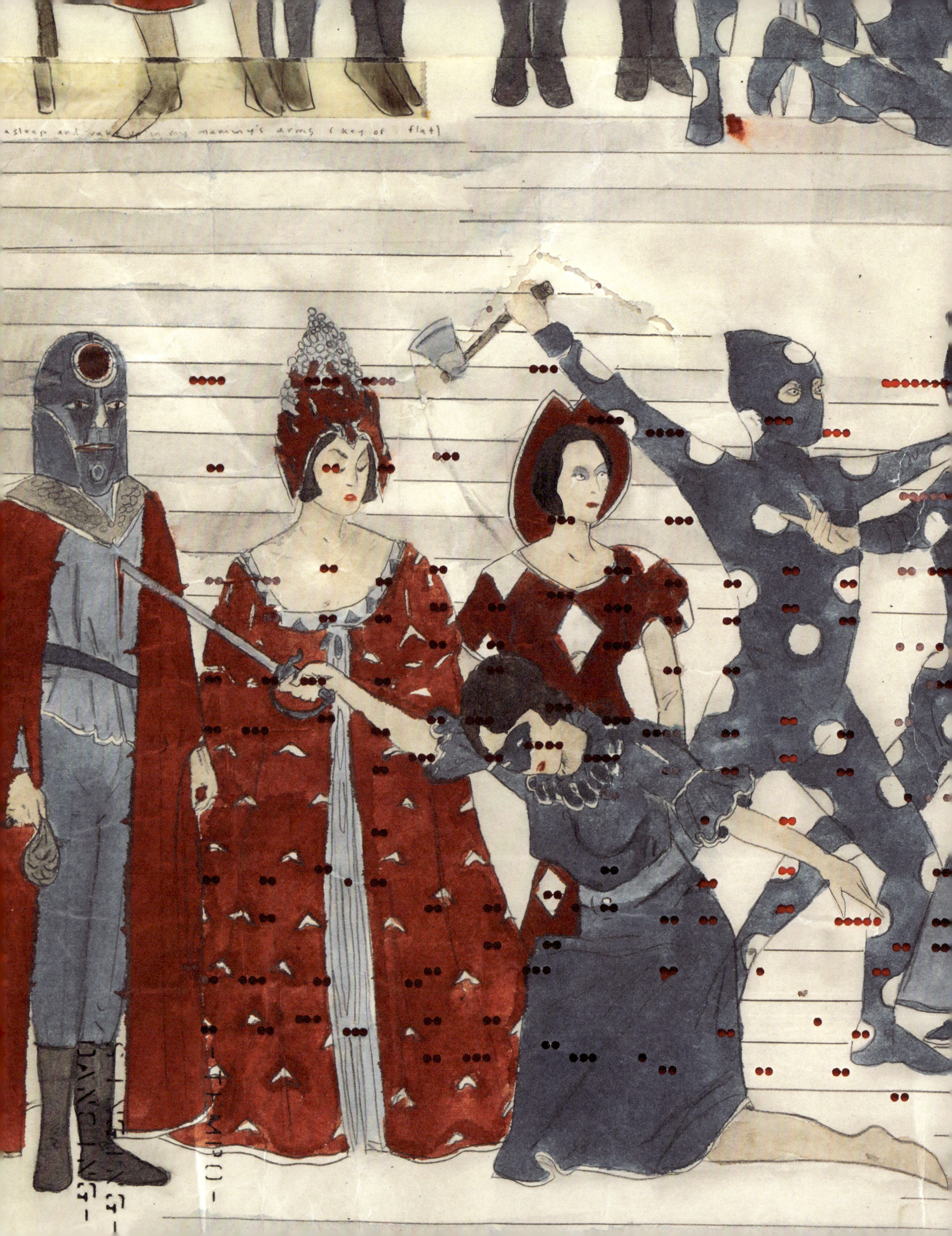

asleep and wake up in my mammy's arms (key of flat)
DANCING
TEMPO

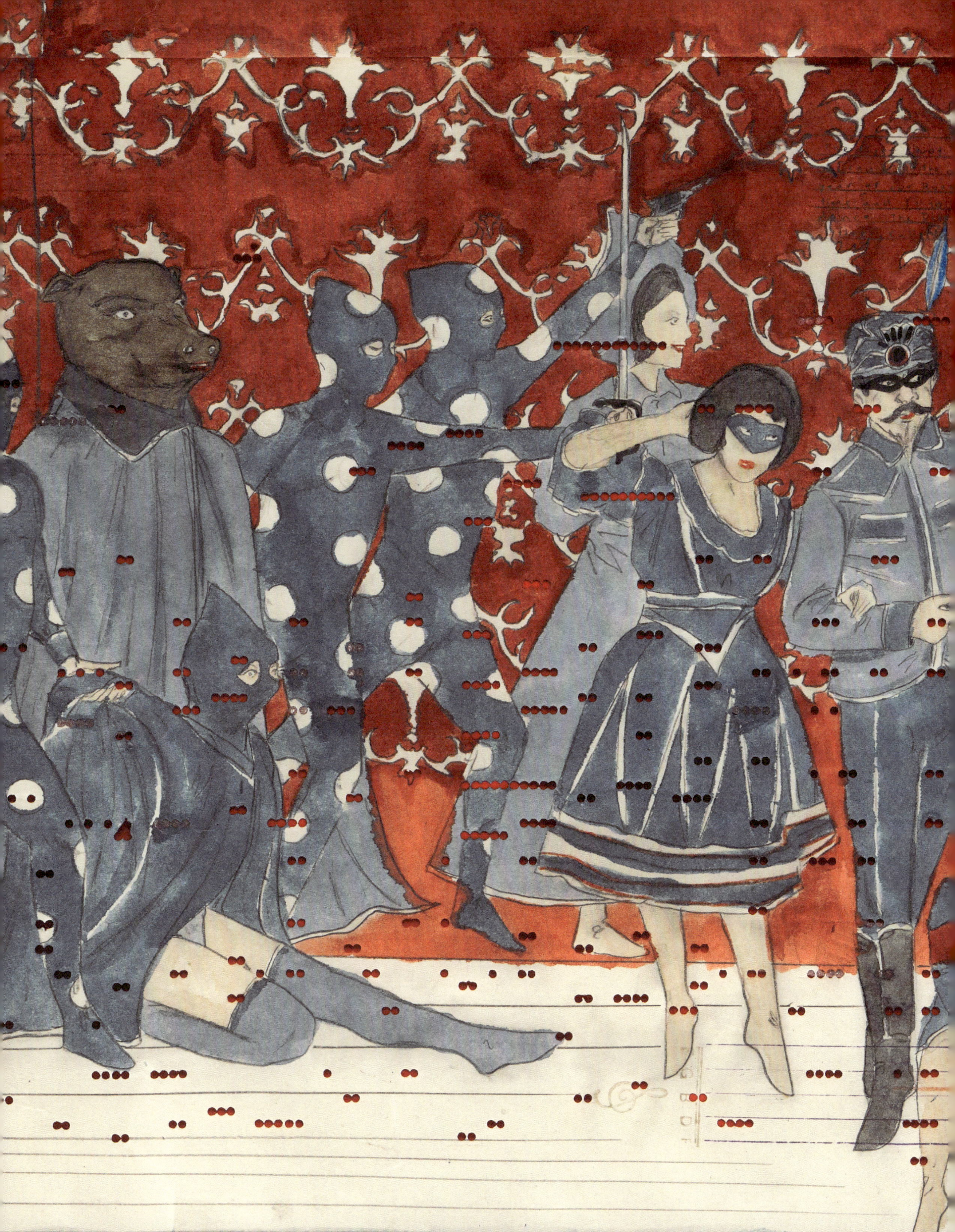

As innocent as grace itself, 2012

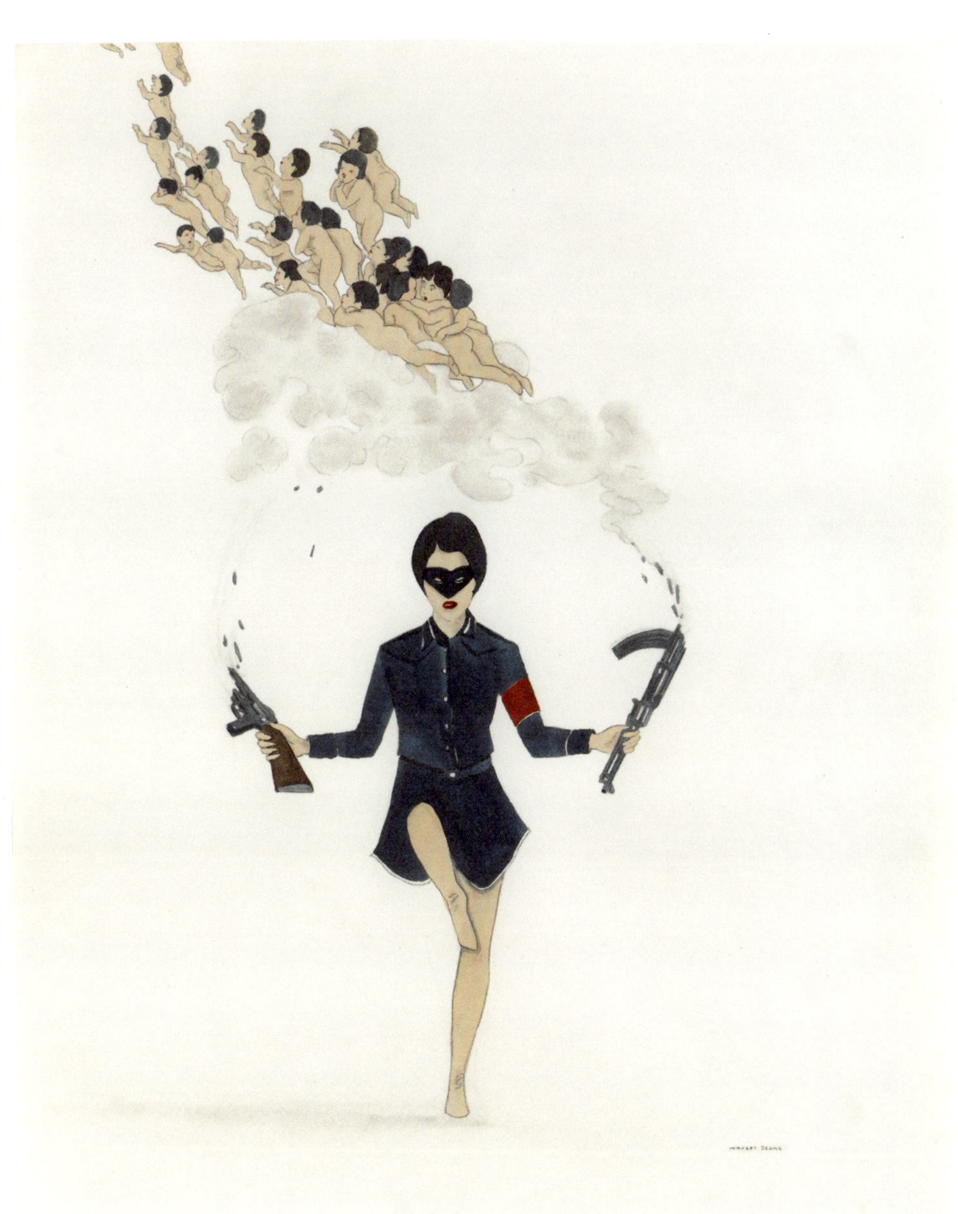

Was he not born of woman, 2013

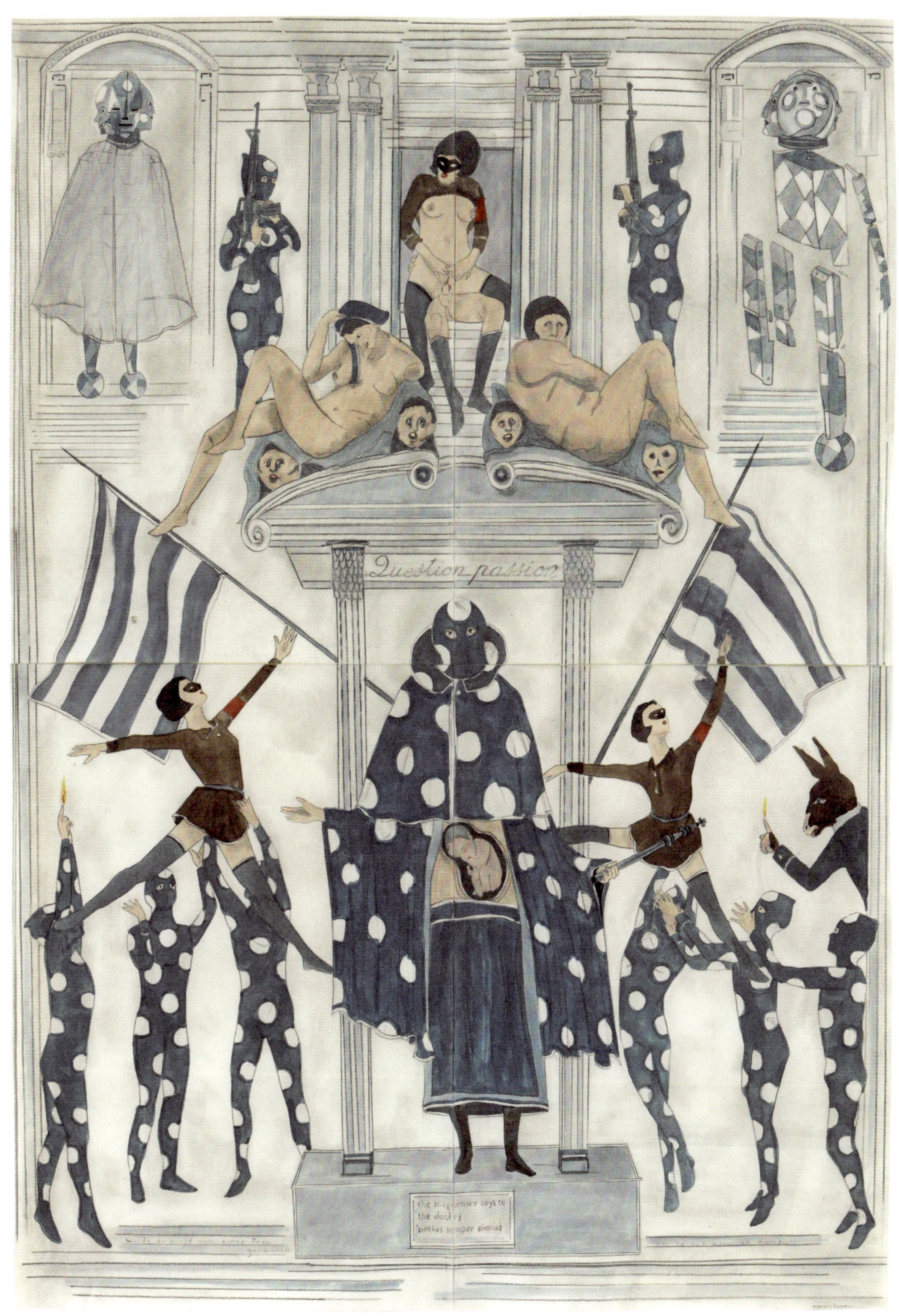

Question passion
the magnetiser says to
the donkey
'simius semper simius

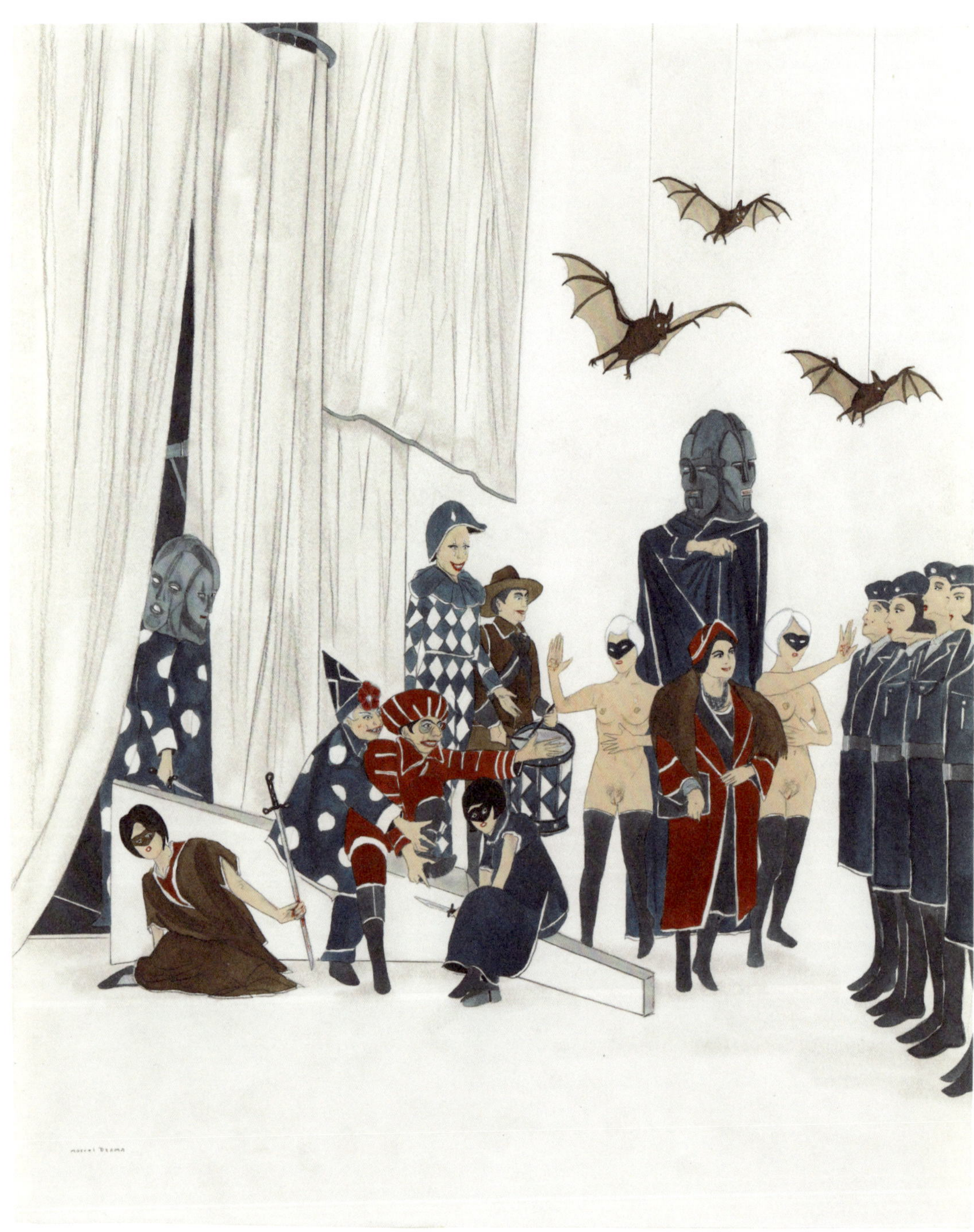

I am queen in title and in style, 2013

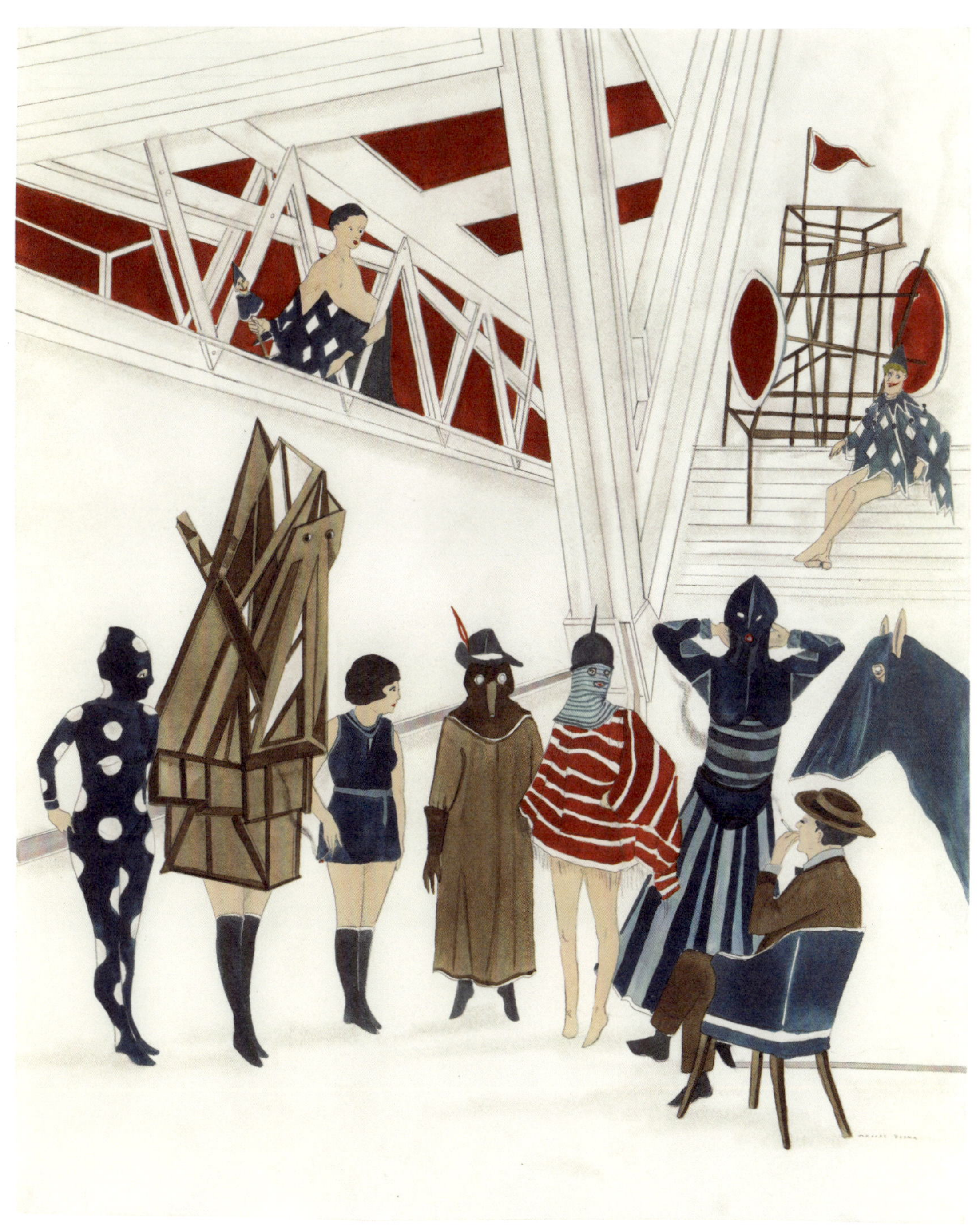

Waiting to be anointed, 2013

A creature, that did bear the shape of man, 2013

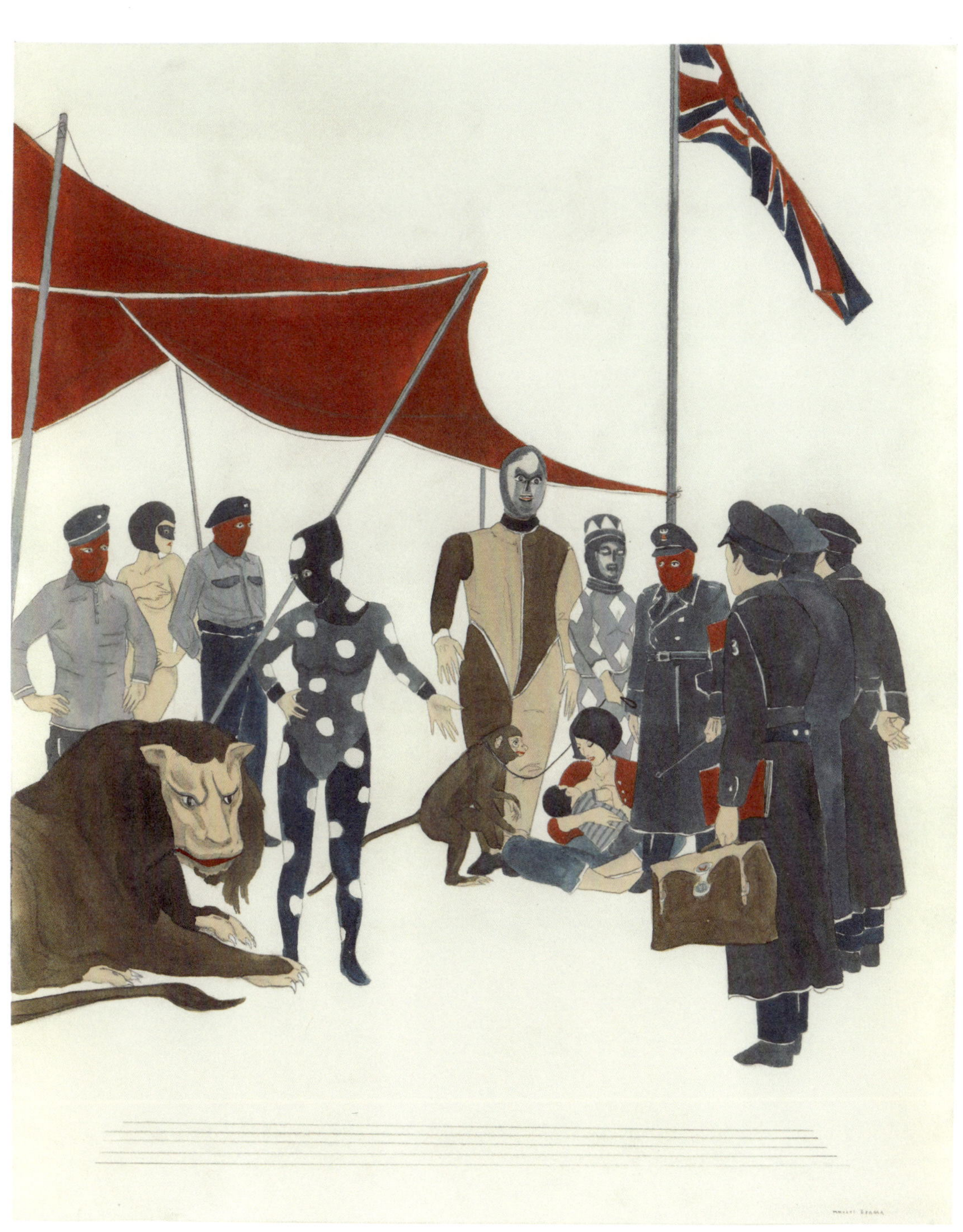

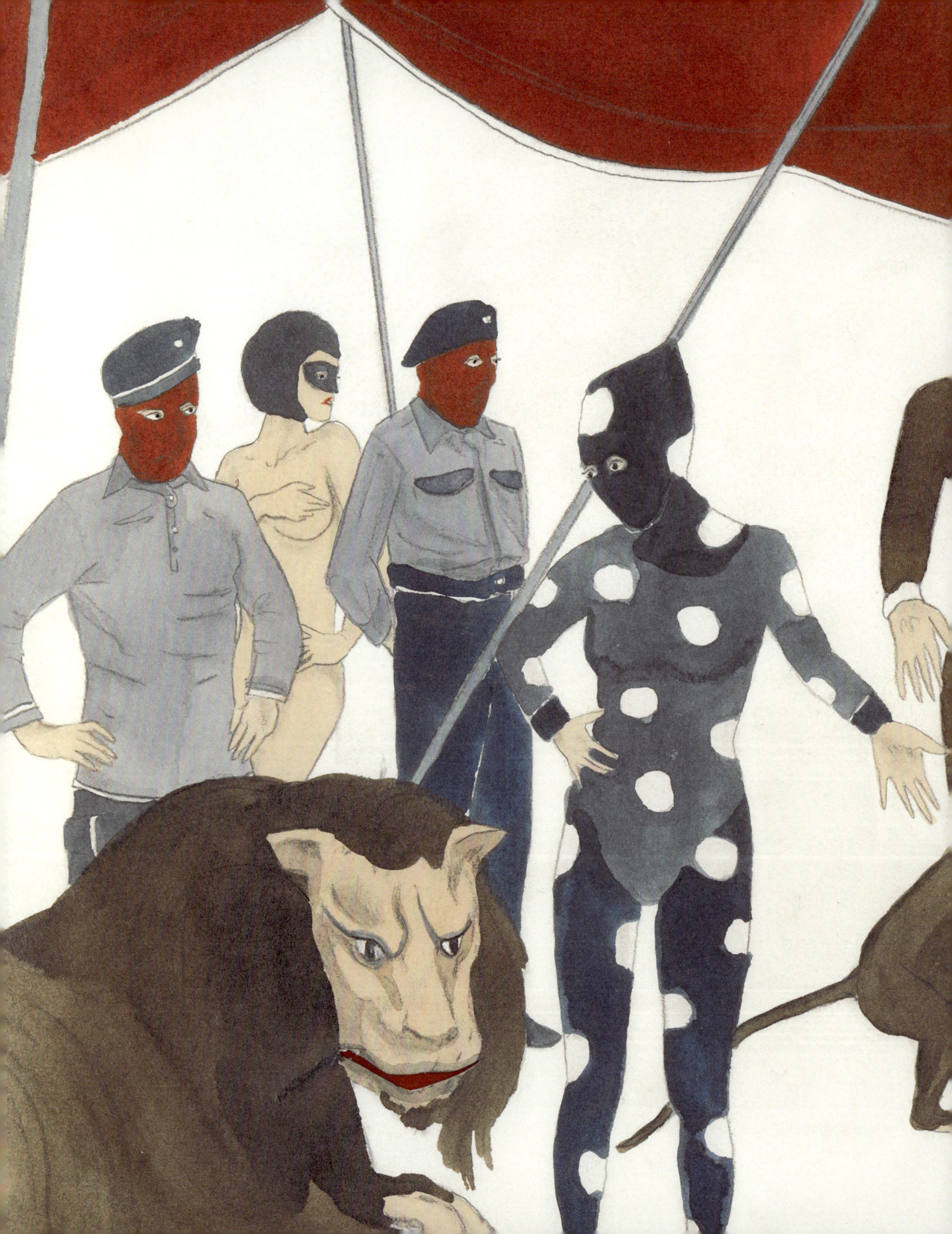

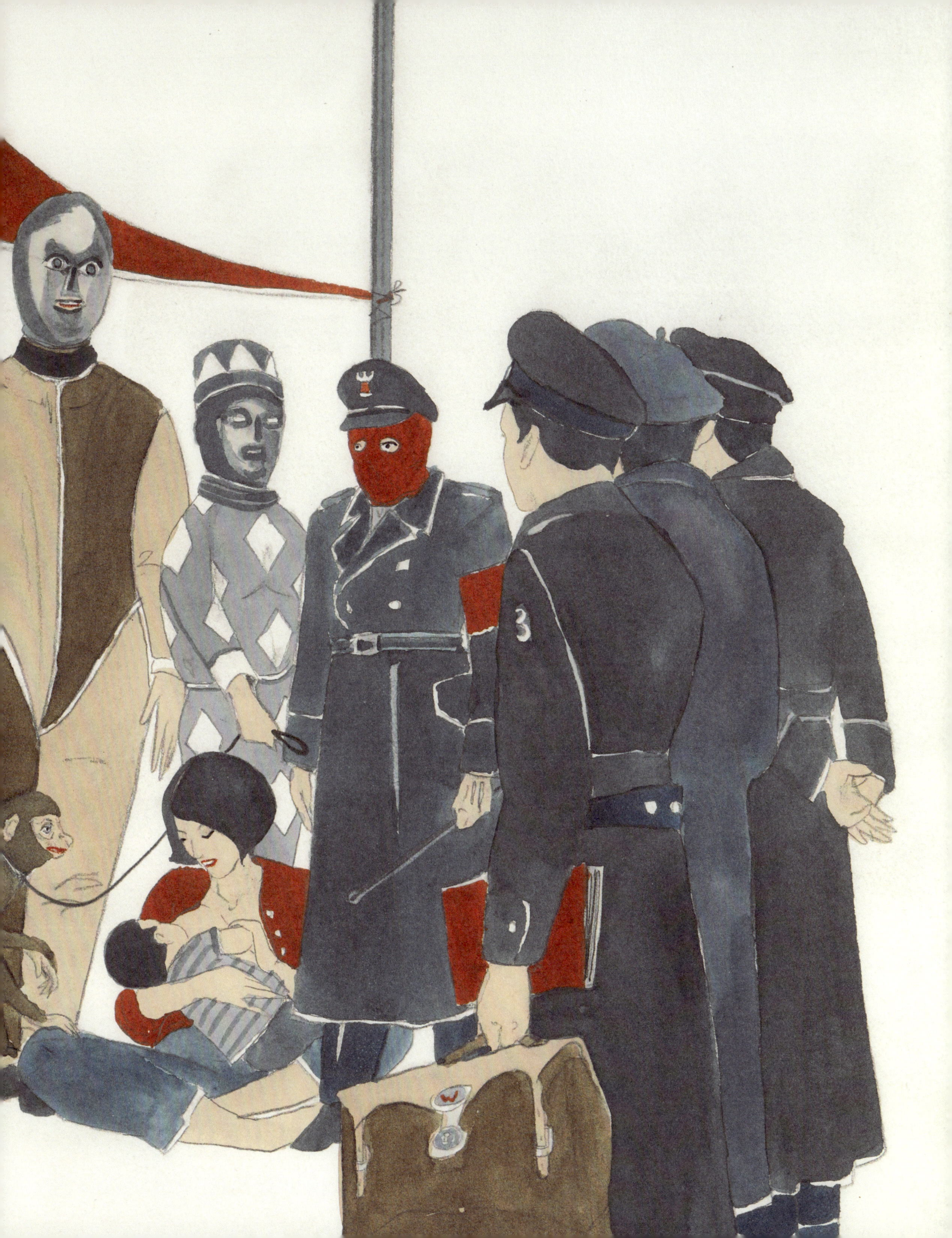

Perhaps they are gods, 2013

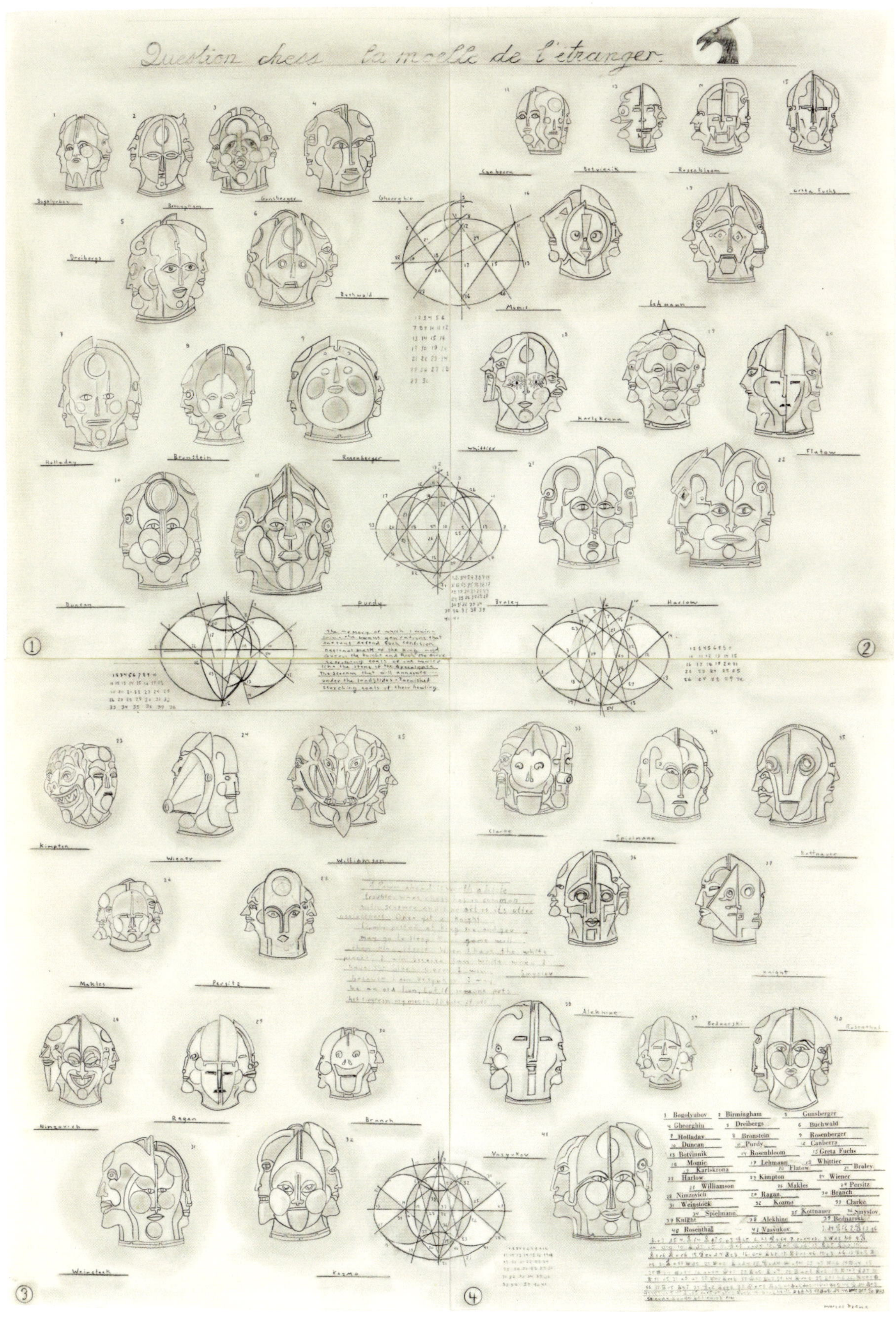

Question chess   La moelle de l'étranger.

1 Bogolyubov   2 Birmingham   3 Gunsberger
4 Gheorghiu   5 Dreibergs   6 Buchwald
7 Holladay   8 Bronstein   9 Rosenberger
10 Duncan   11 Purdy   12 Canberra
13 Botvinnik   14 Rosenbloom   15 Greta Fuchs
16 Momic   17 Lehmann   18 Whittier
19 Karlskrona   20 Flatow   21 Braley
22 Harlow   23 Kimpton   24 Wiener
25 Williamson   26 Makles   27 Pervitz
28 Nimzovich   29 Ragan   30 Branch
31 Weinstock   32 Kozmo   33 Clarke
34 Spielmann   35 Kottnauer   36 Spryolov
37 Knight   38 Alekhine   39 Bednarski
40 Rosenthal   41 Vasyukov

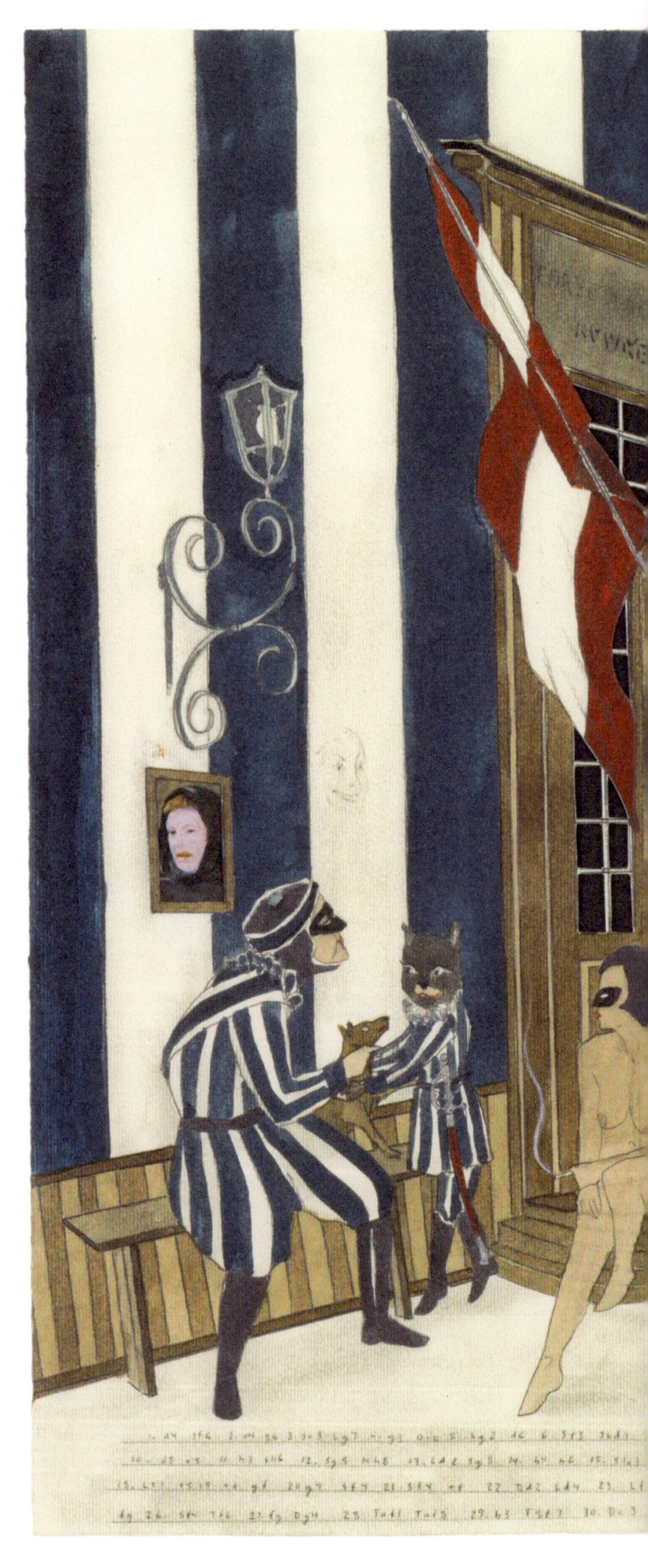

Opportunists mingling with combatants, 2012

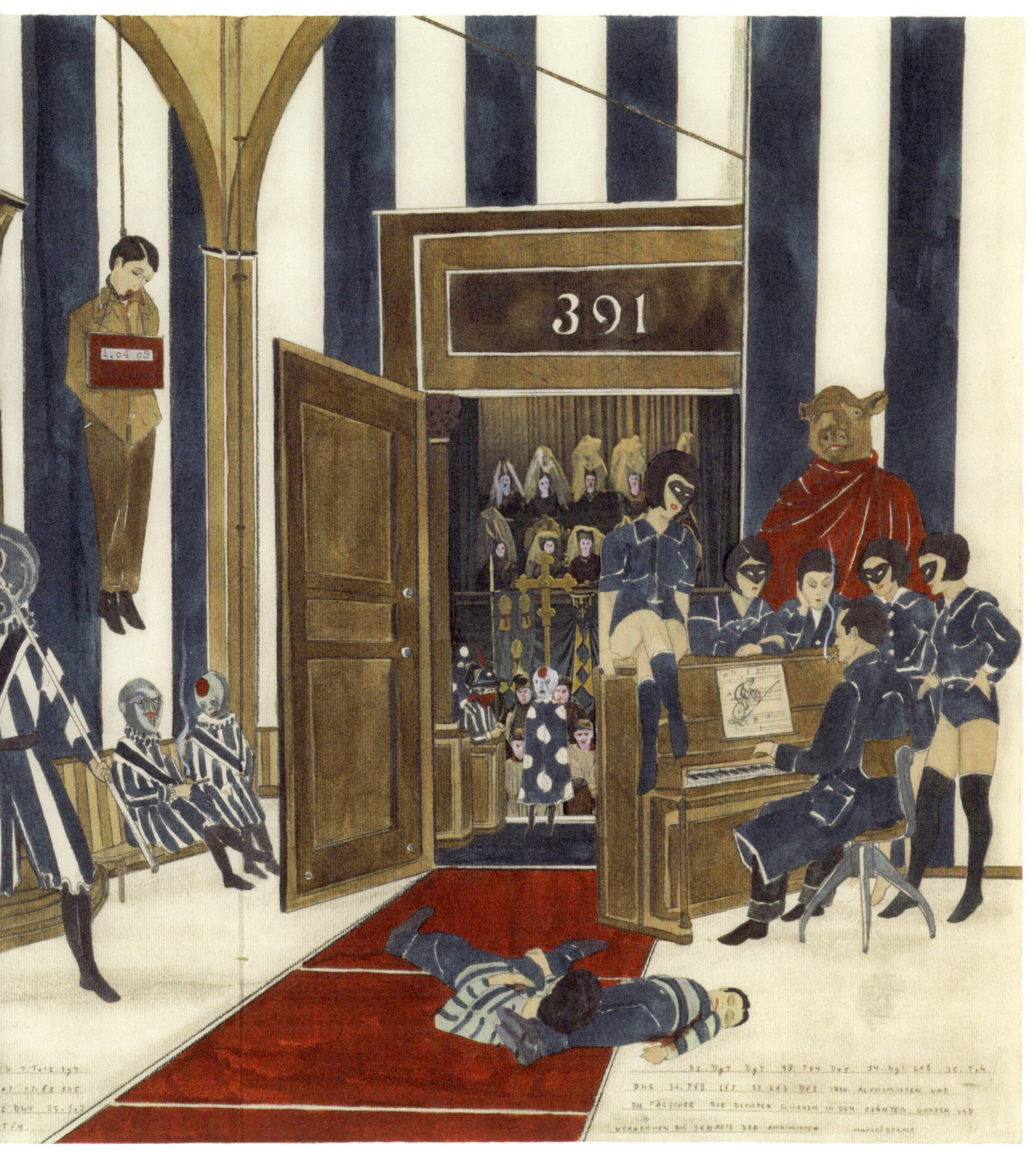
391
1.c4 c5
marcel DZAMA

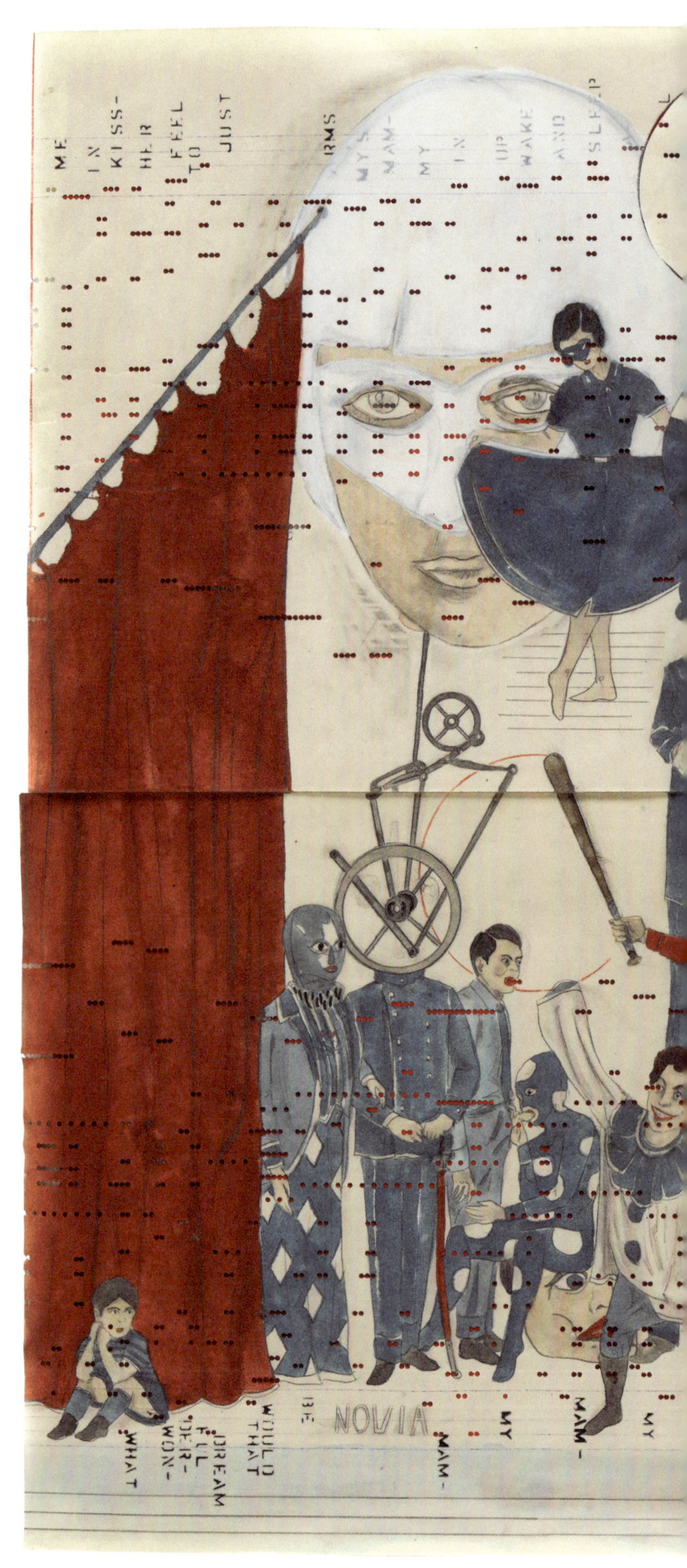

The queen's ghost vanish'd from our sight, 2013

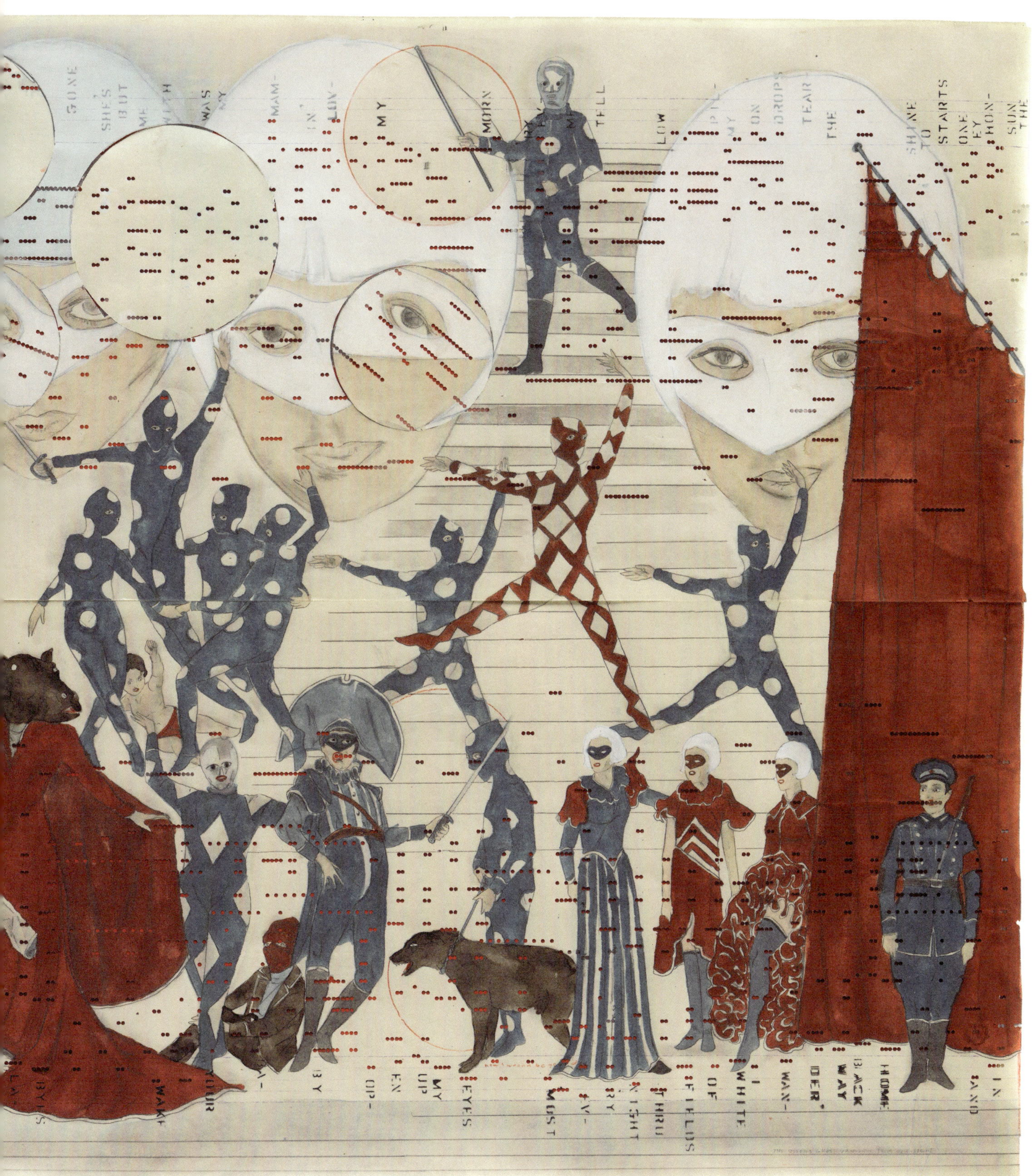

The factious feast, 2013

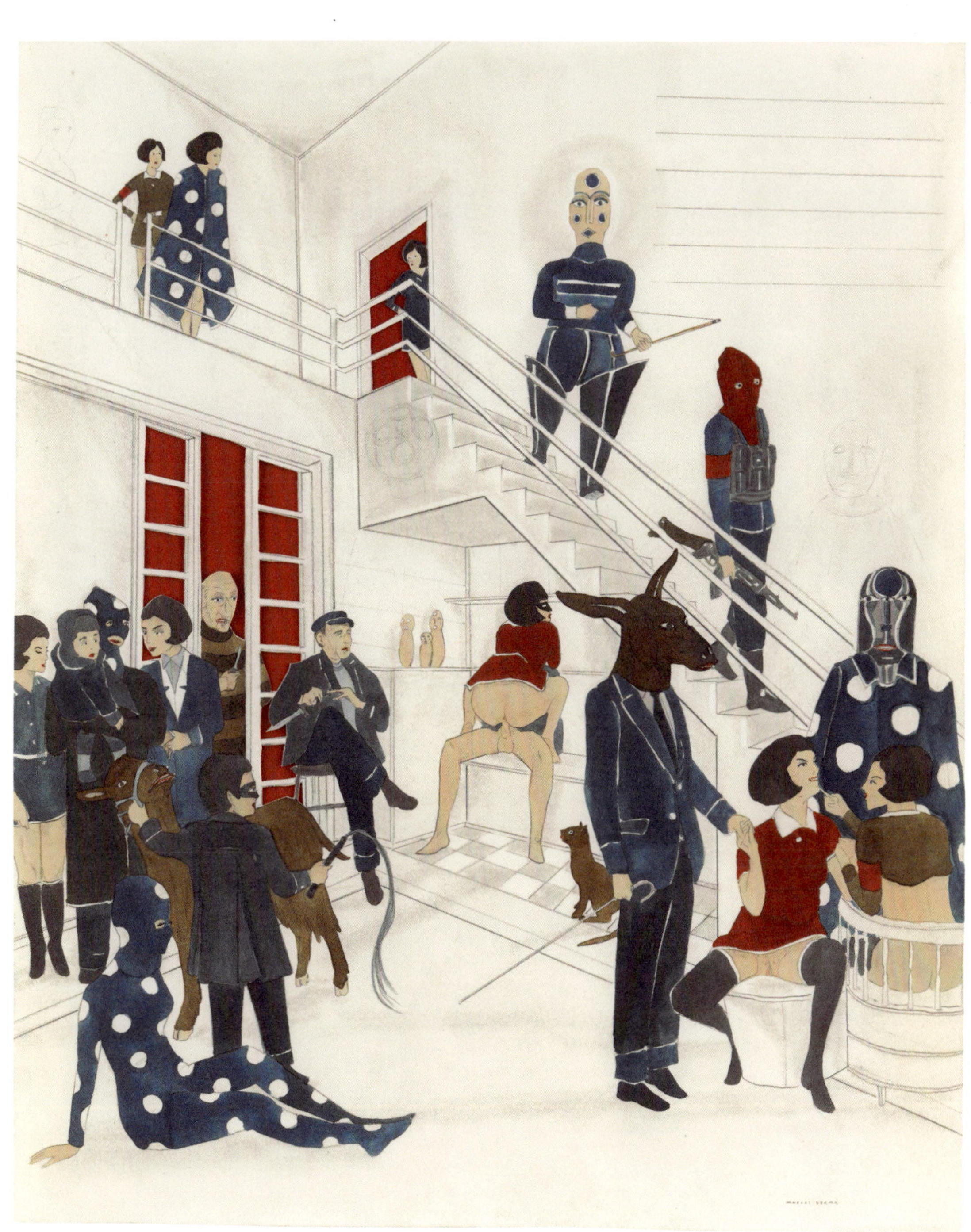

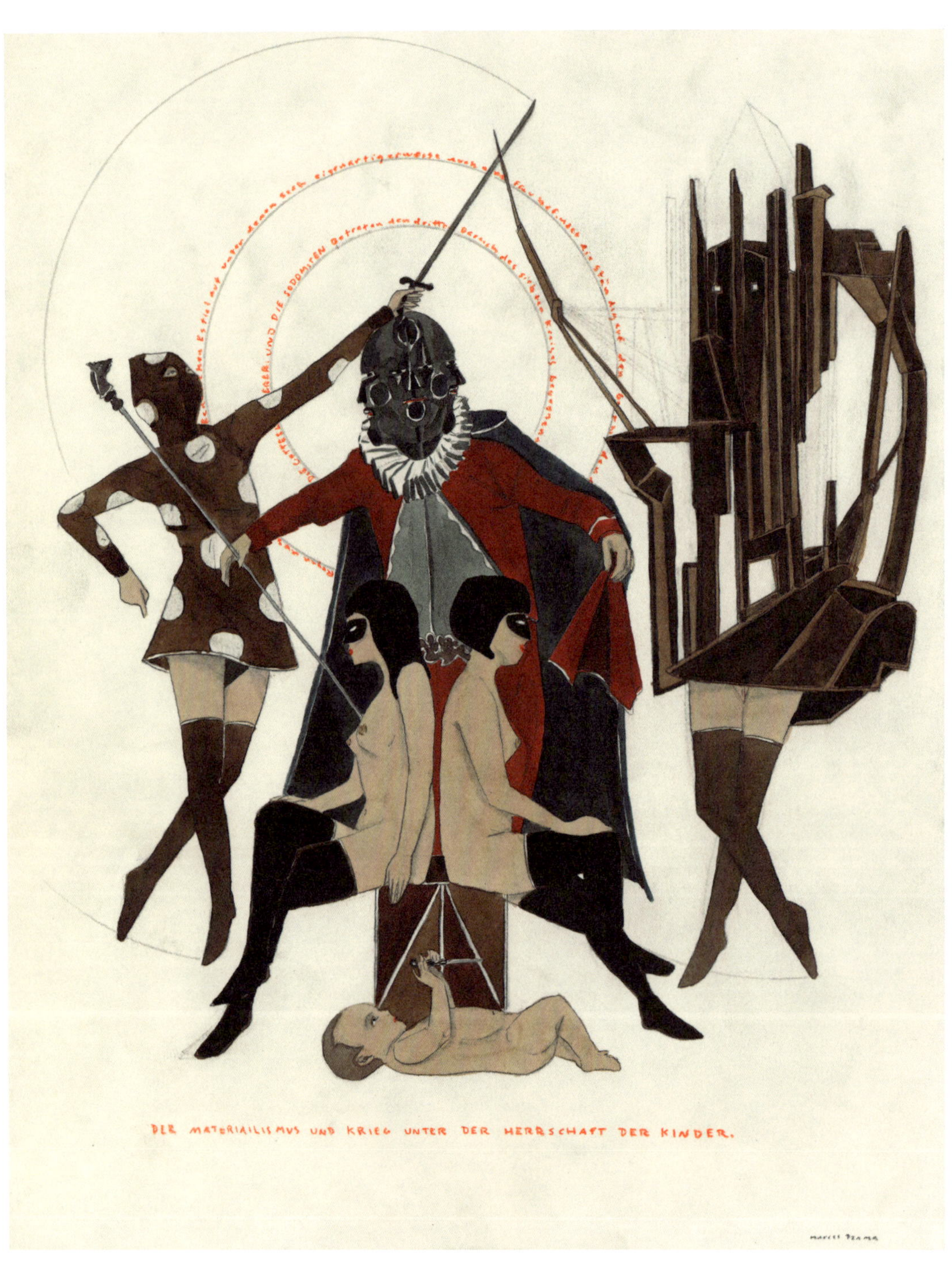

I fear I am attended by spies, 2012

58

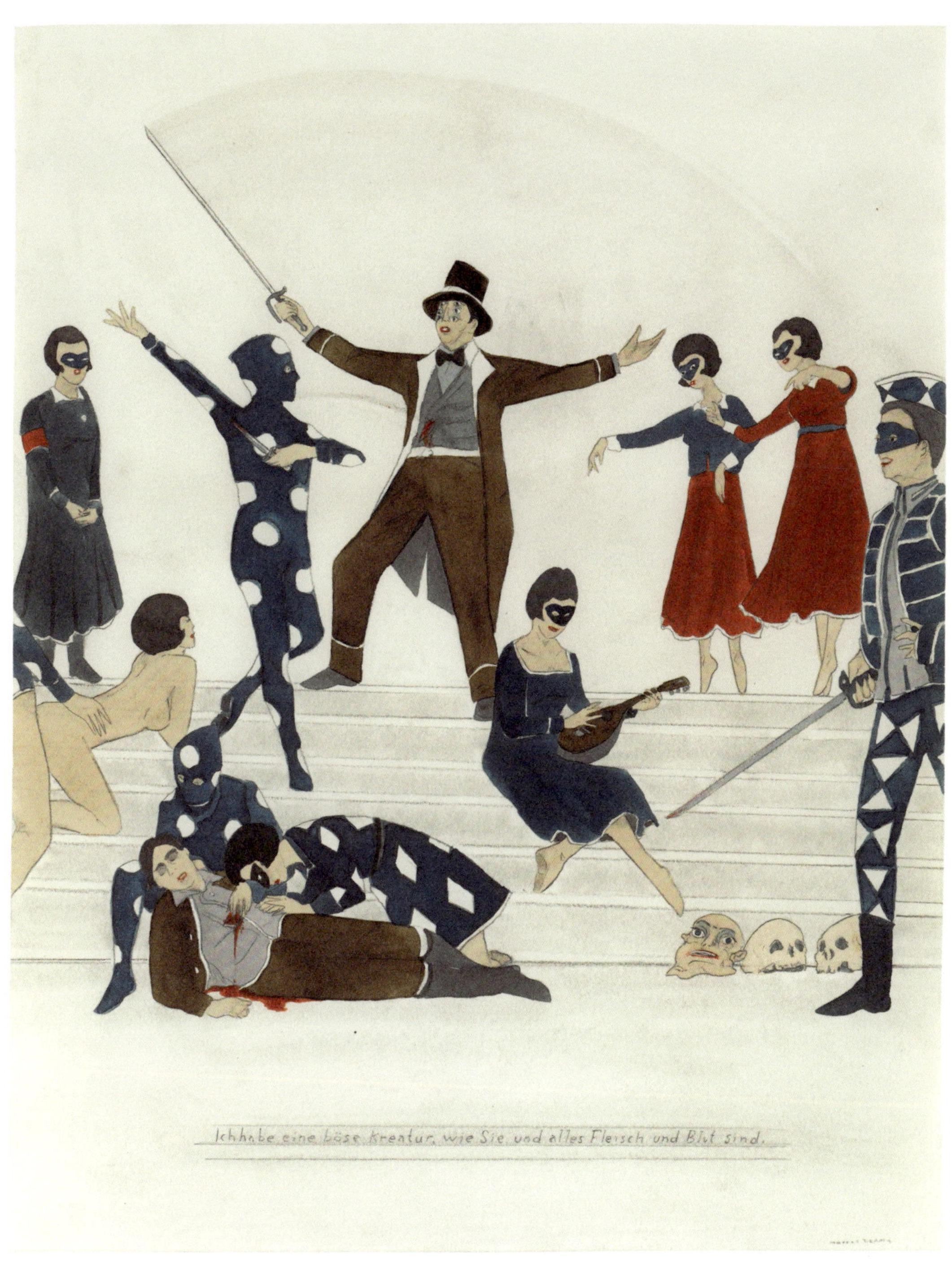

I have been a wicked creature, as you and all flesh and blood are, 2013

Picasso's cock fight, 2013

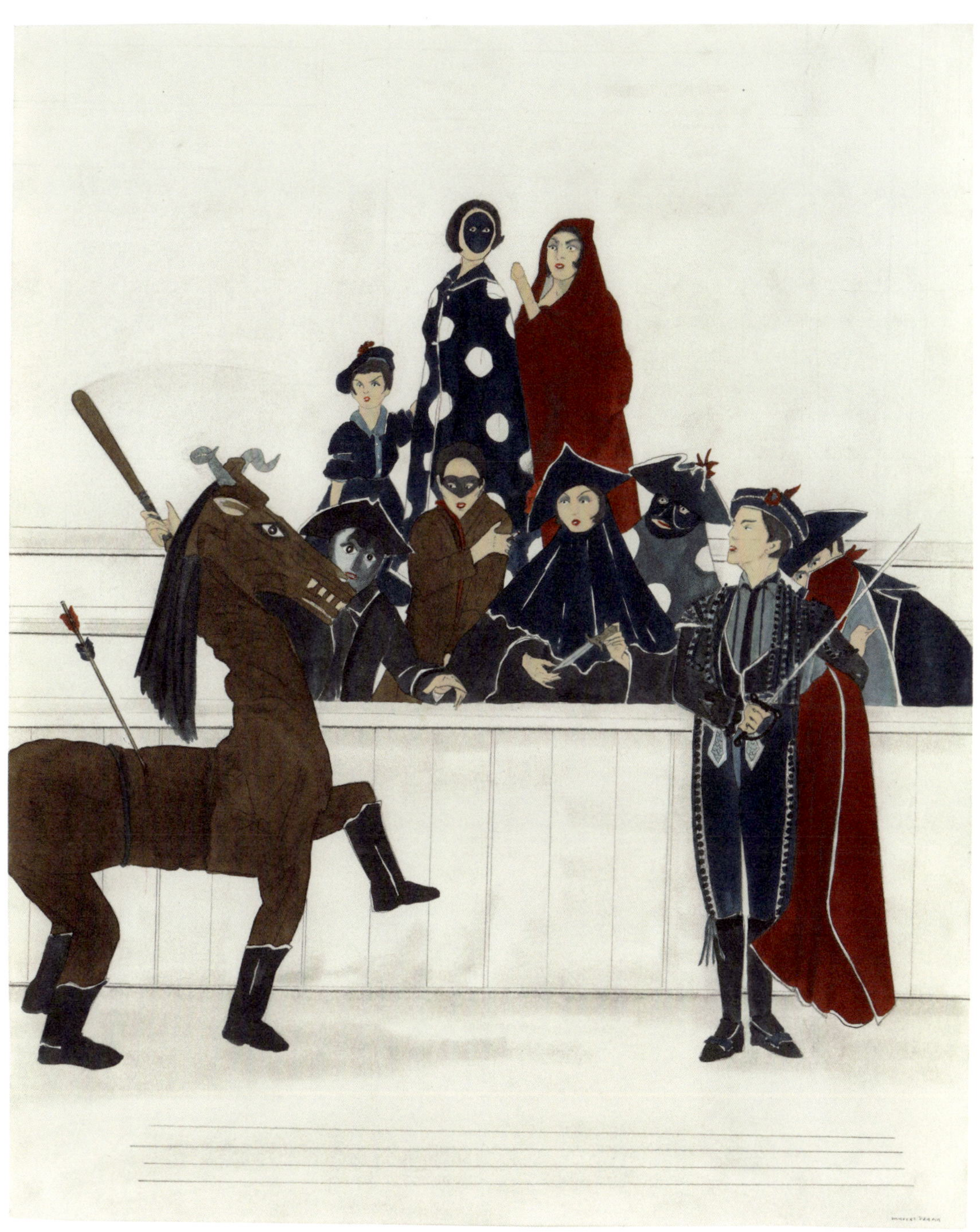

The Ned Kelly armour defense, 2013

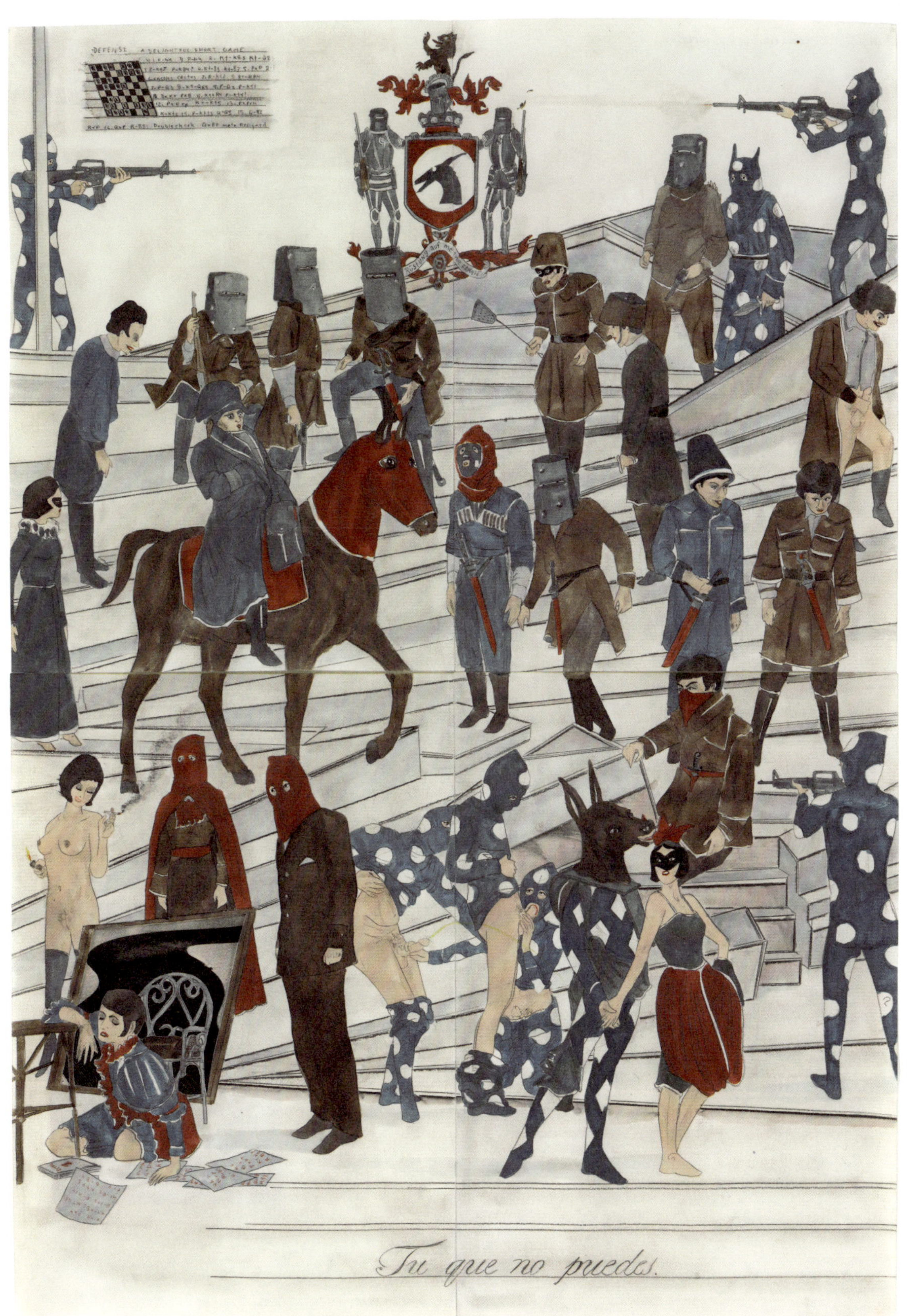

Tu que no puedes.

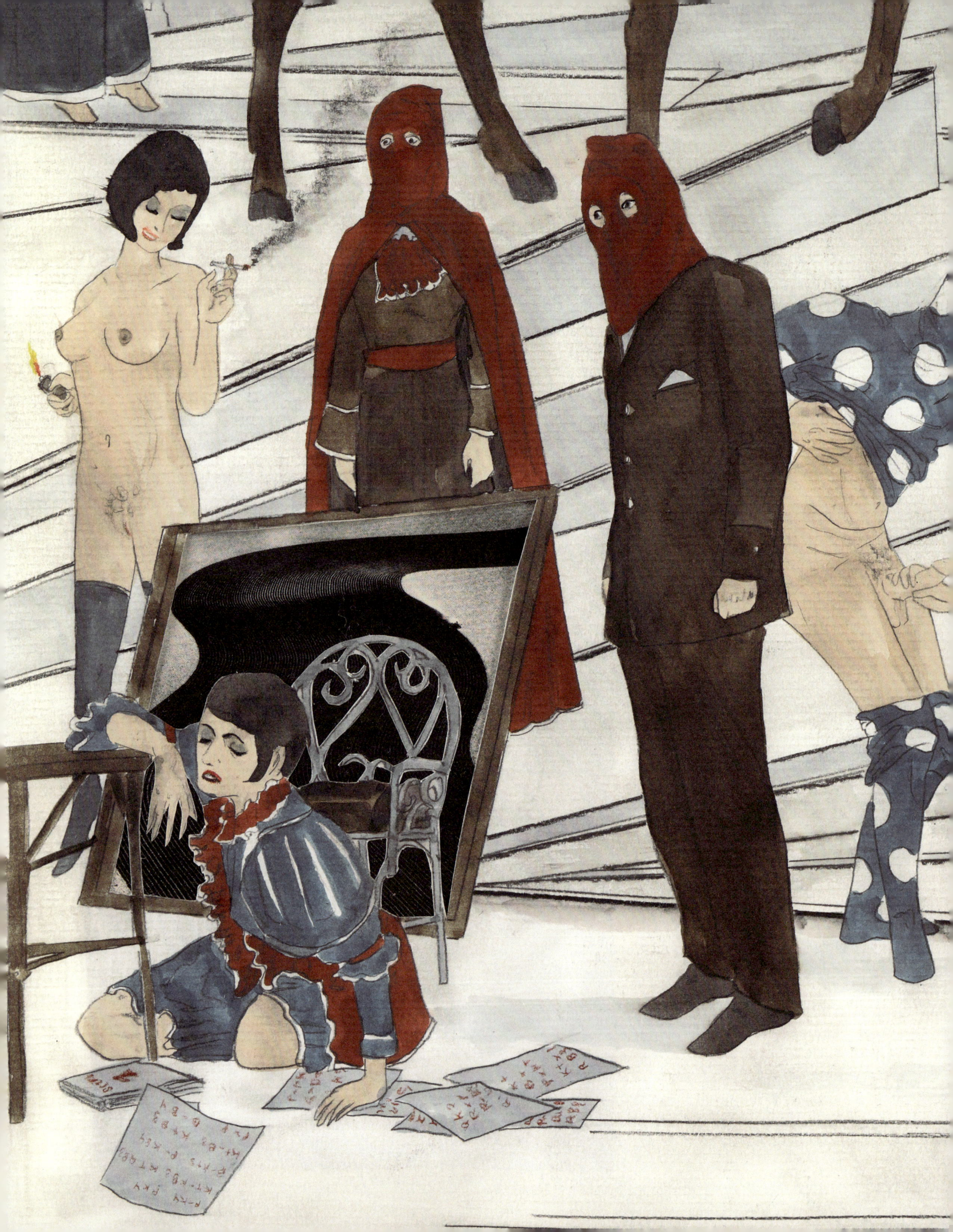

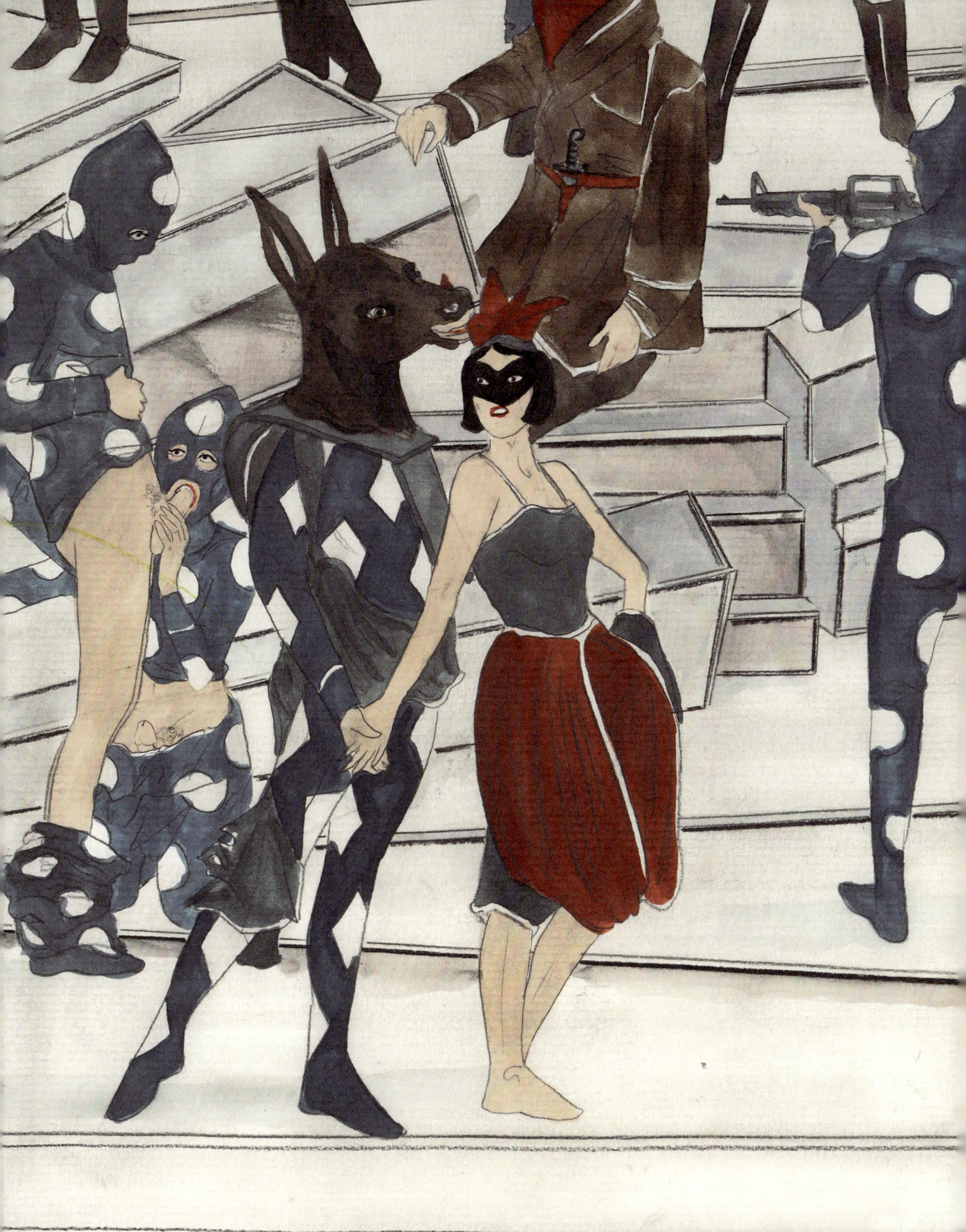

The photo shoot or (Blood has fingers), 2013

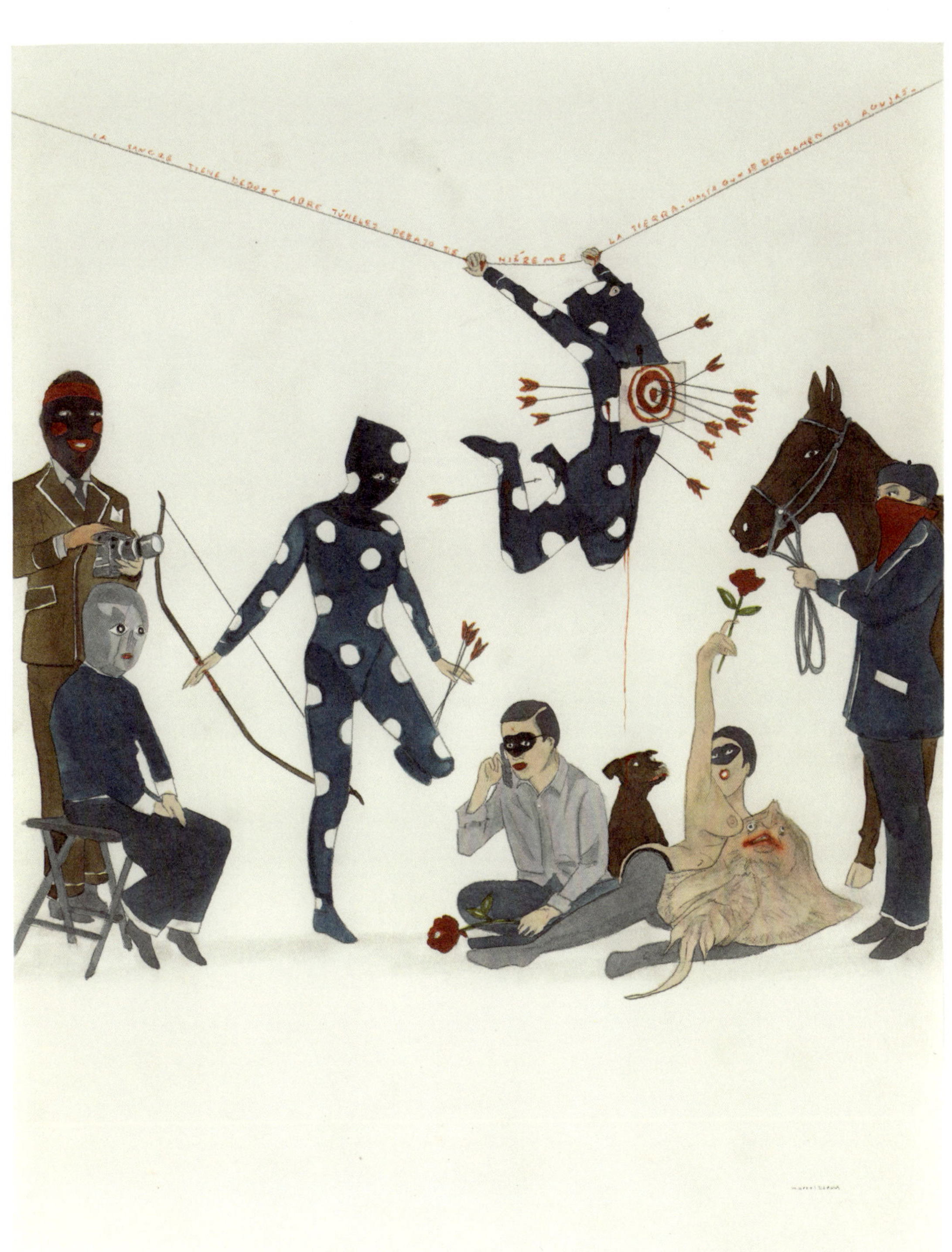

LA SANGRE TIENE DEDOS Y ABRE TÚNELES DEBAJO DE HIÉREME LA TIERRA. HASTA QUE SE DERRAMEN SUS AGUJAS.

The chessmen, 2010

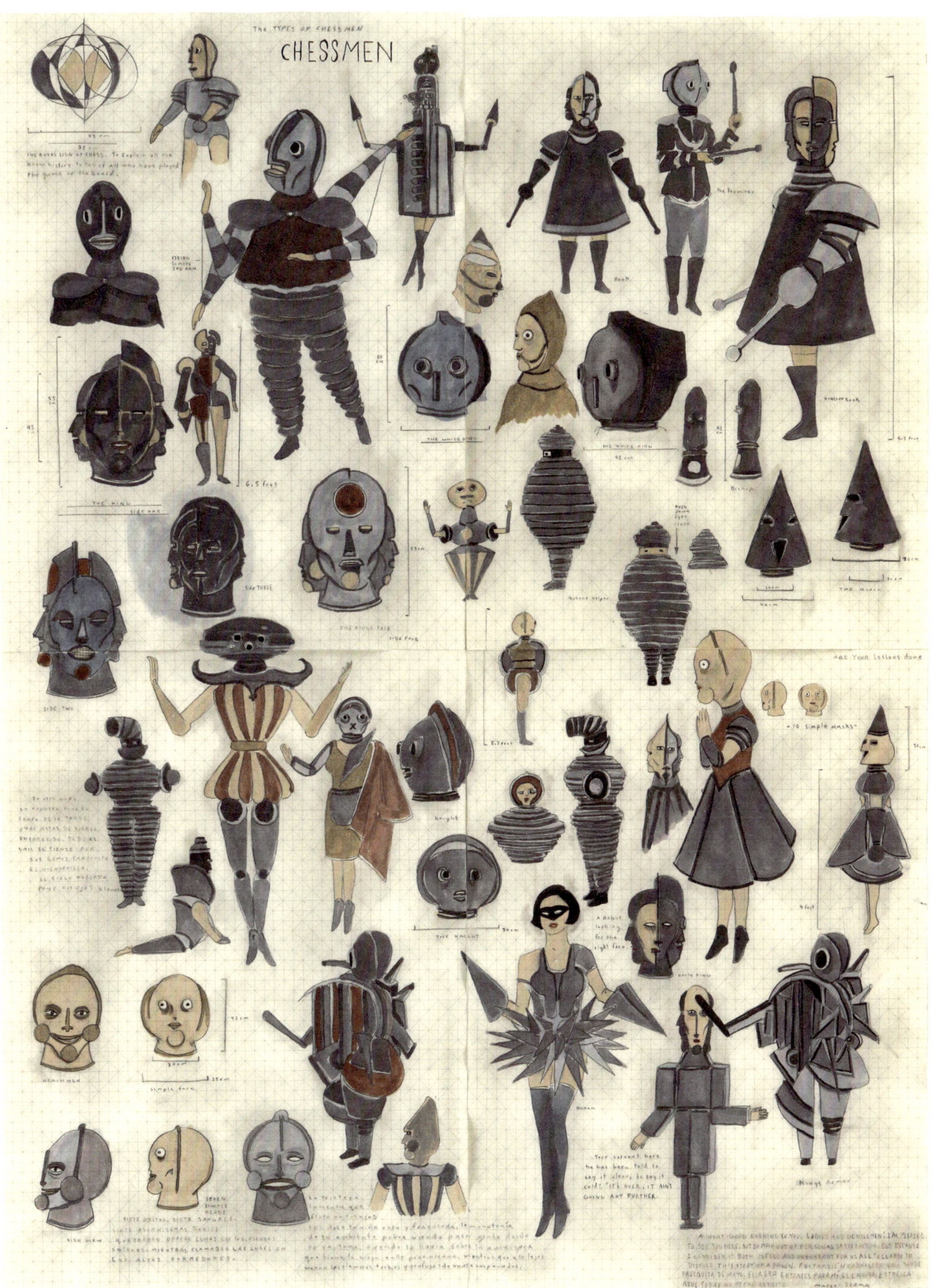
THE TYPES OF CHESSMEN
CHESSMEN
CHESSMEN
ARE YOUR LESSONS DONE
"10 SIMPLE MAIDS"
THE WHITE KING
THE KNIGHT
THE QUEEN

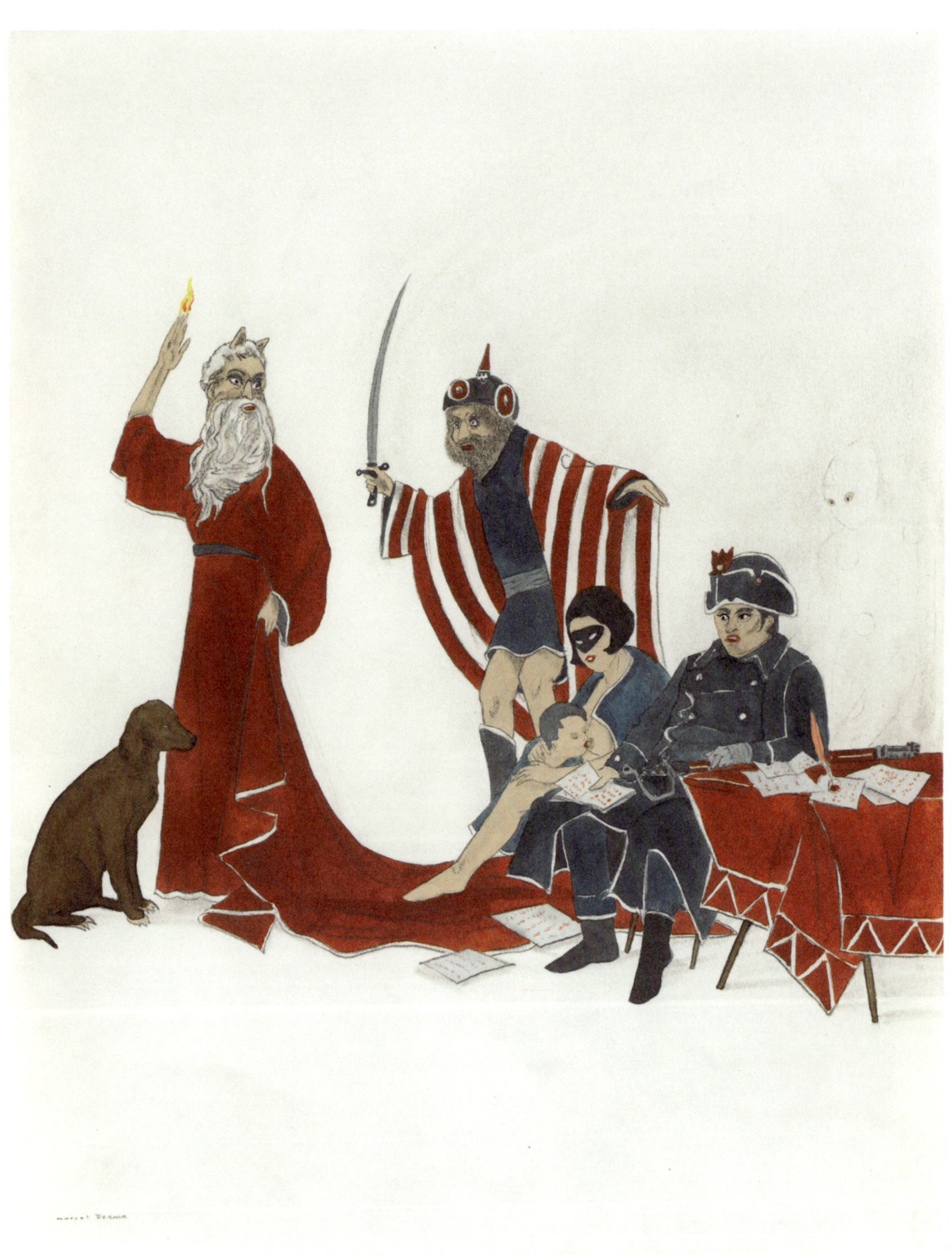

Who will lead forth, 2013

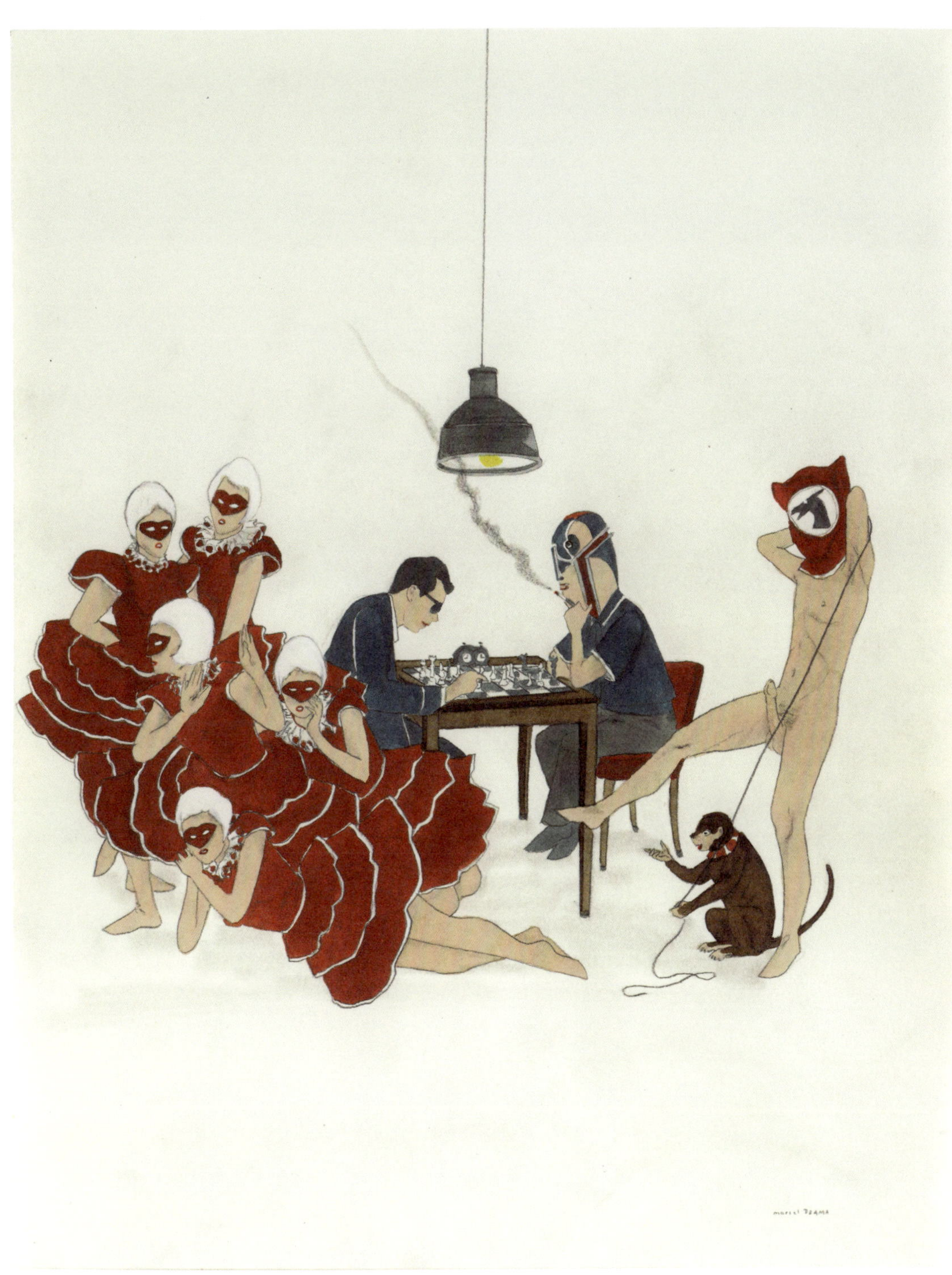

Let me be cruel, not unnatural, 2013

Sculptures

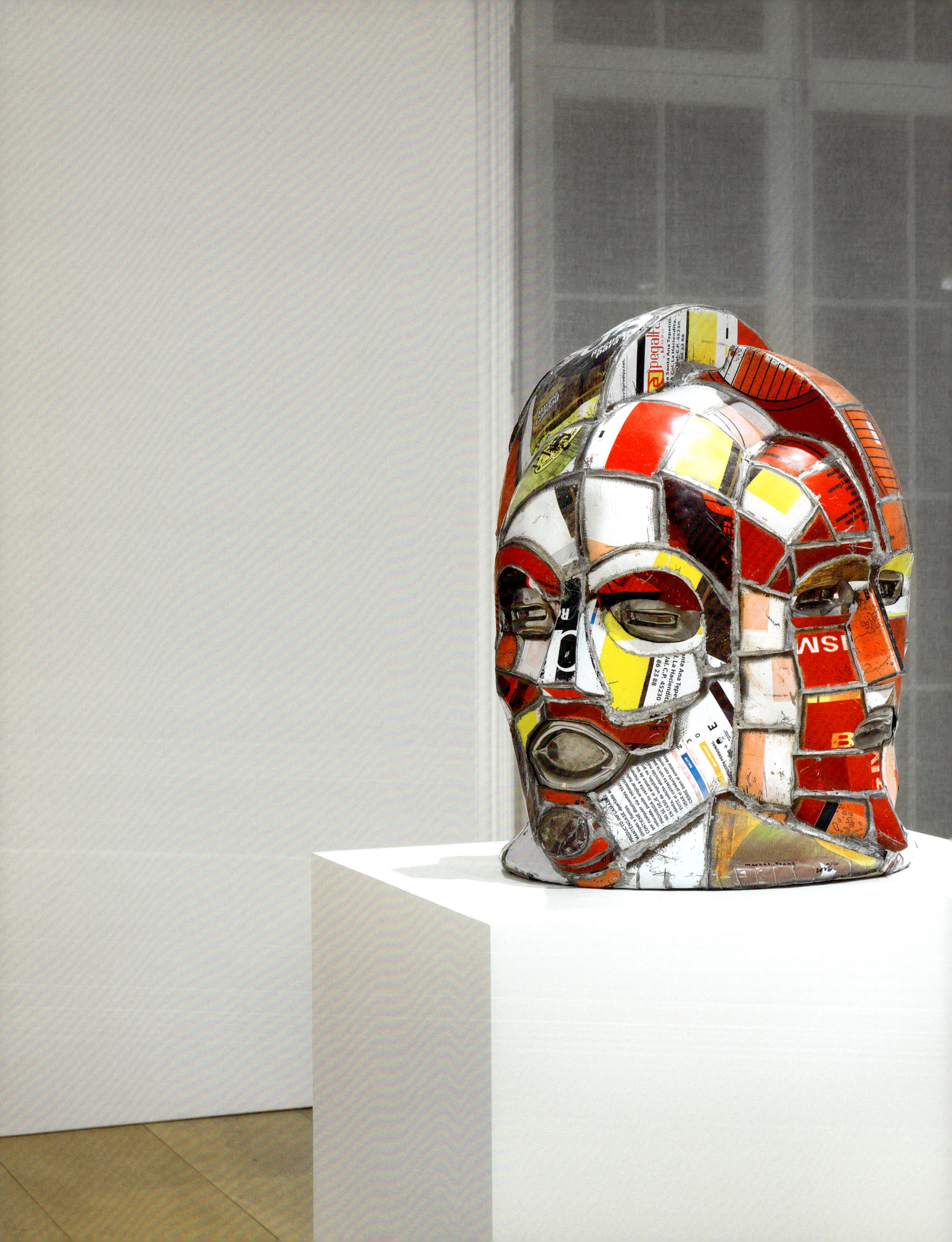

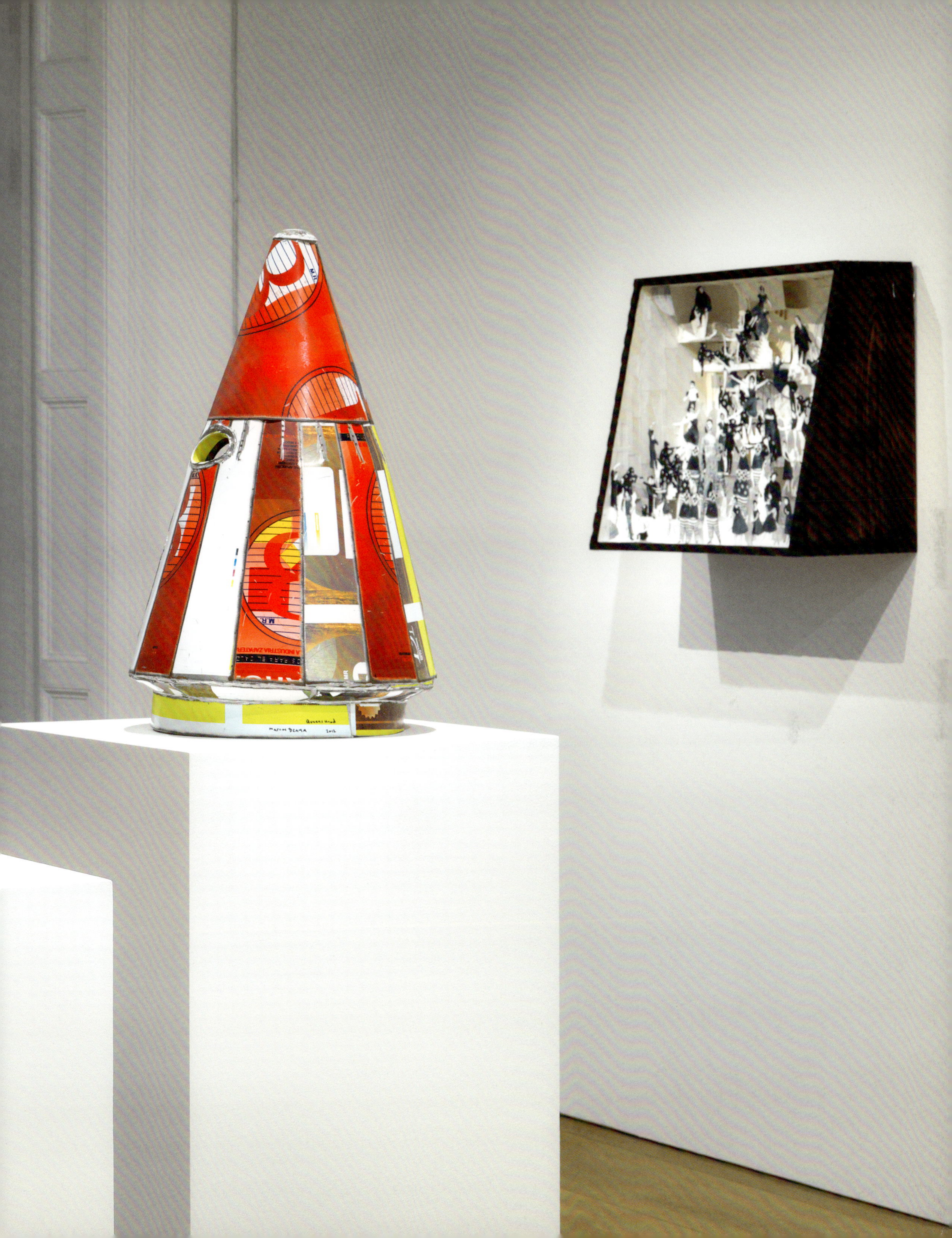

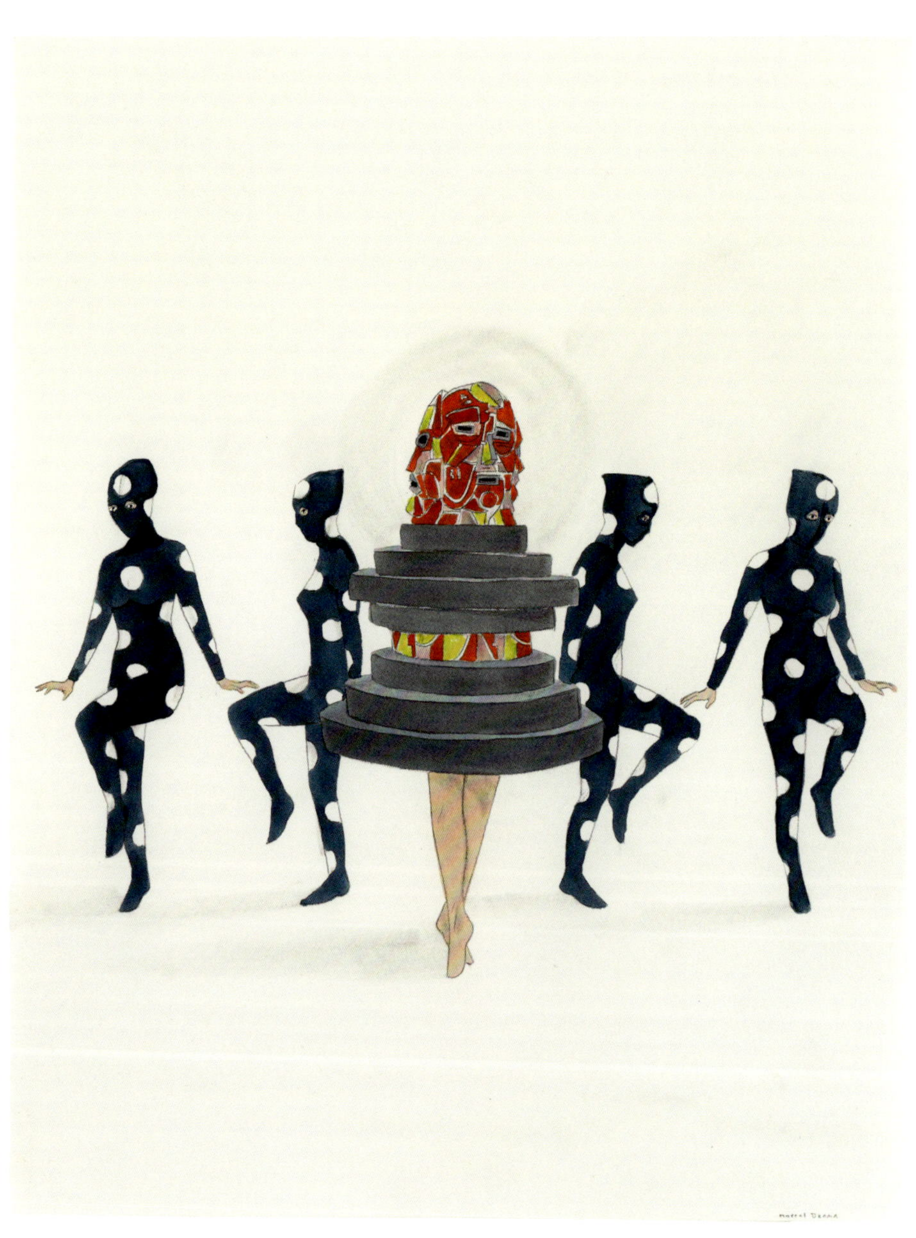

The king's Janus times two, 2012

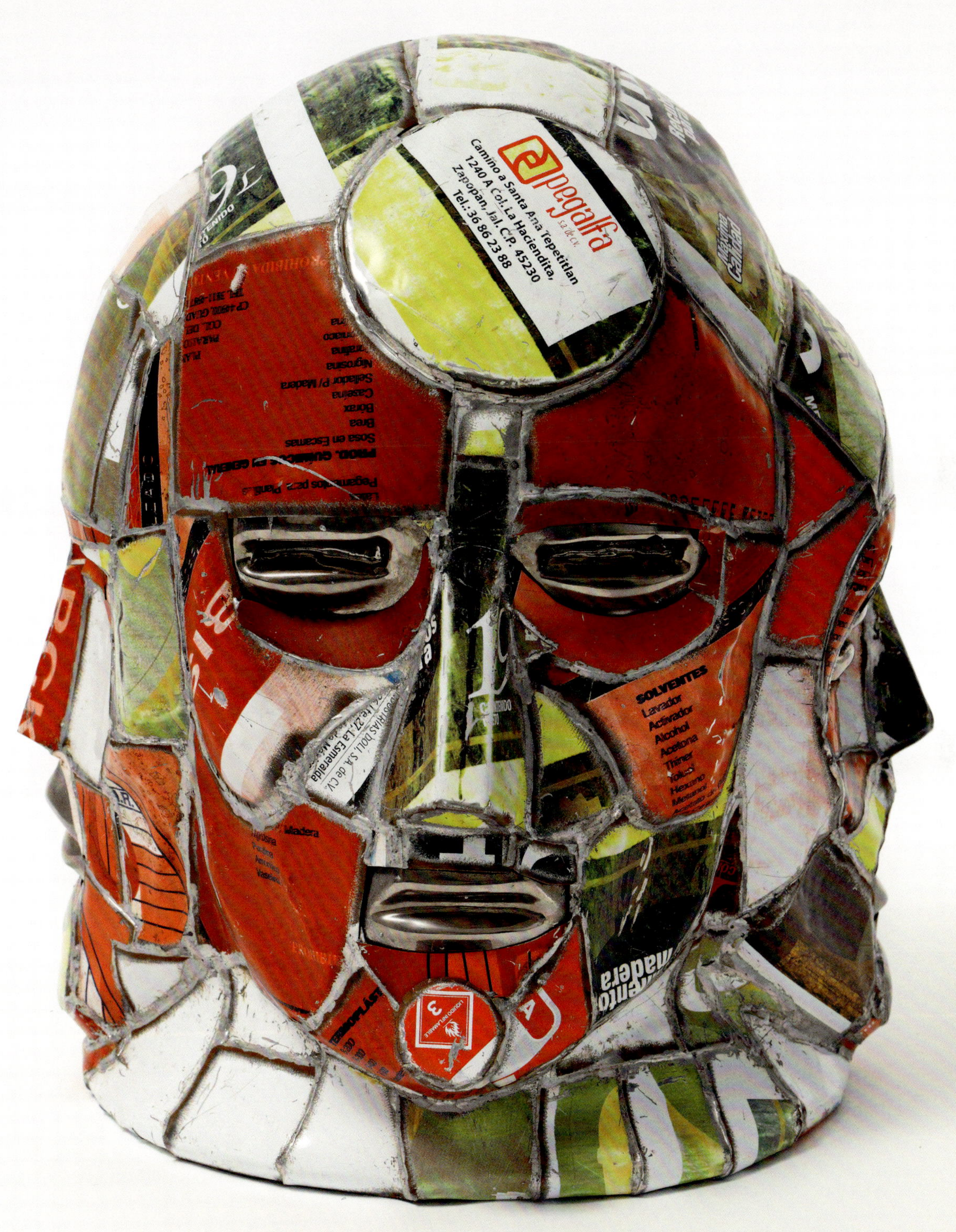

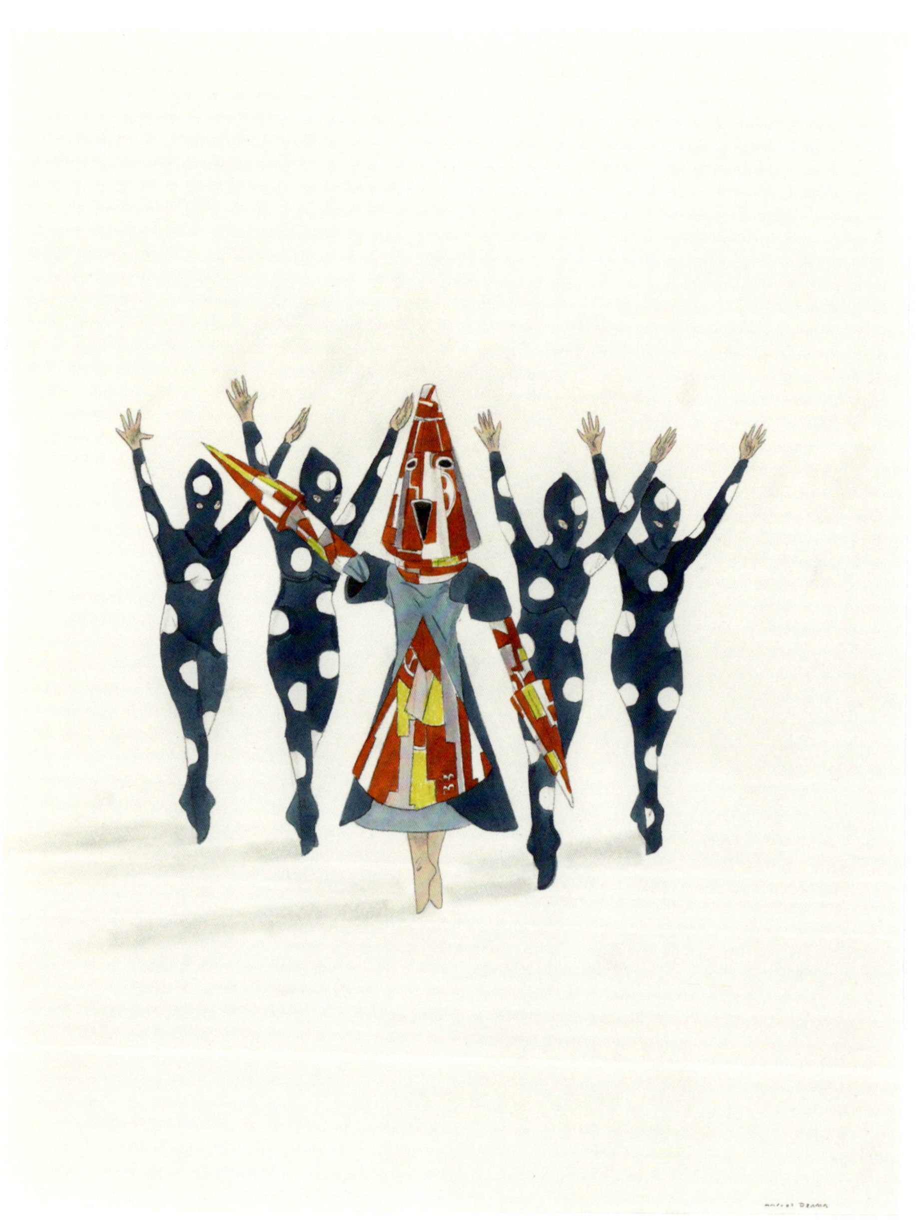

The queen's head, 2012

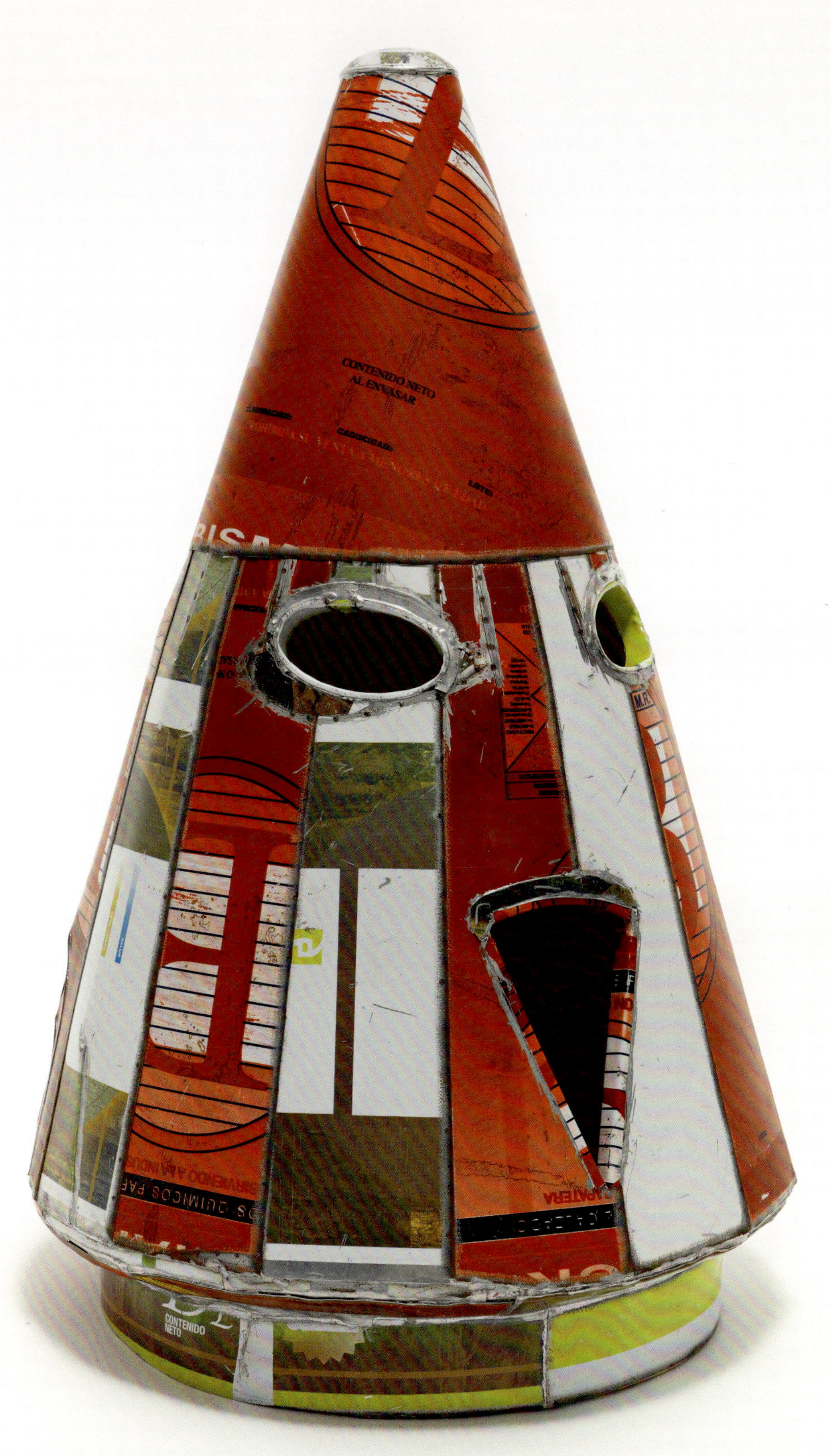
CONTENIDO NETO
AL ENVASAR
CONTENIDO
NETO

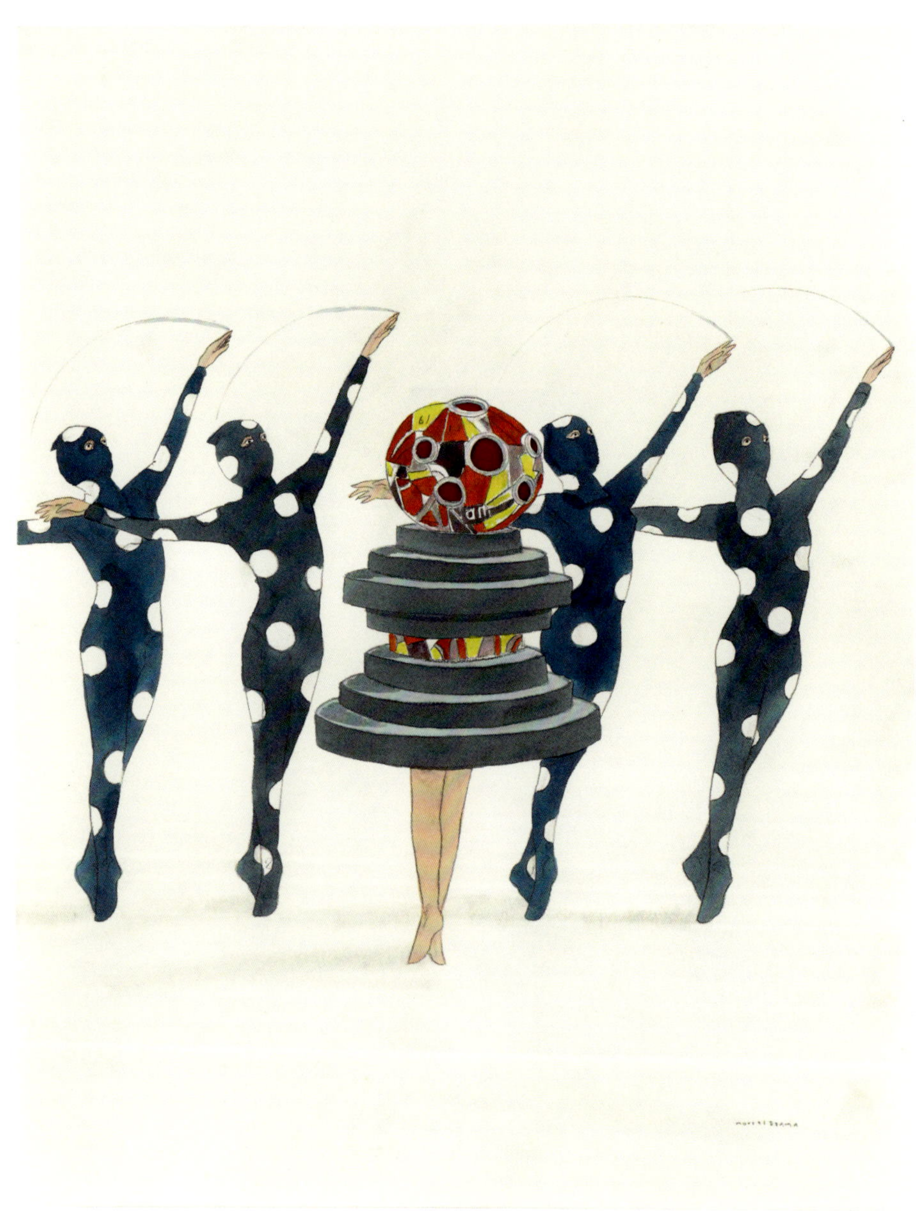

The rook's head, 2012

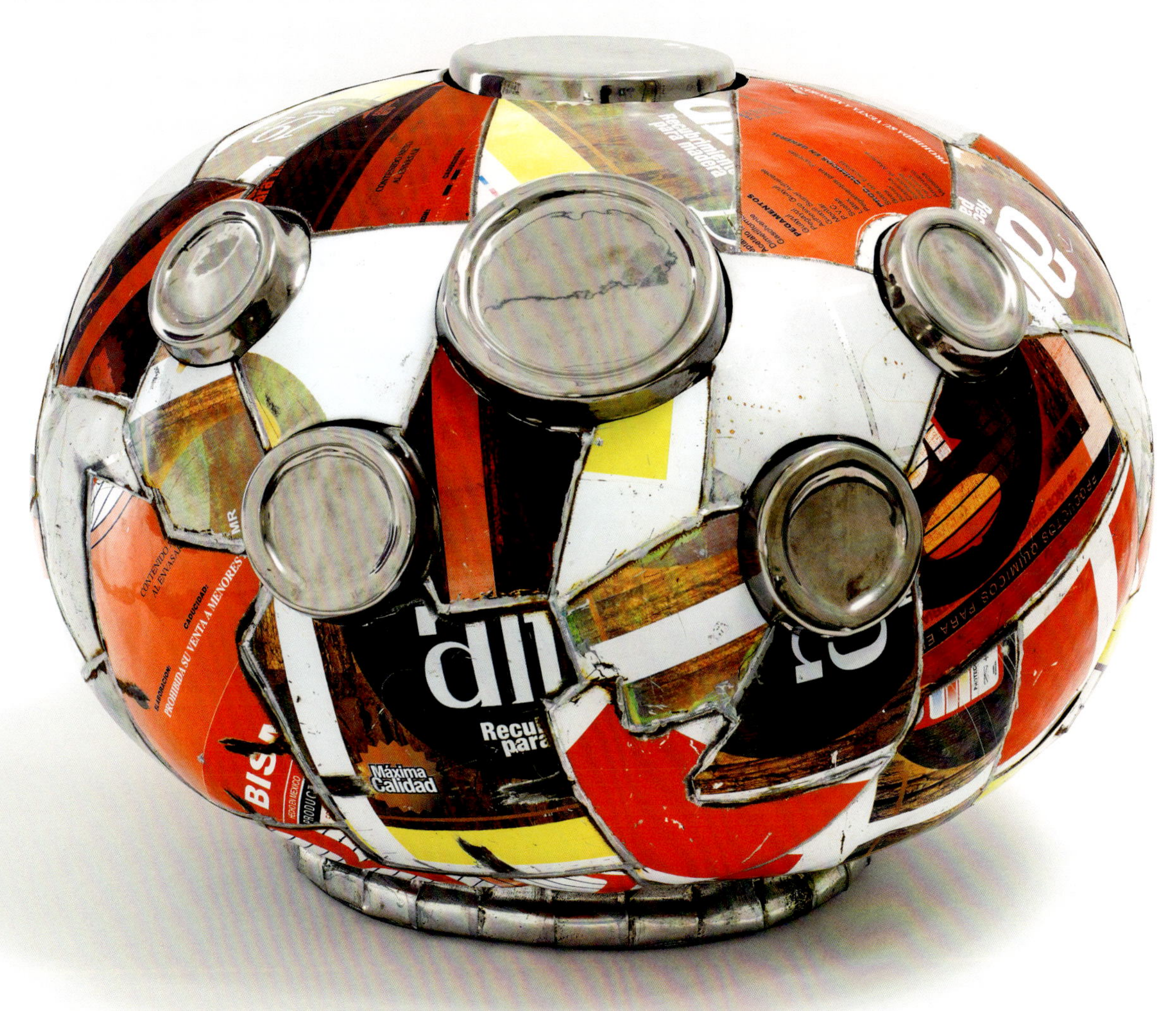

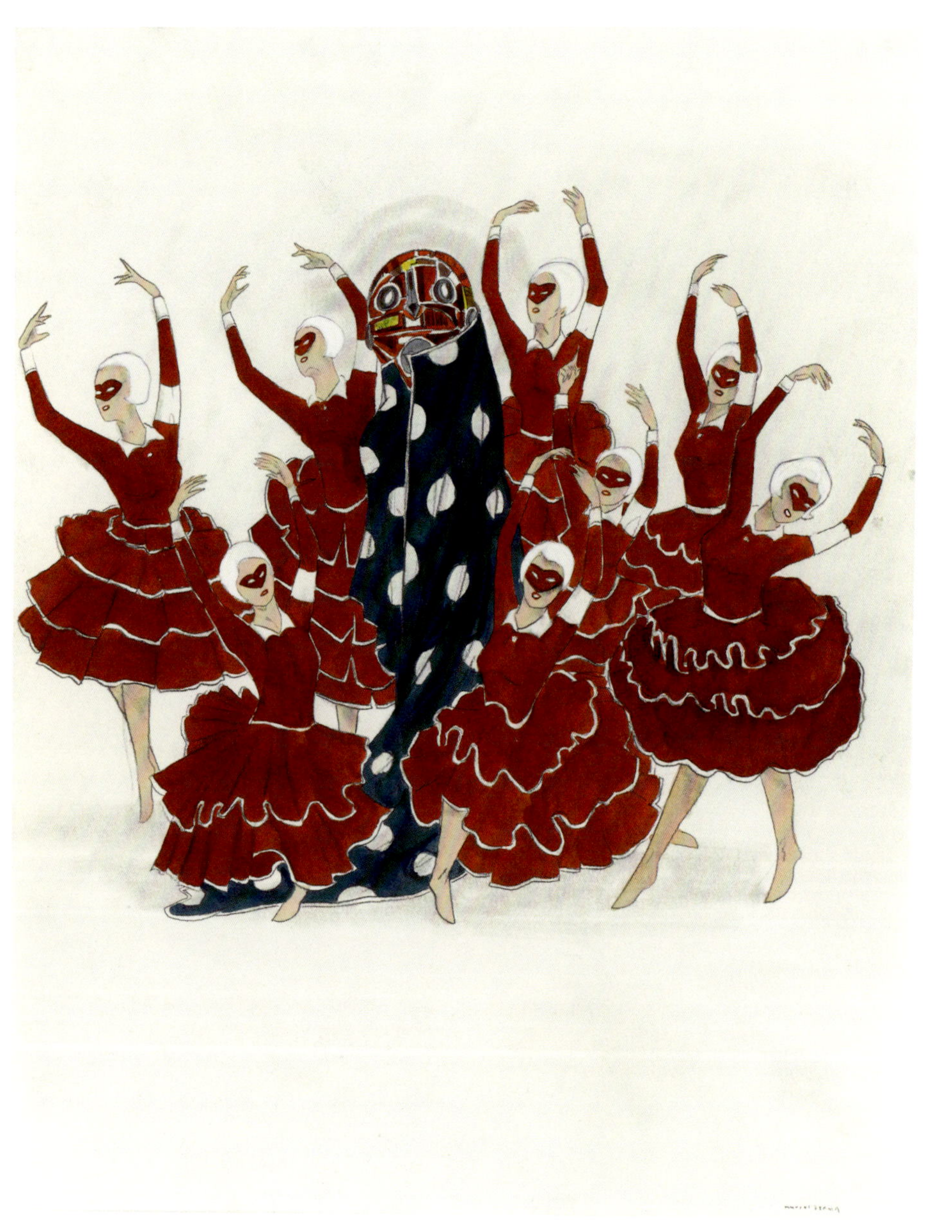

The jester's head, 2012

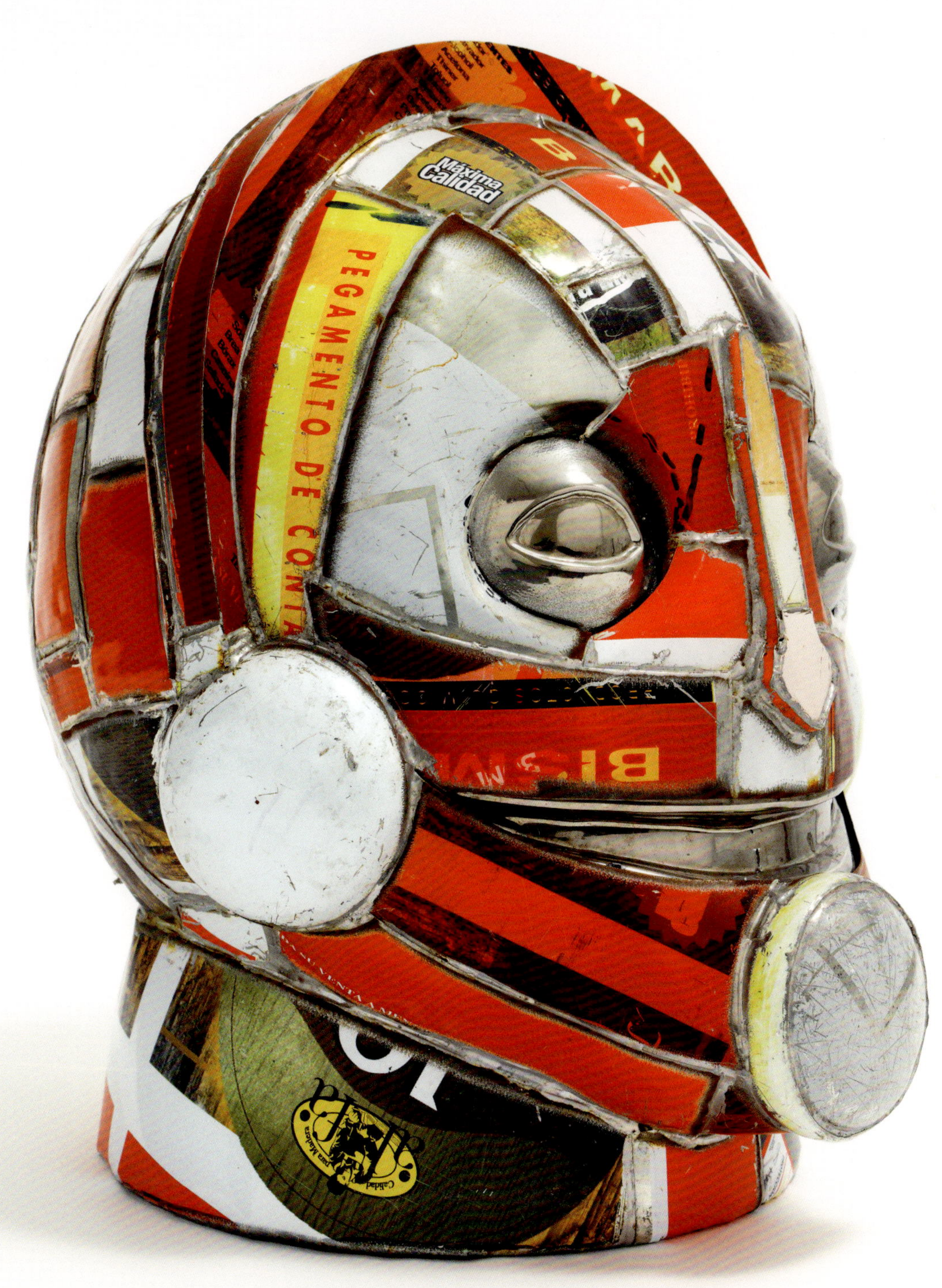

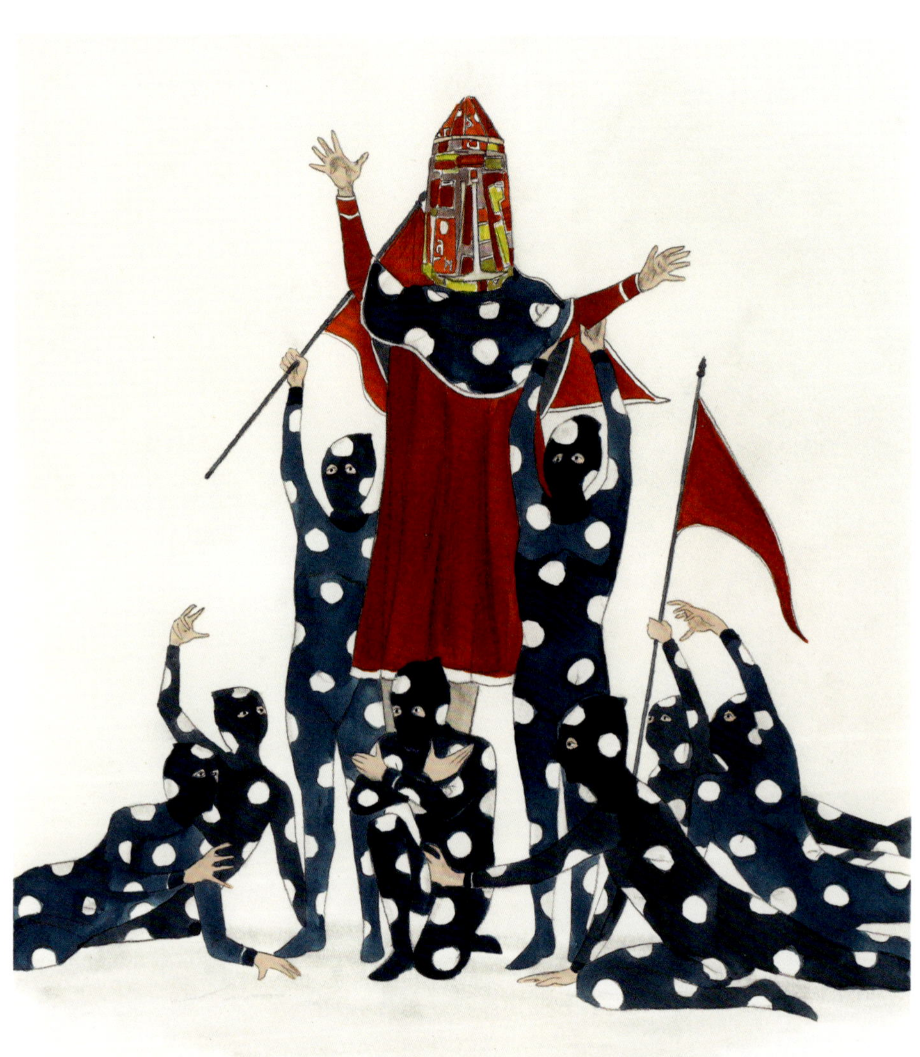

The bishop's head, 2012

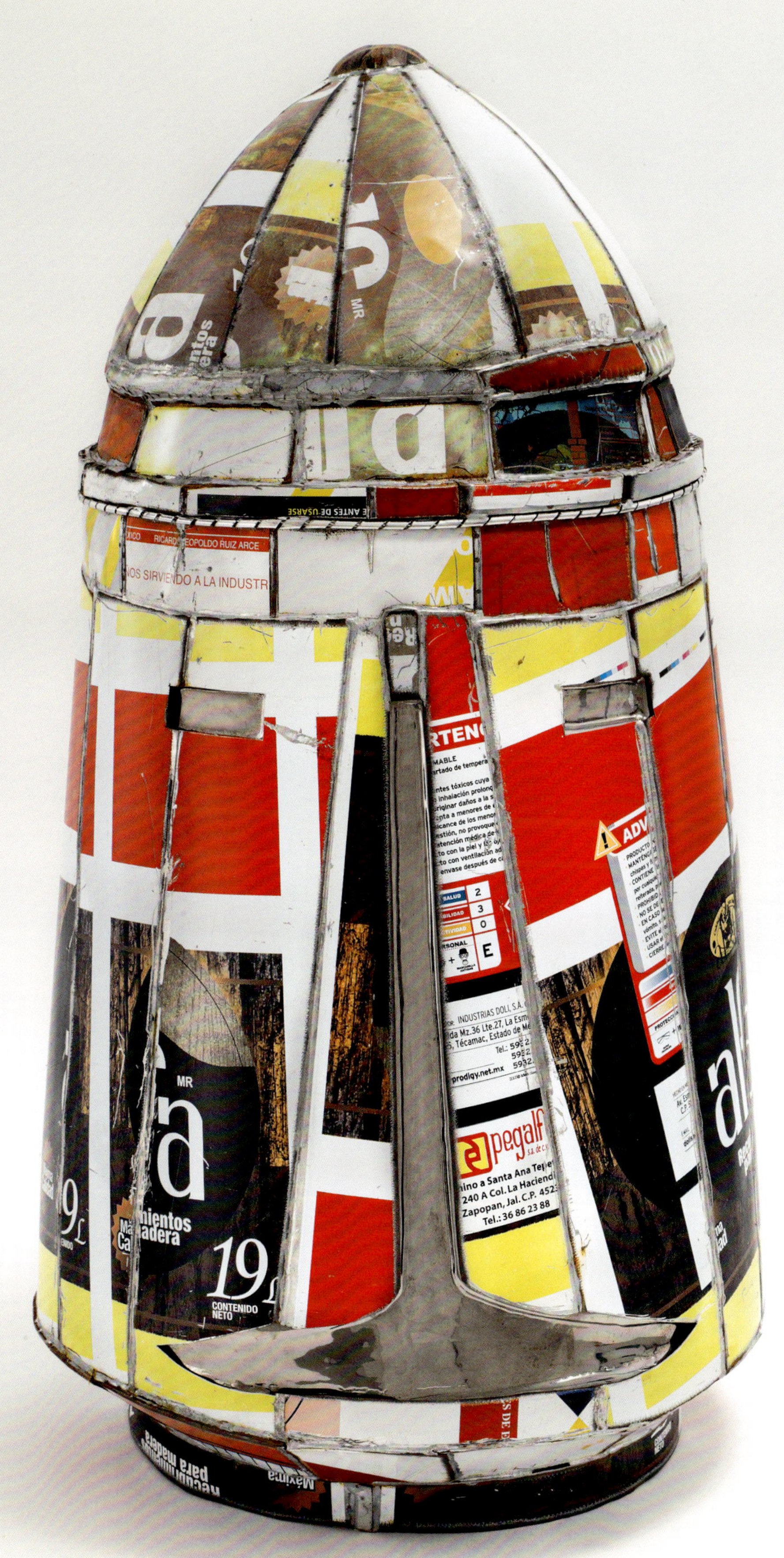

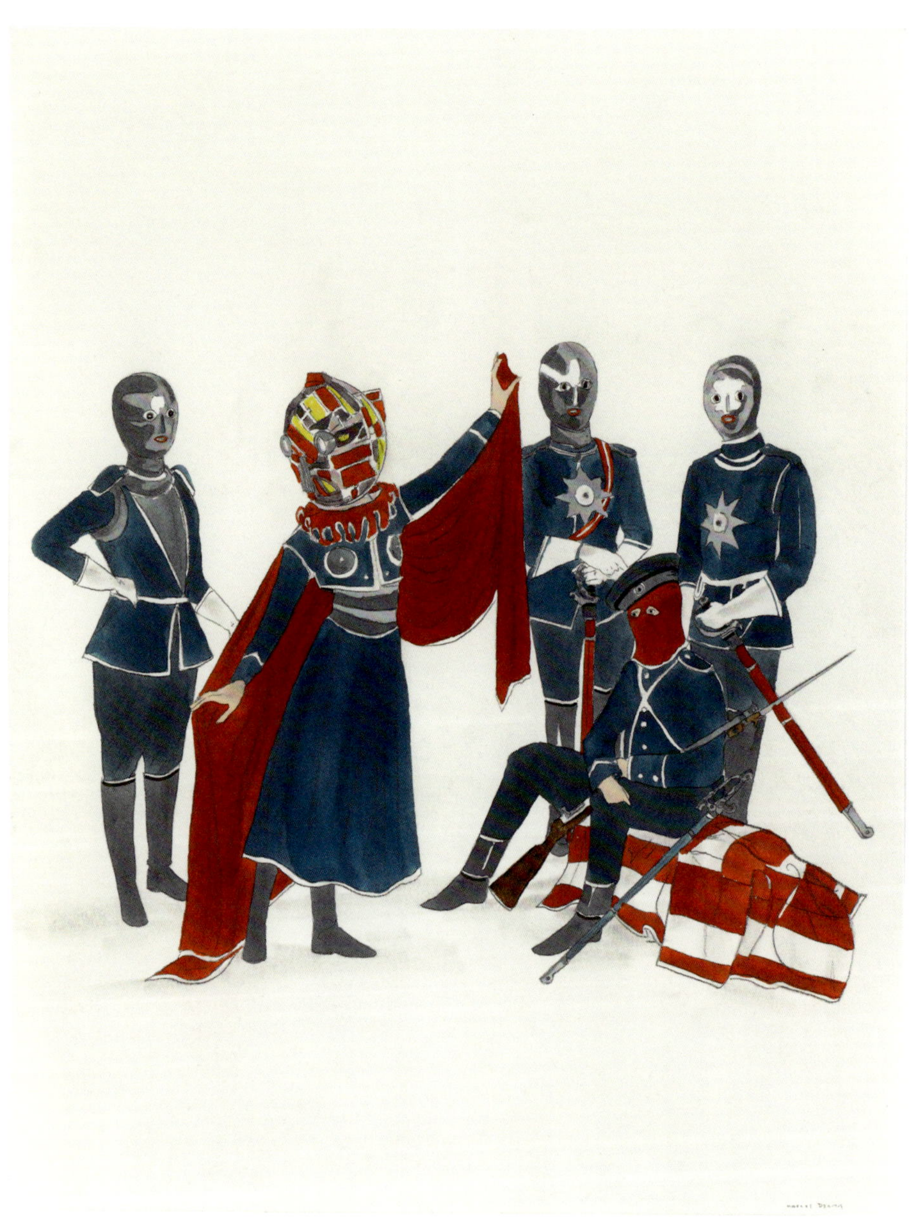

The king's head, 2012

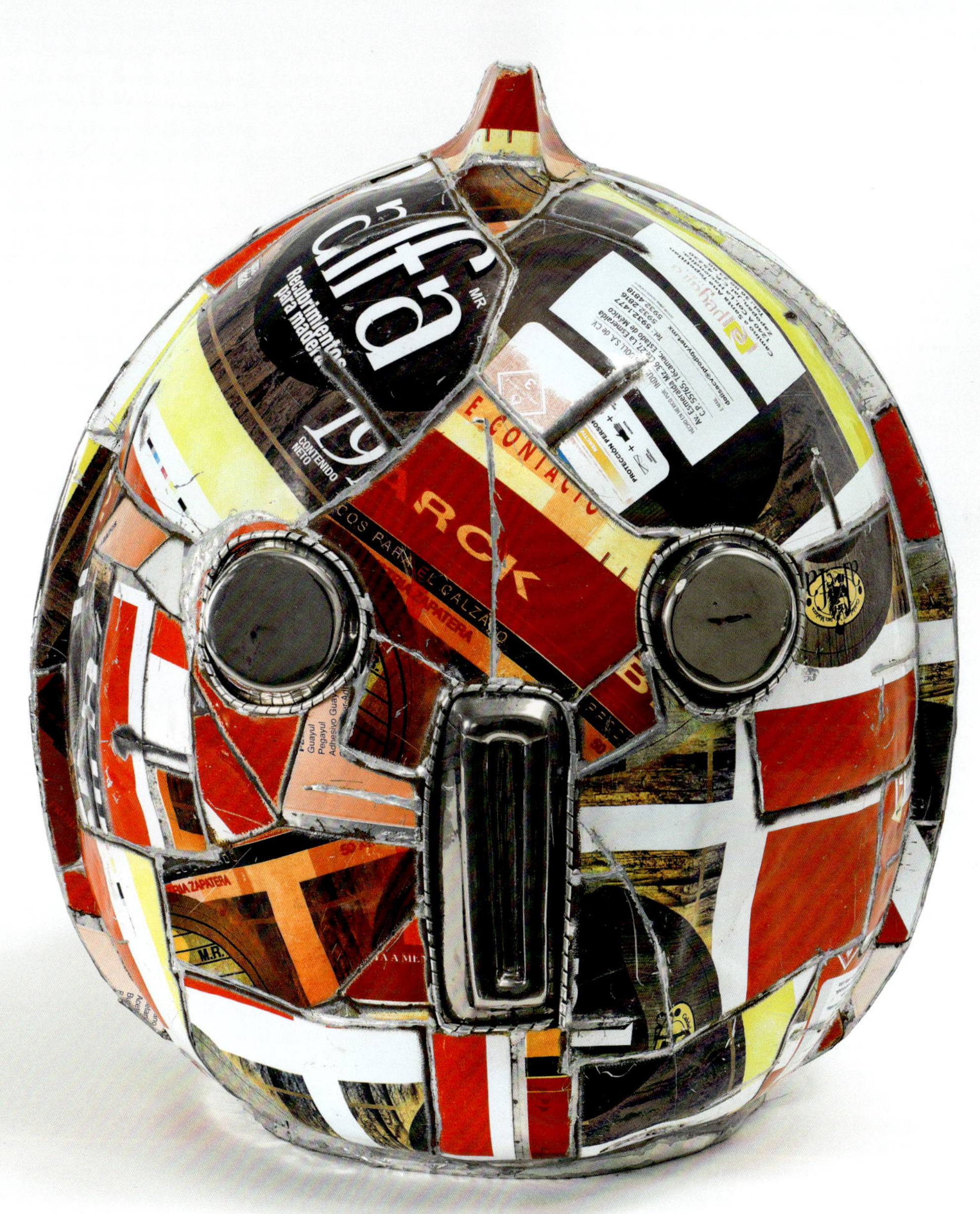

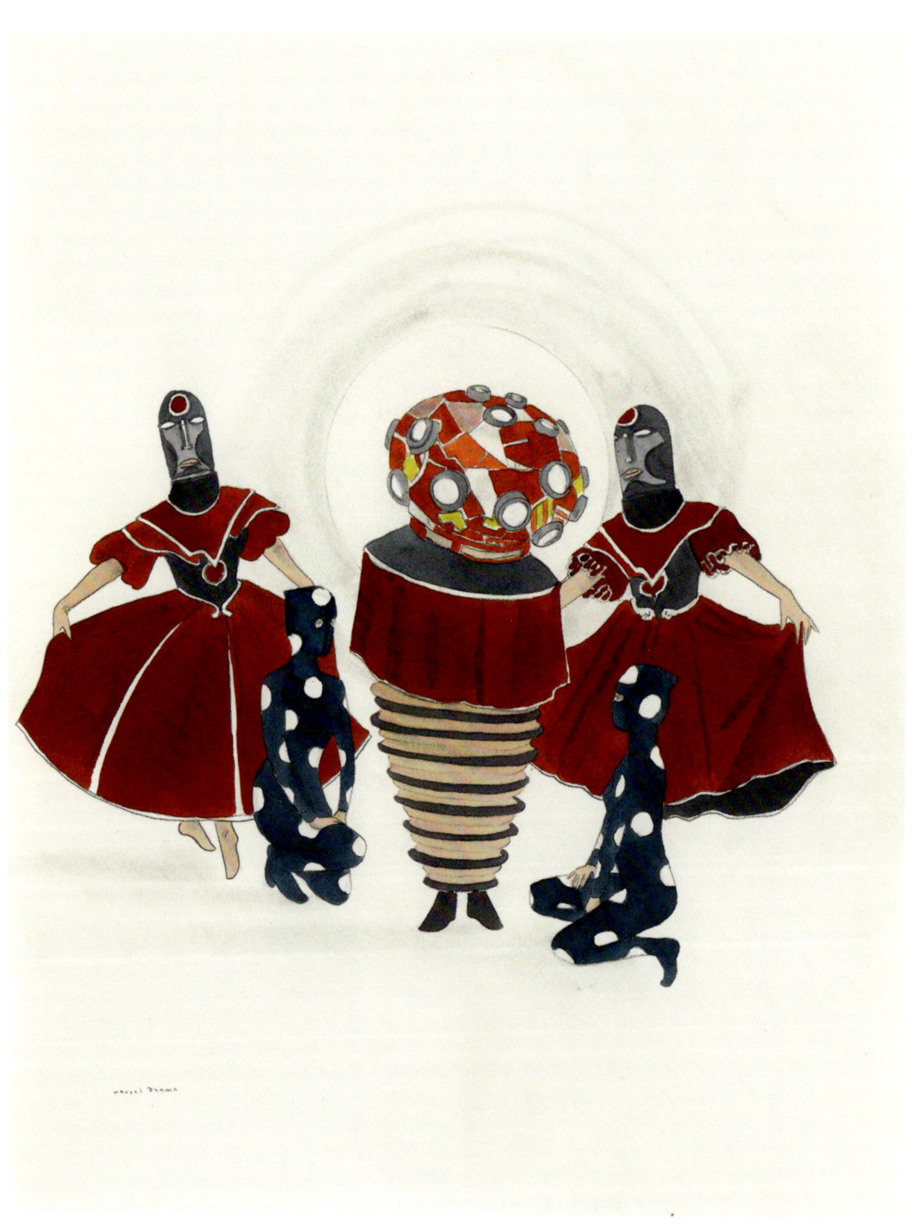

The rook's head, 2012

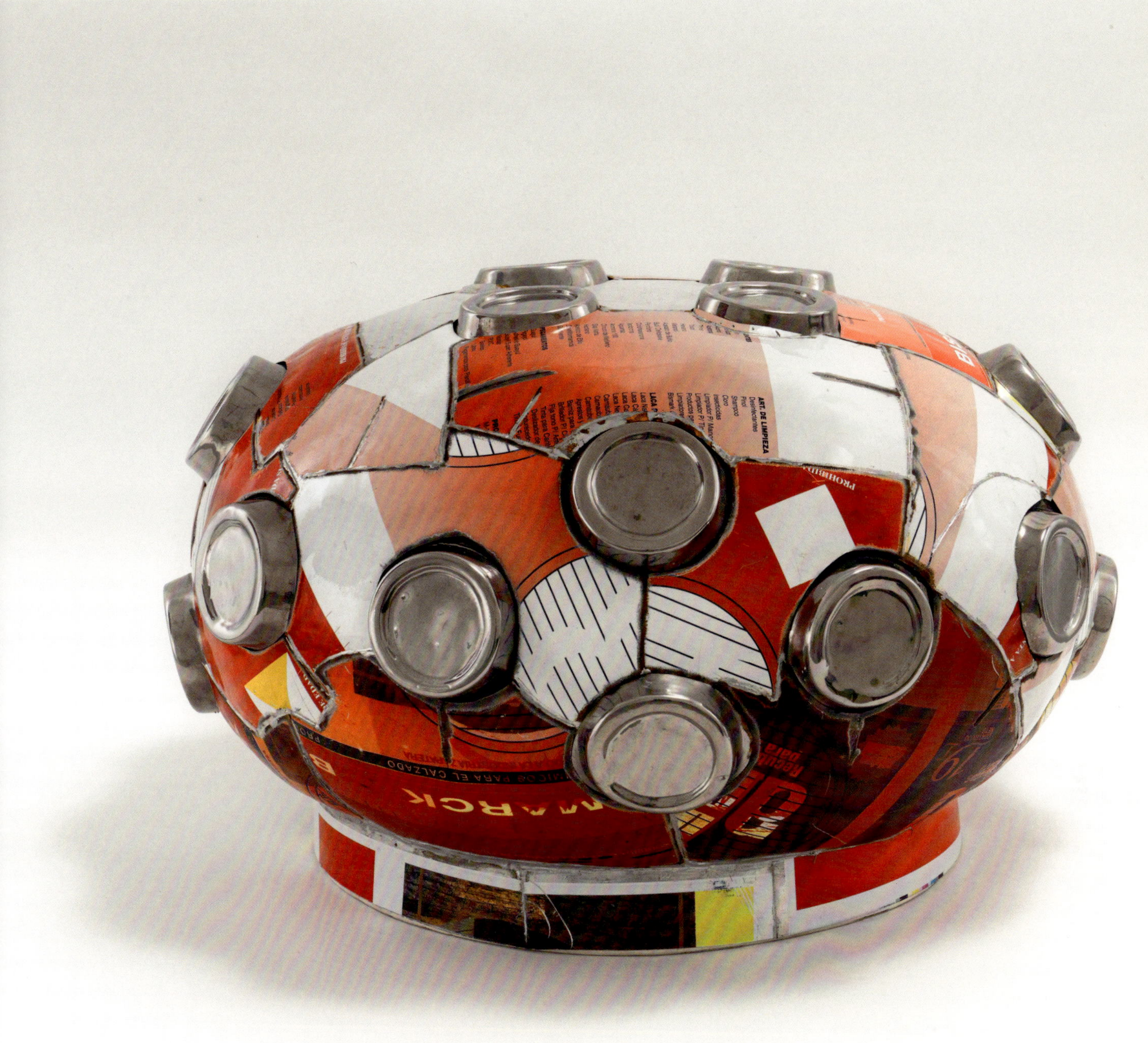

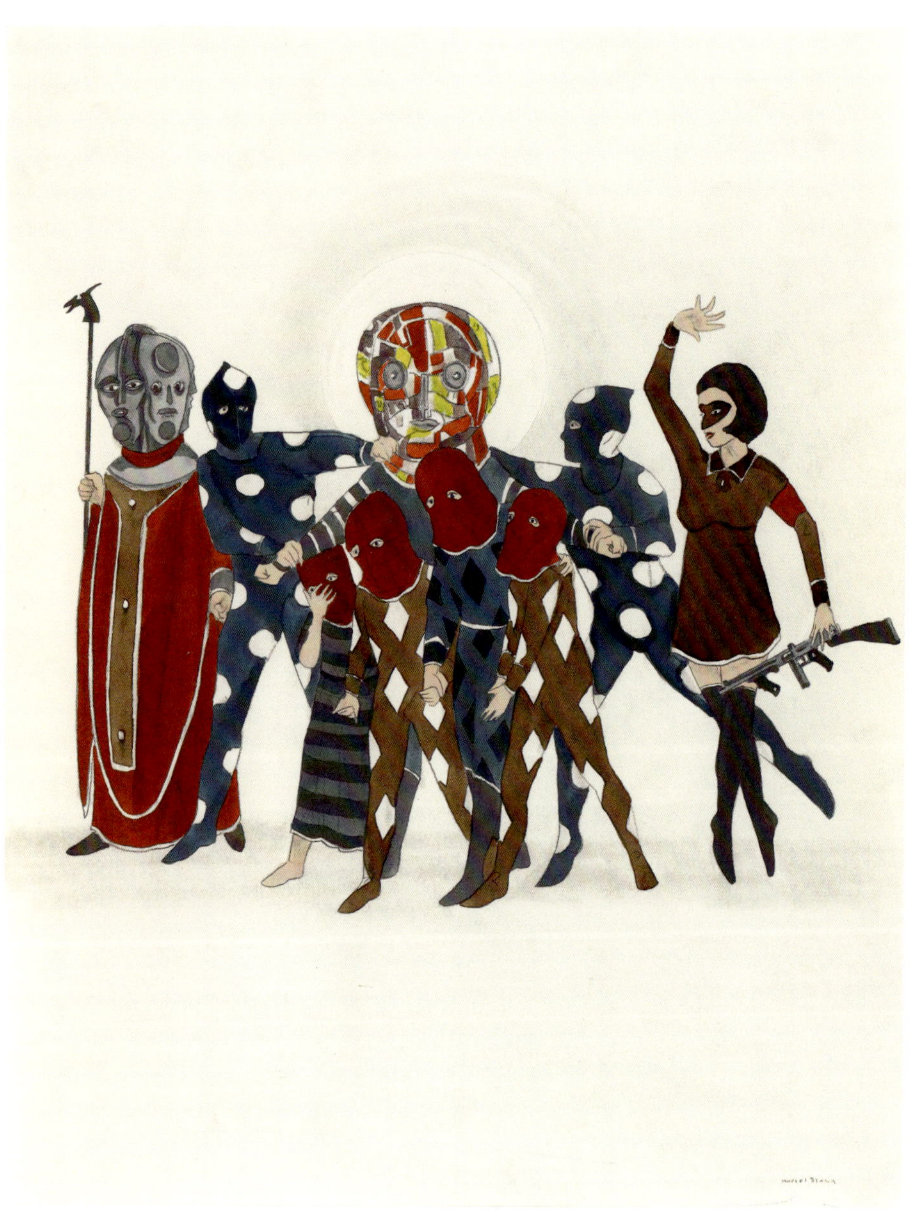

The pawn's head, 2012

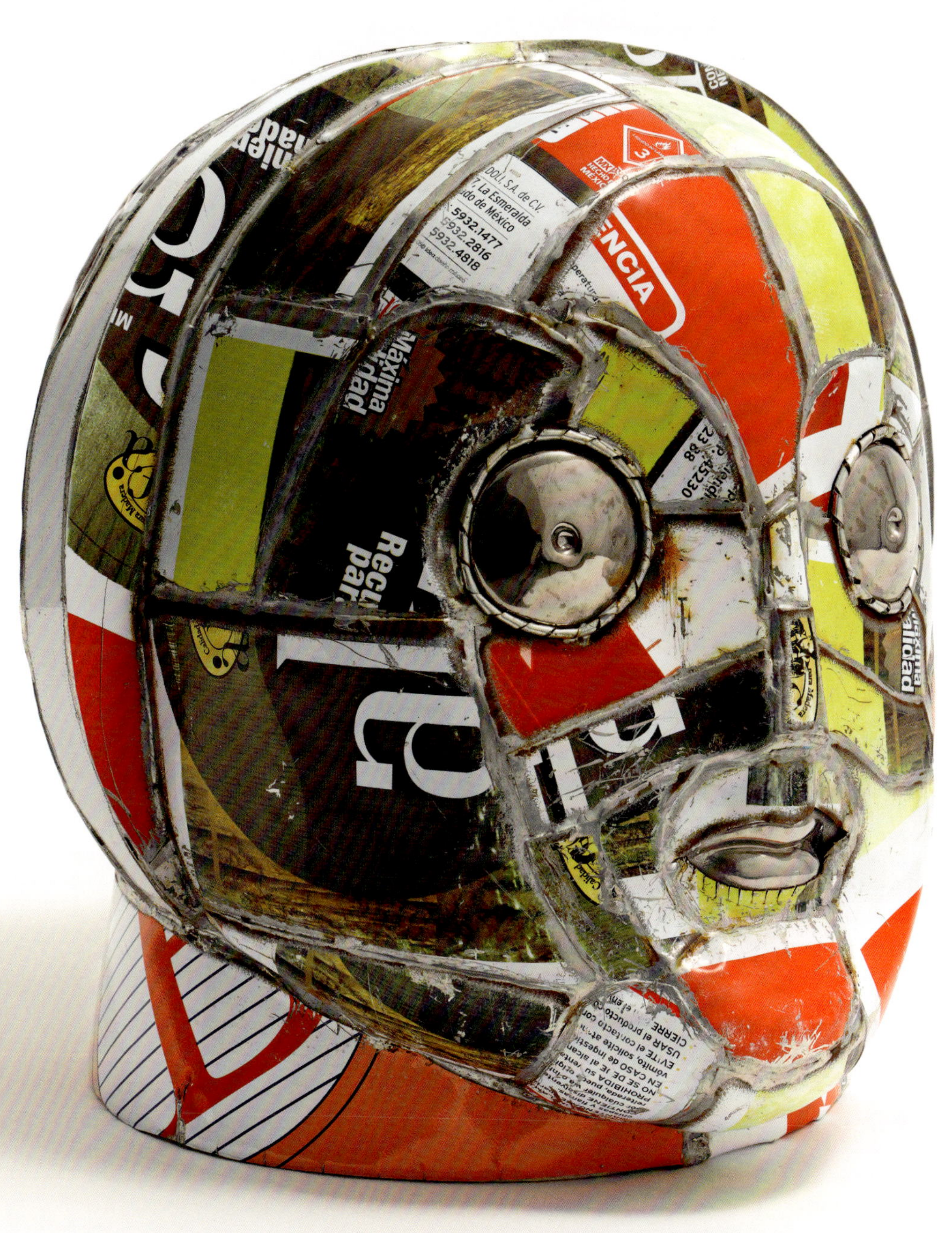

The king's Janus times two puppet for all the Sister Squares, 2013

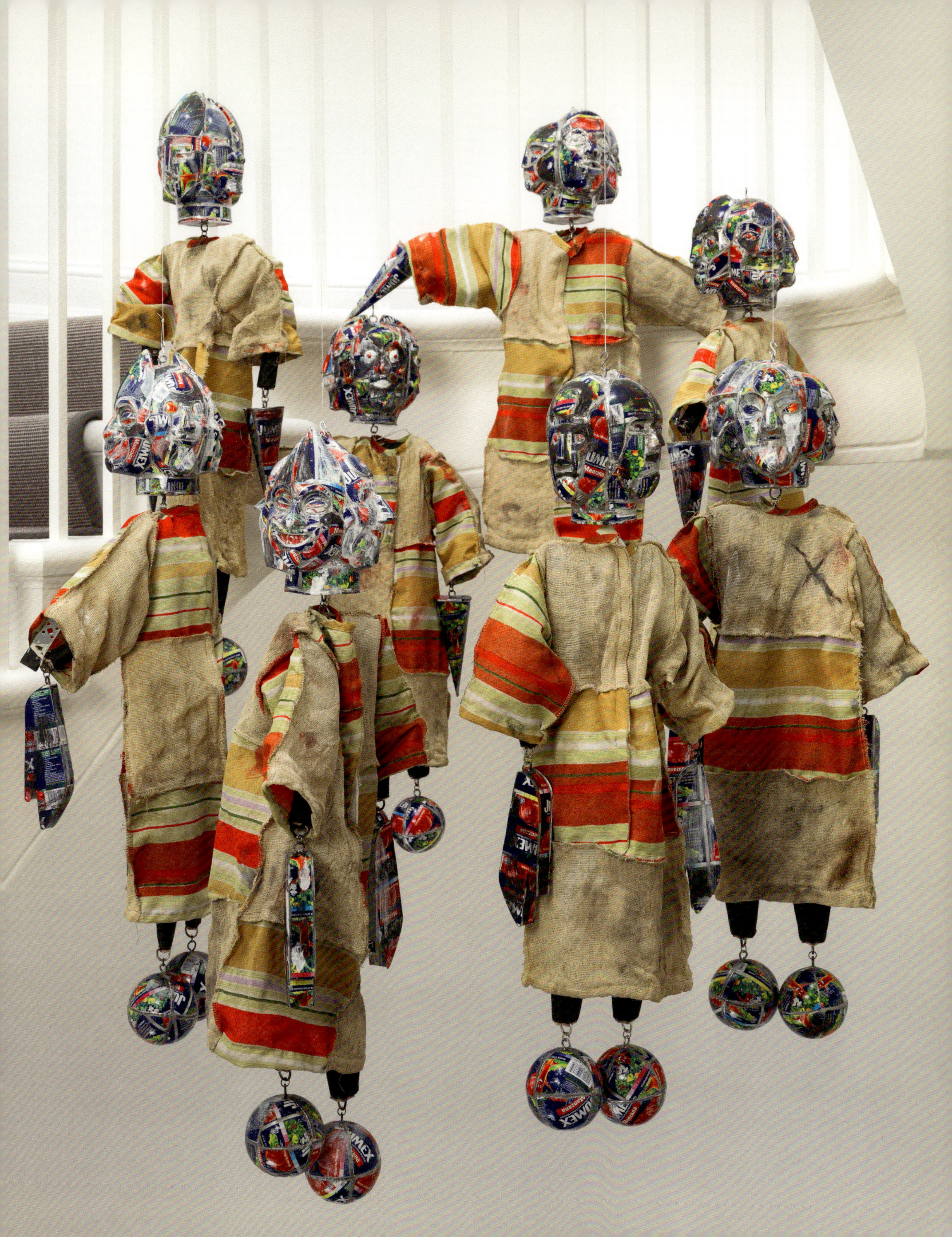

A red box for Marcel, 2013

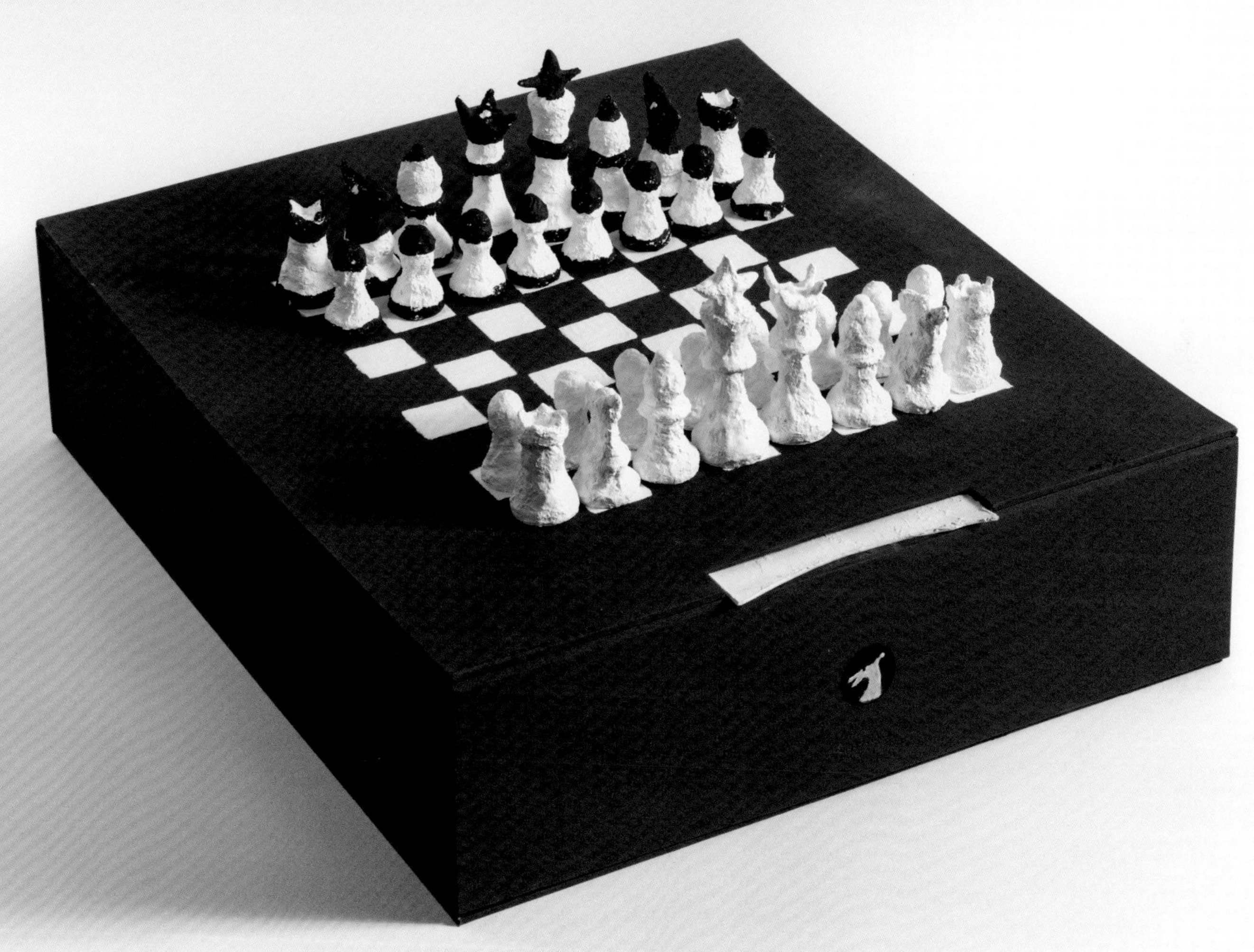

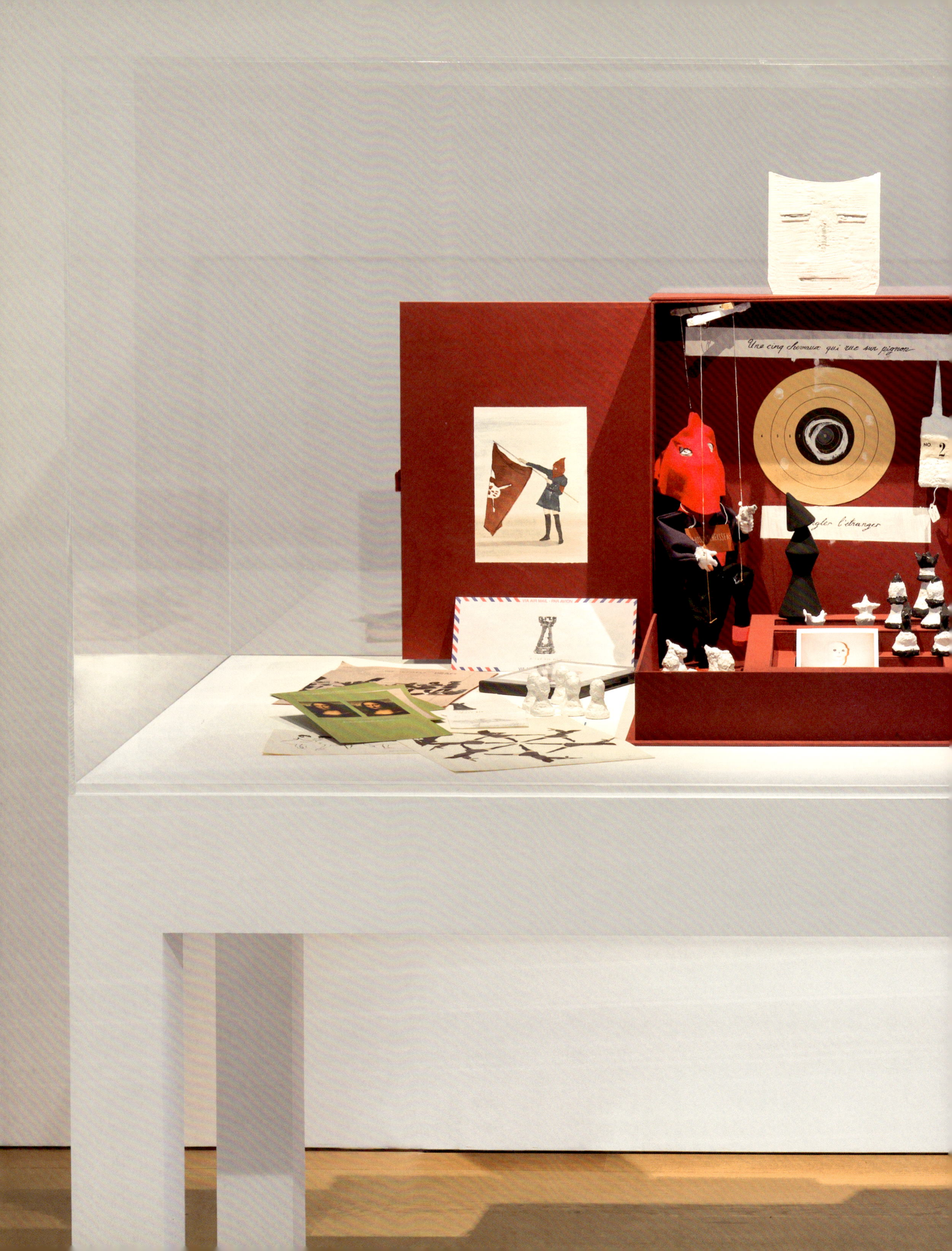
Une cinq chevaux qui rue sur pignon

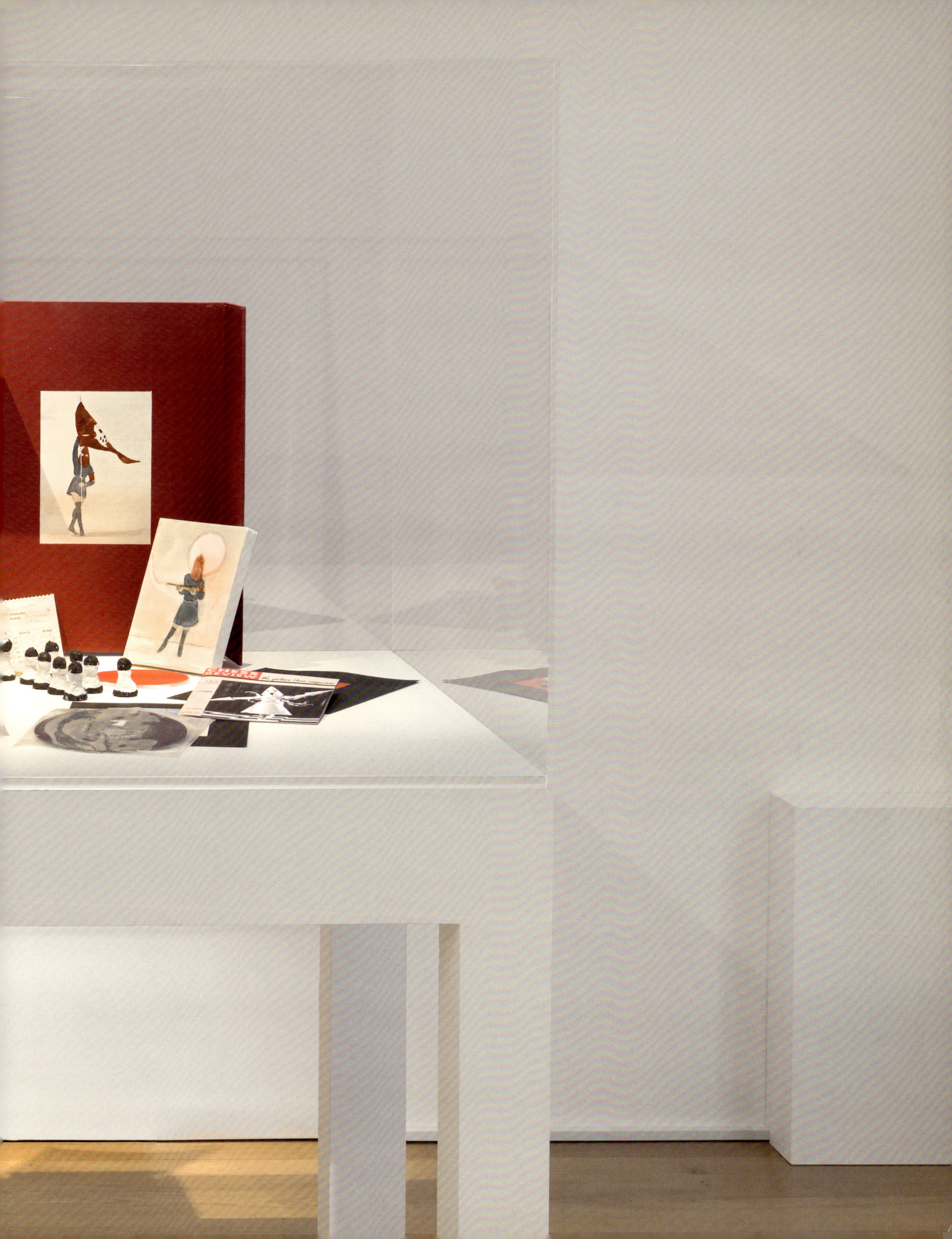

Wooden box (Death Disco Dance), 2013

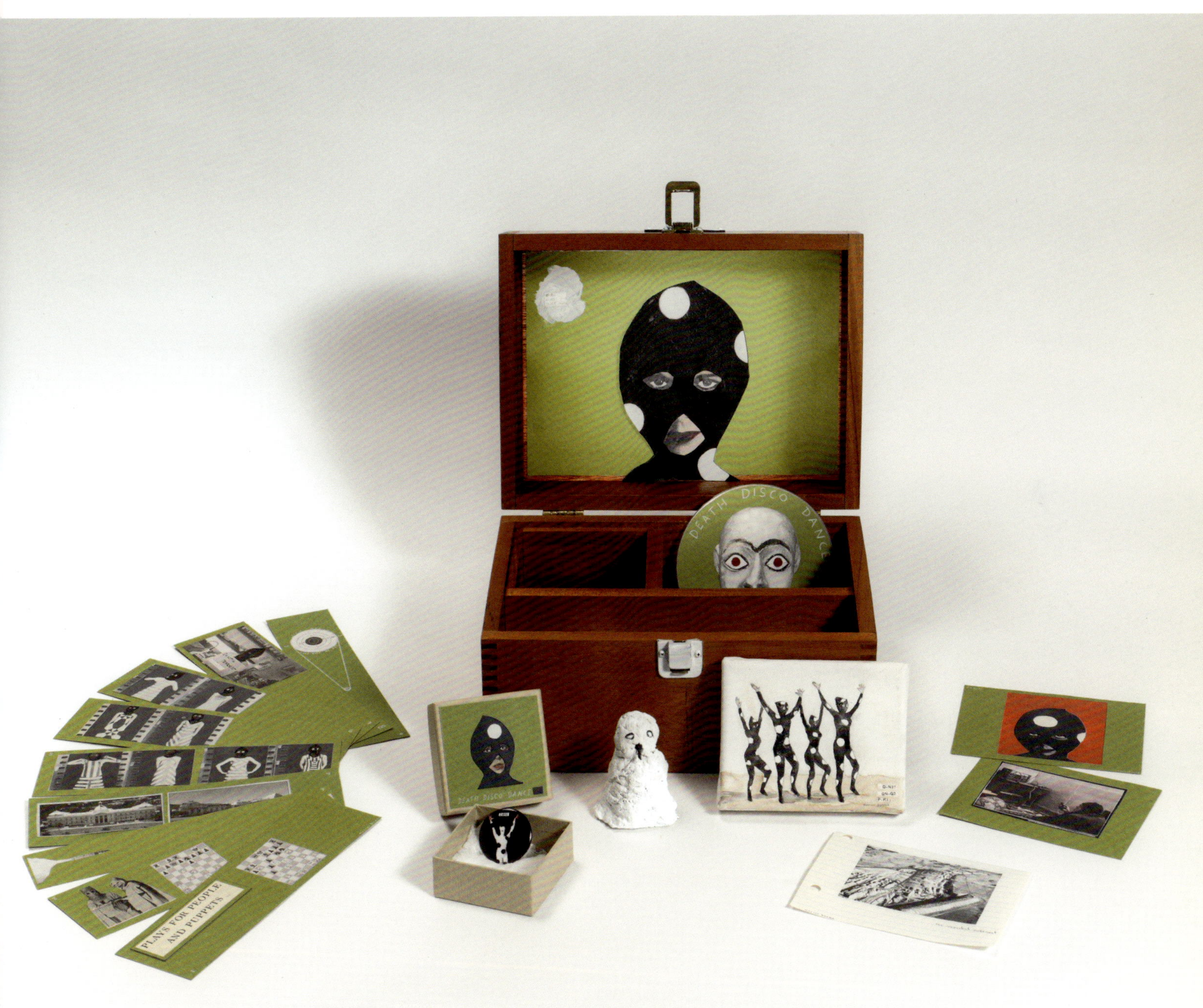

If you think this is just a game, you're wrong, 2013

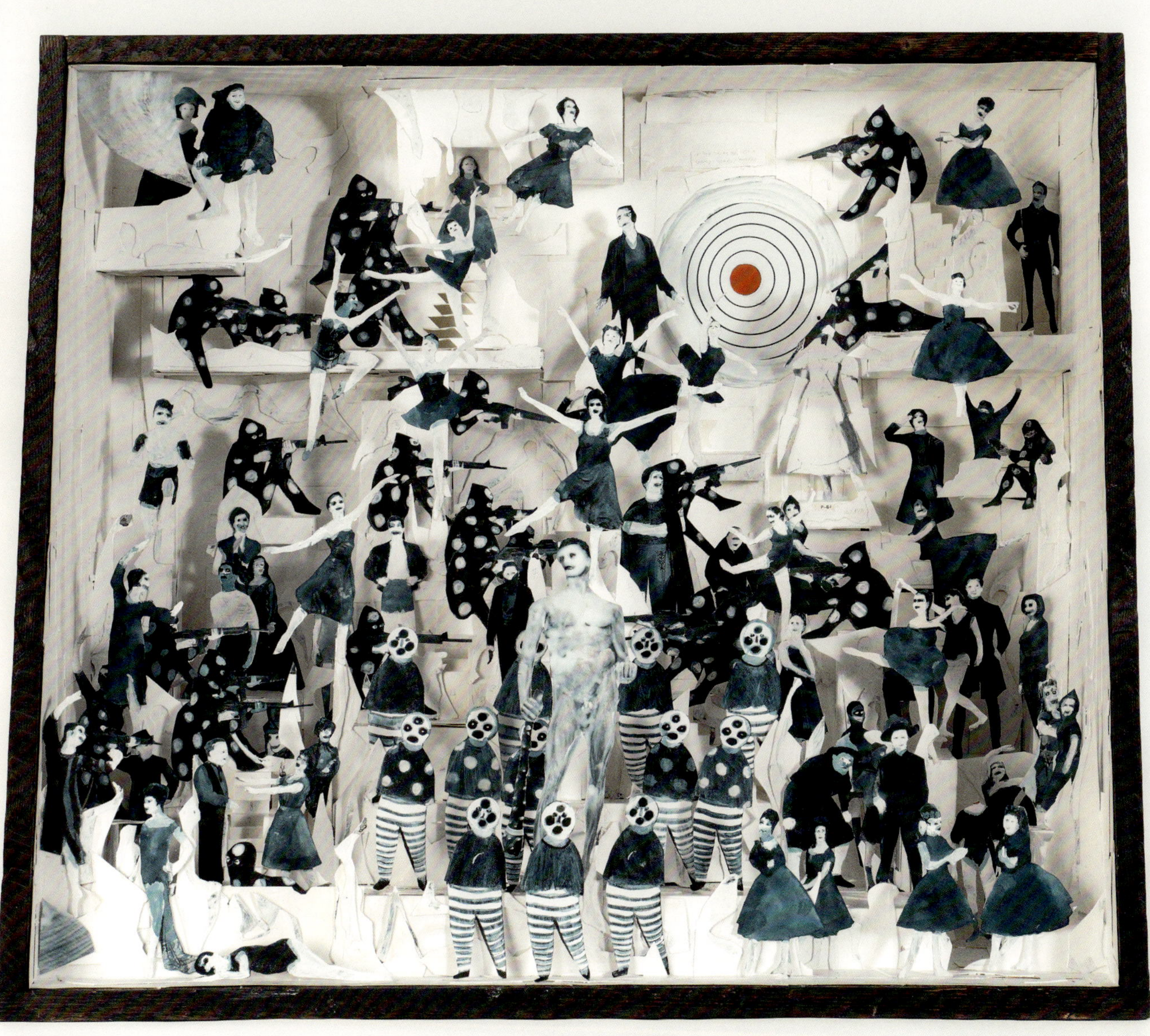

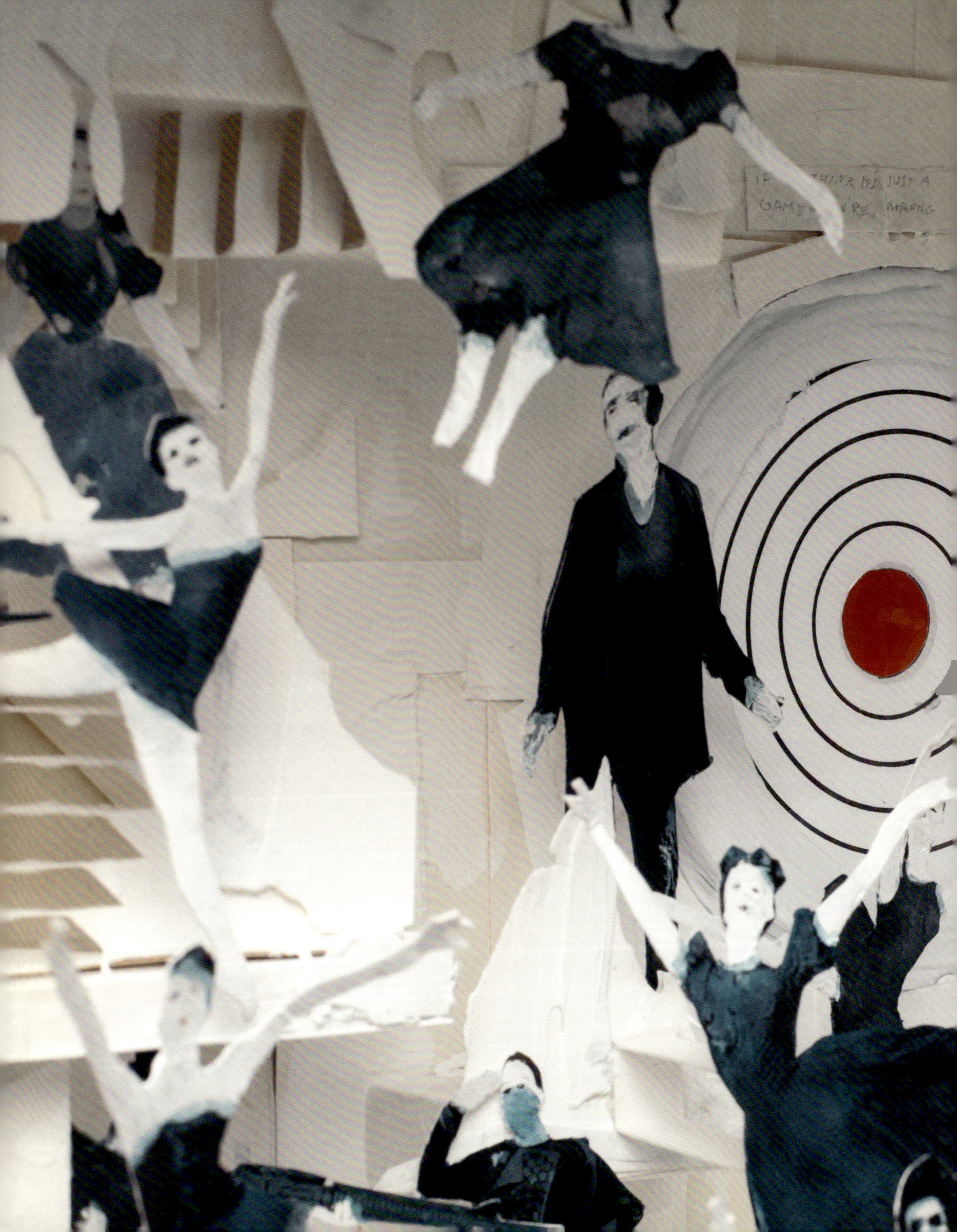

IF YOU THINK IT'S JUST A
GAME YOU'RE WRONG

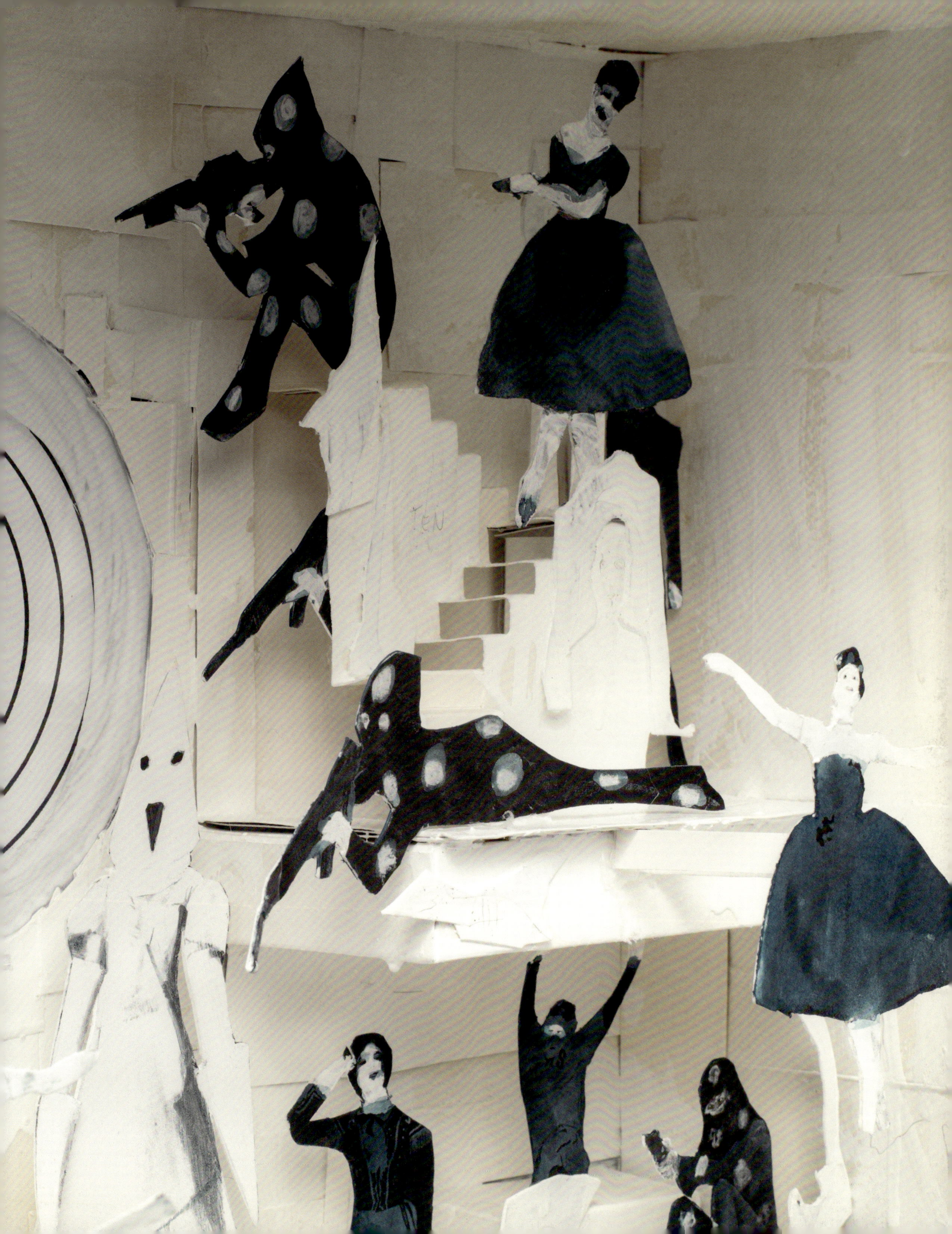

Hastily grabbing those innocent pawns, 2013

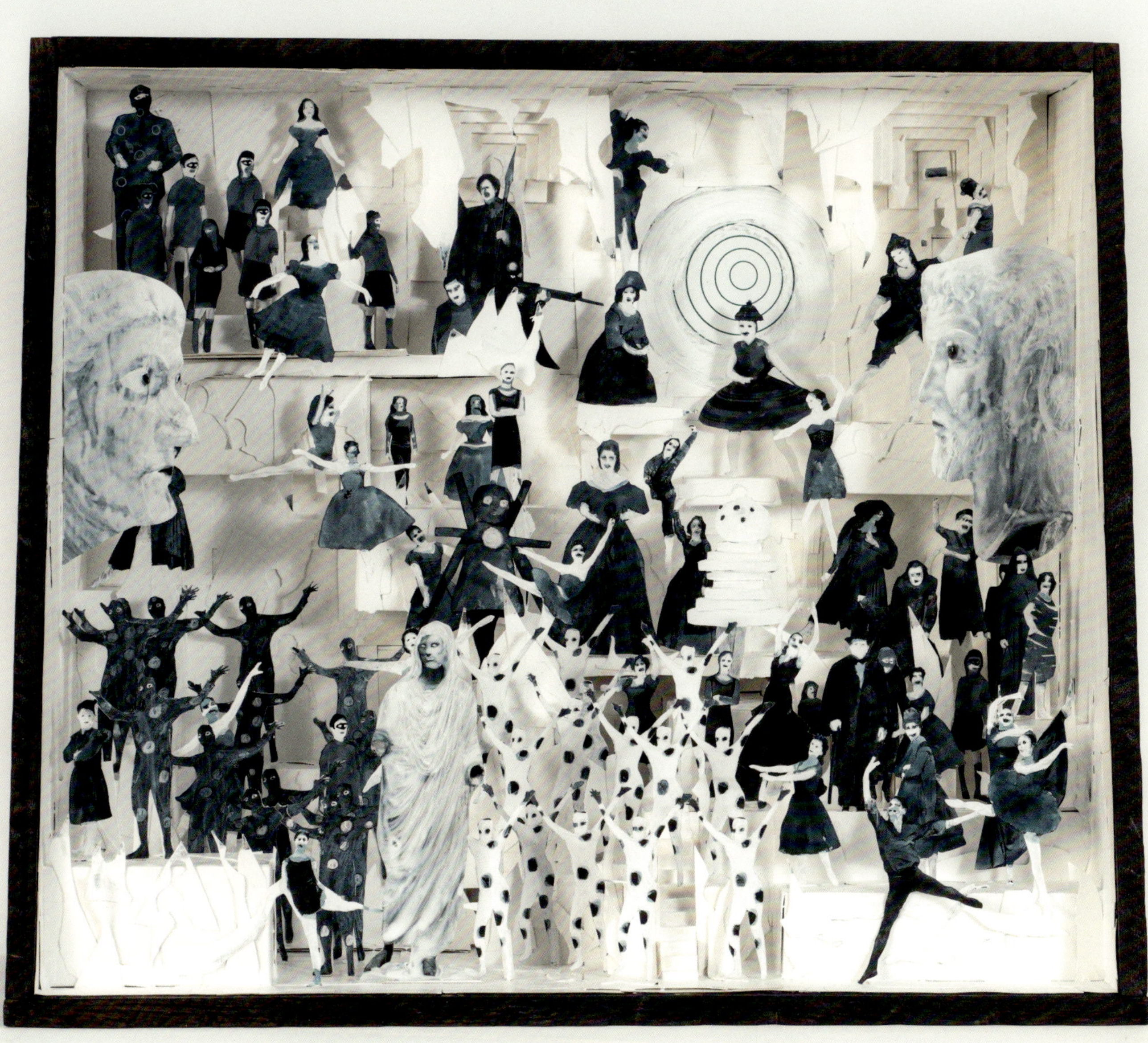

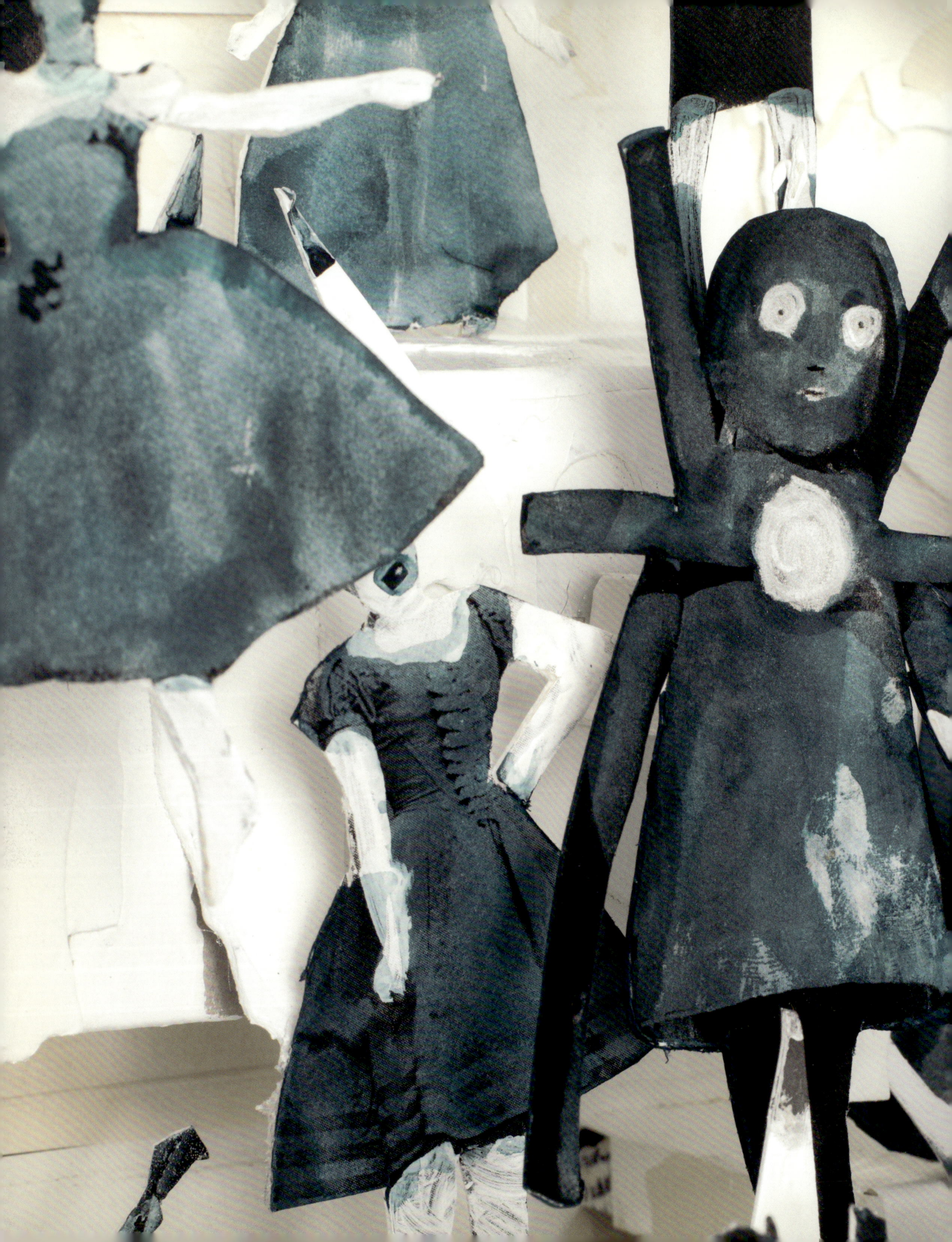

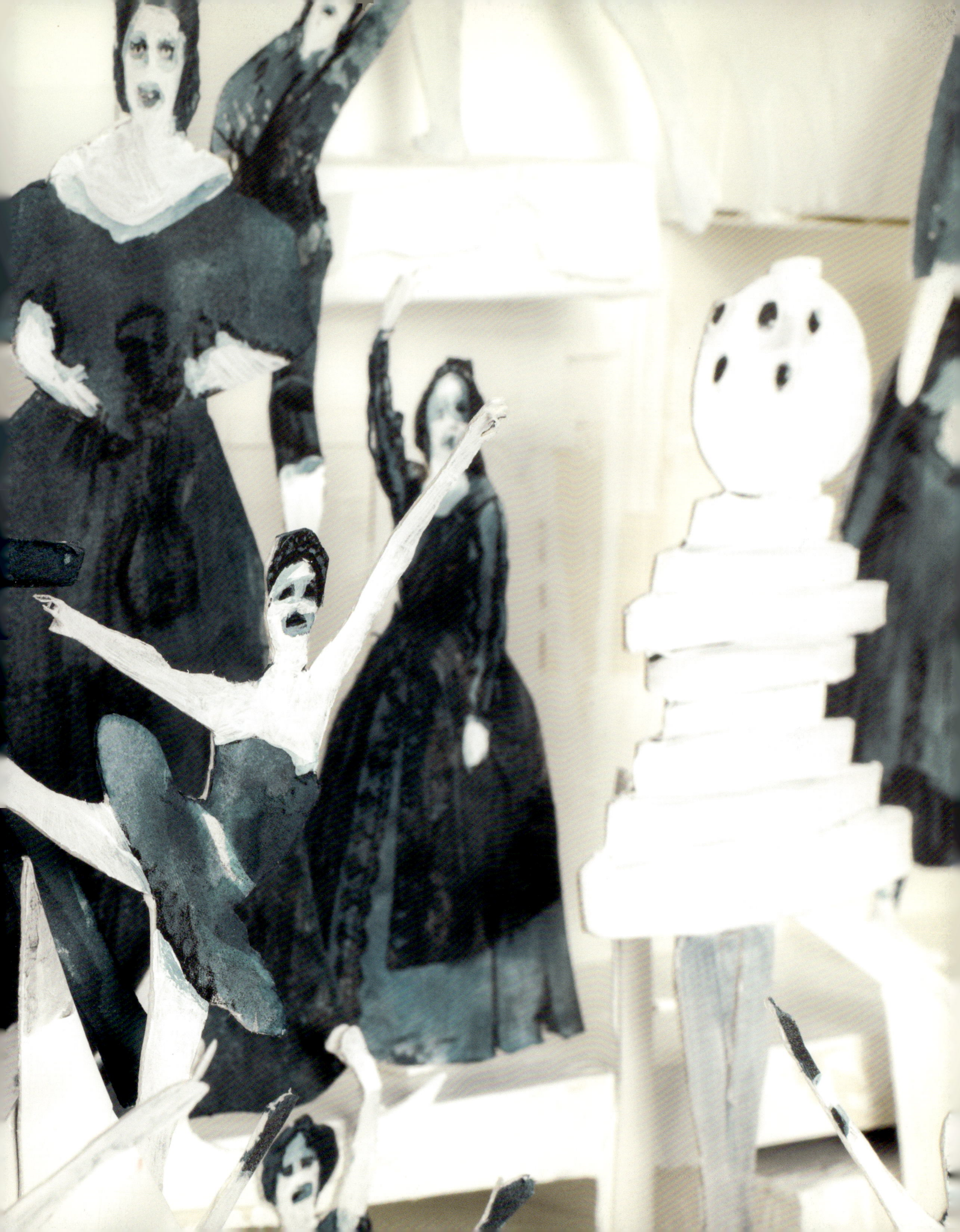

Forgotten terrorists (Unknown 1–5), 2011

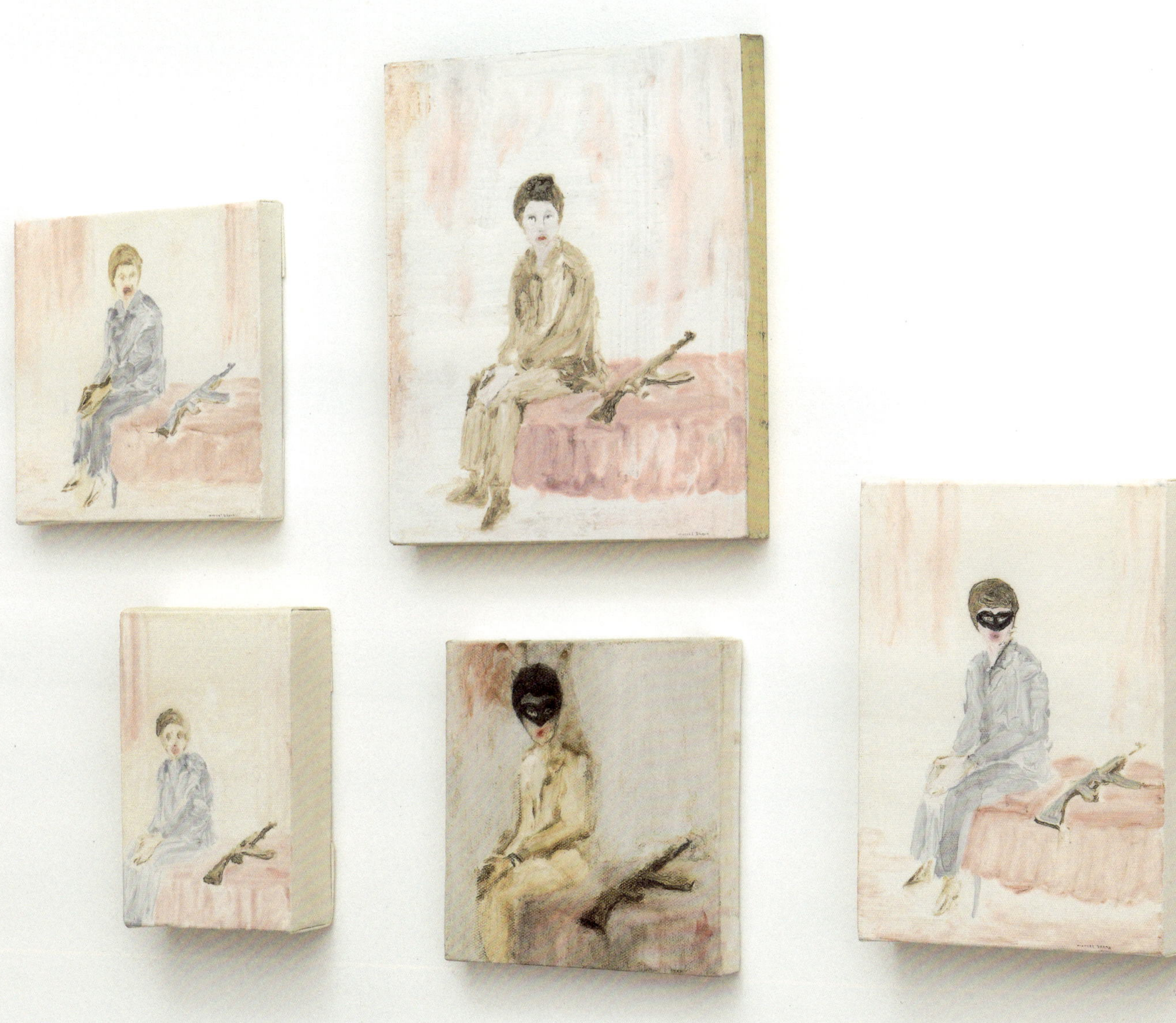

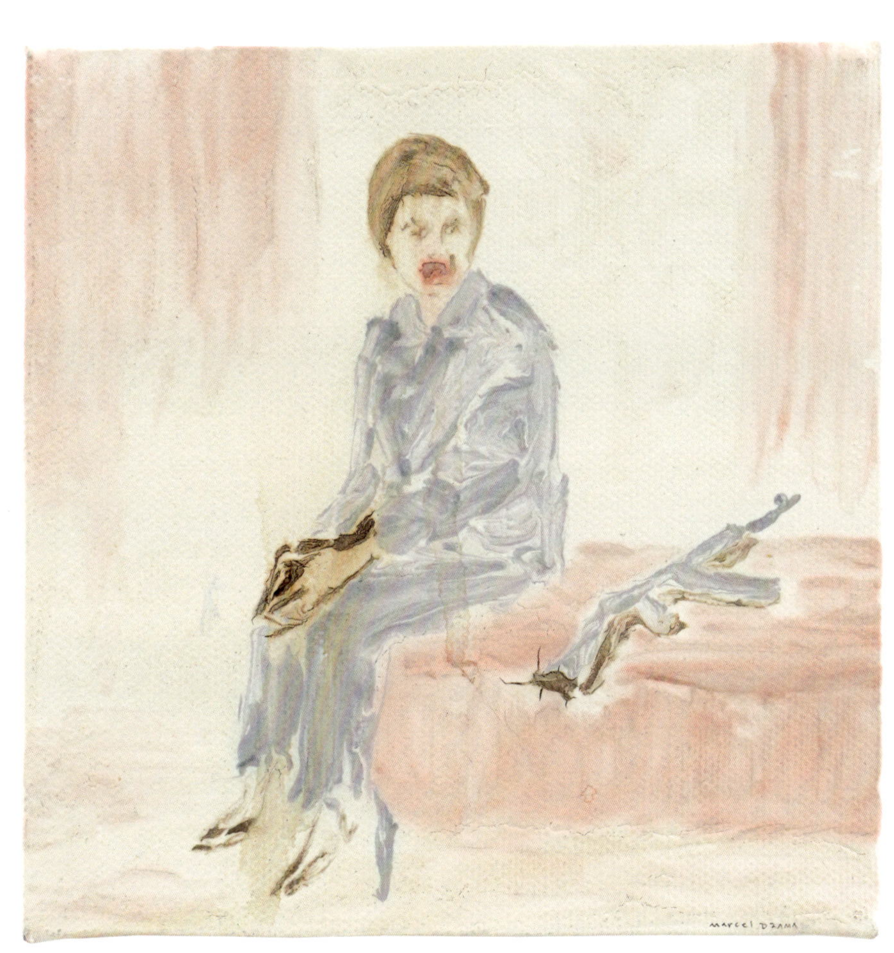

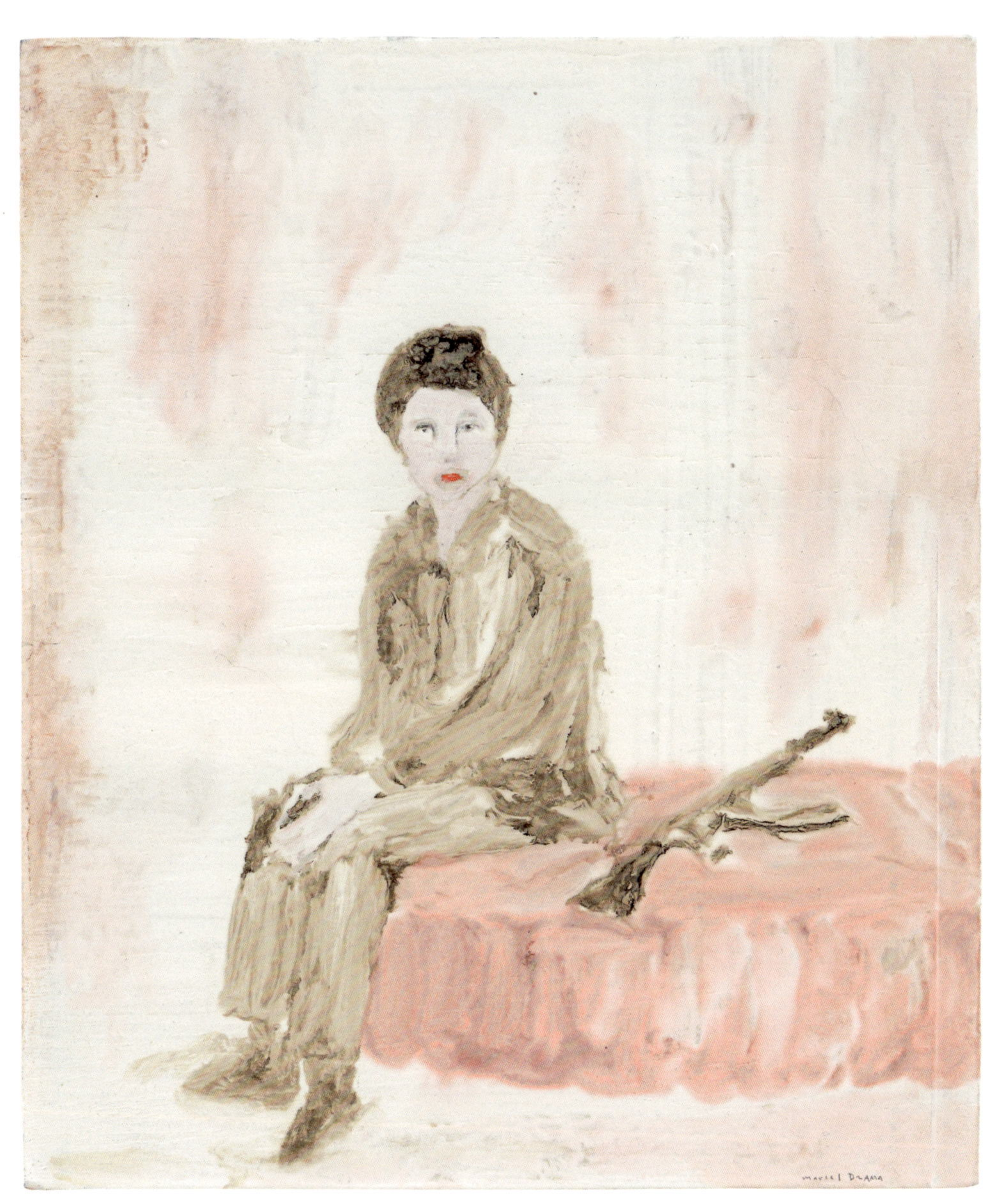

Collages

Andy's Death Disco, 2012

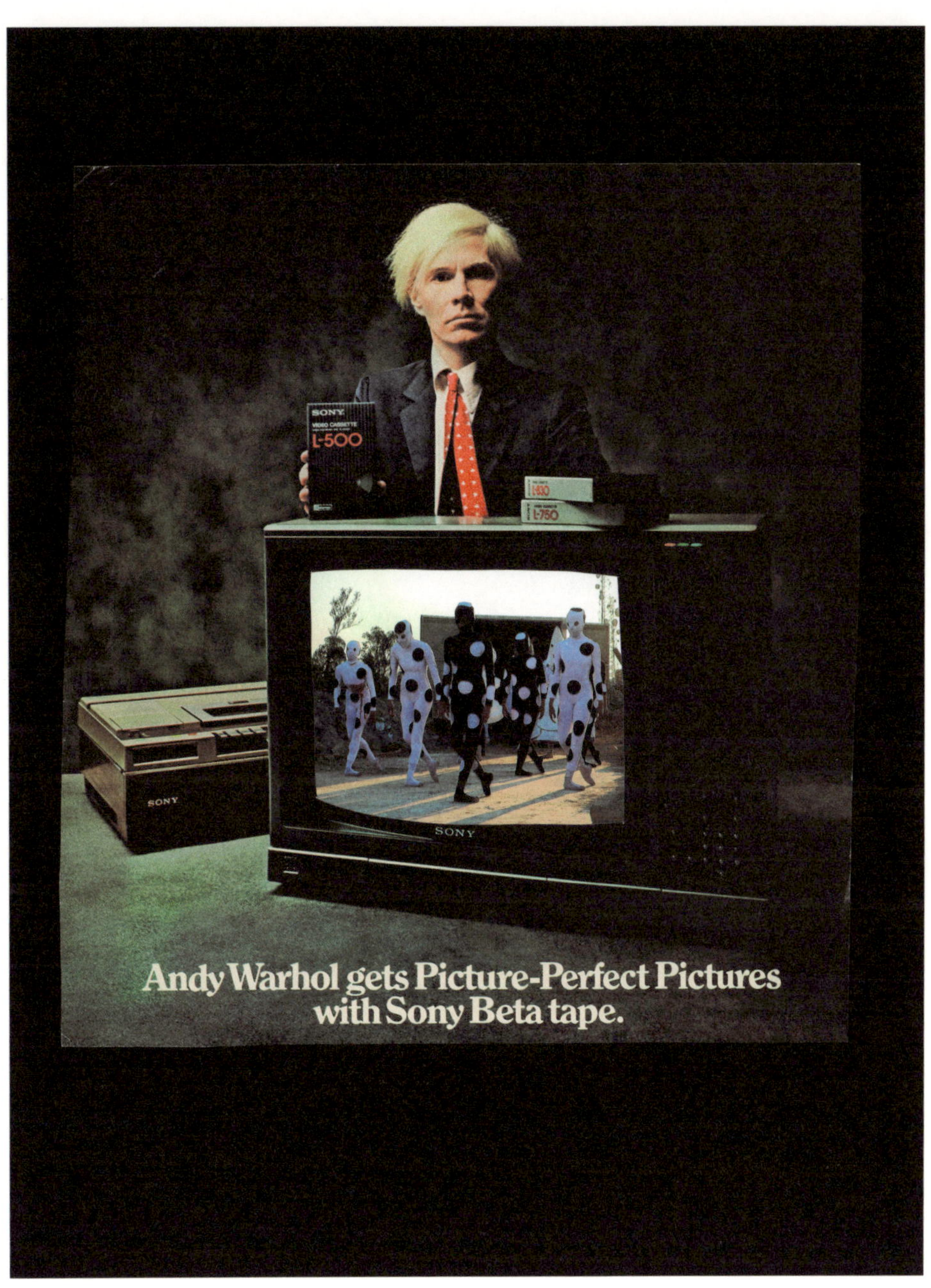

SONY
VIDEO CASSETTE
L-500
Andy Warhol gets Picture-Perfect Pictures
with Sony Beta tape.

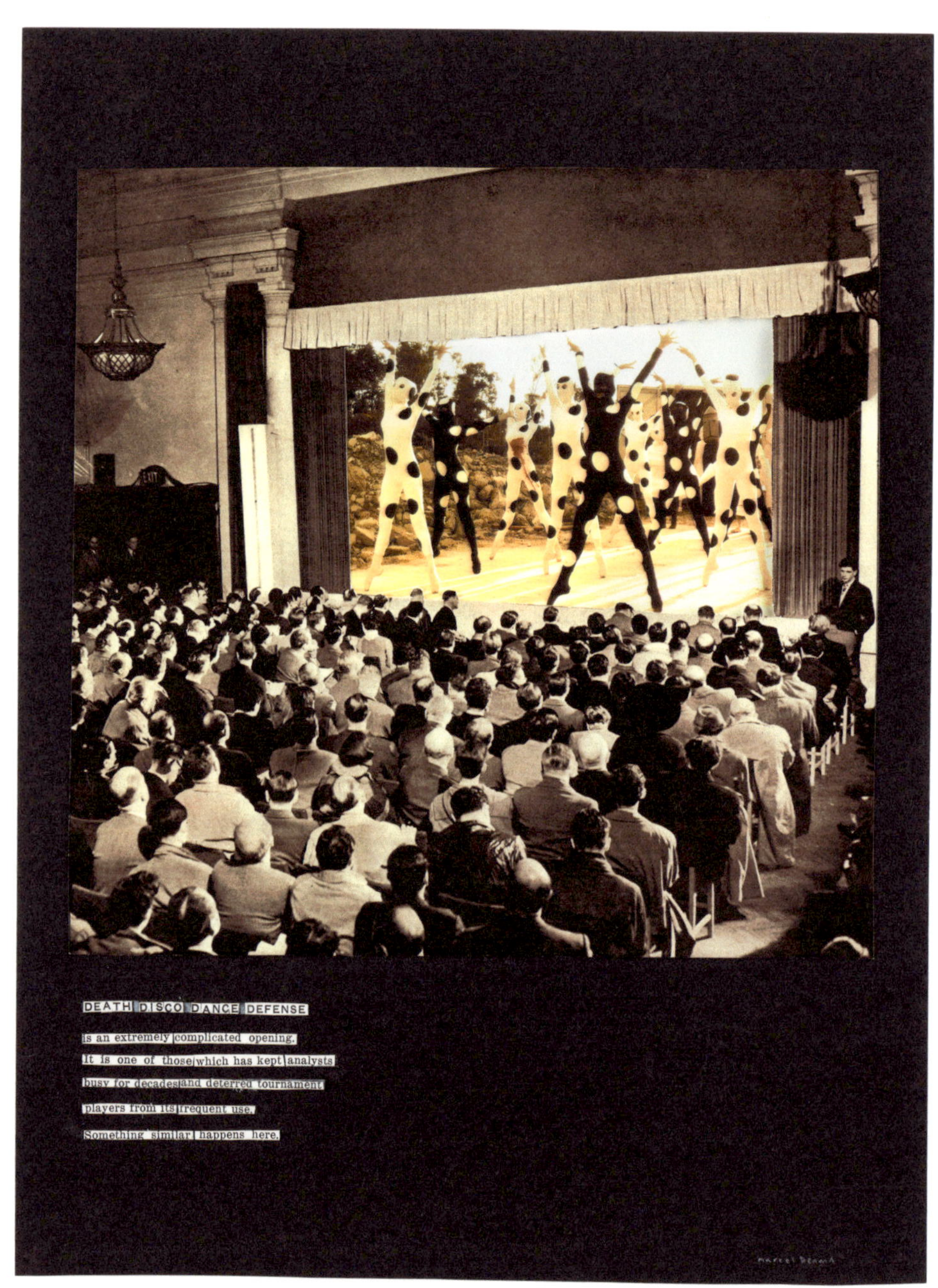

Death Disco Dance defense, 2013

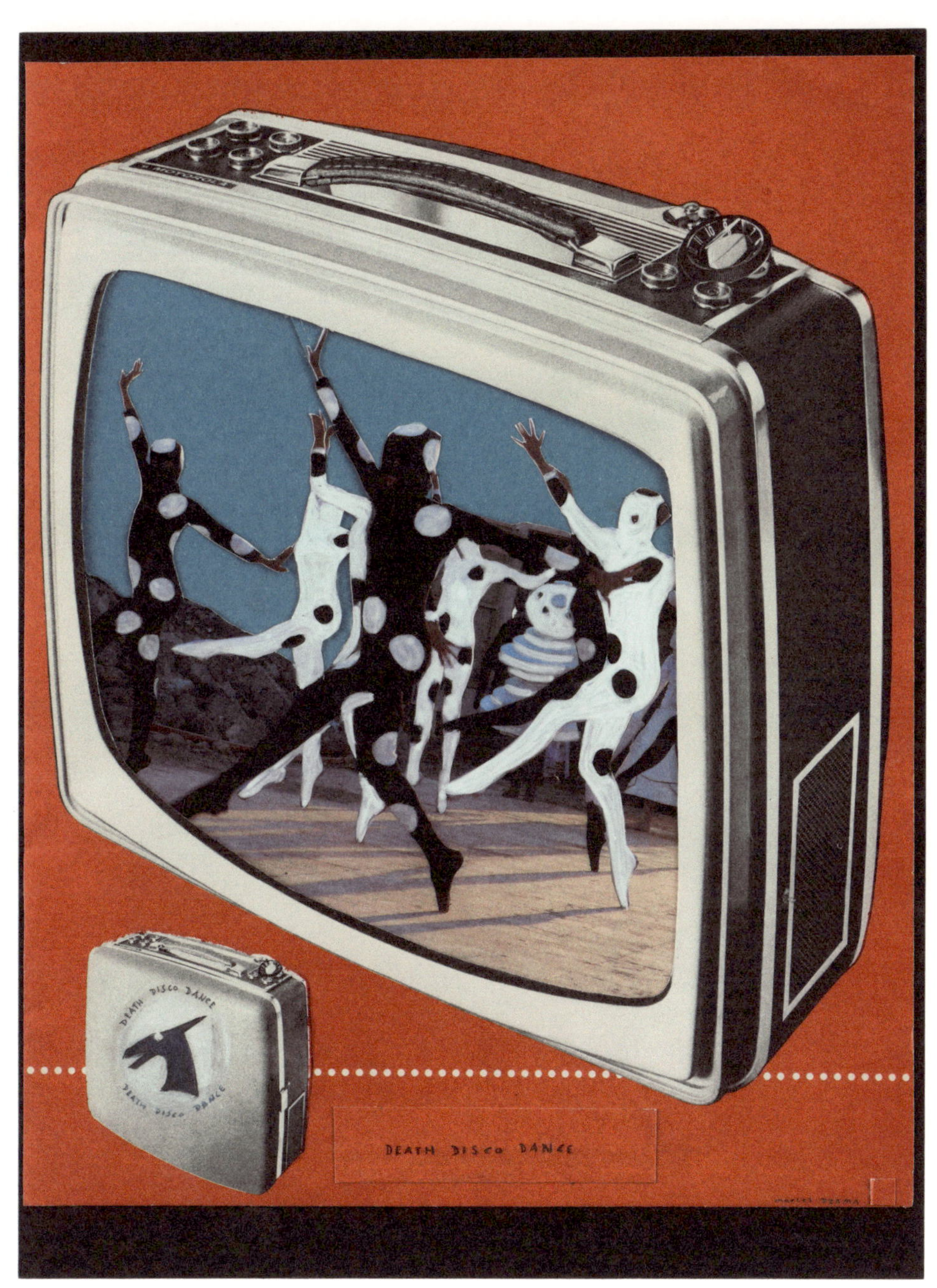

The portable Death Disco Dance, 2013

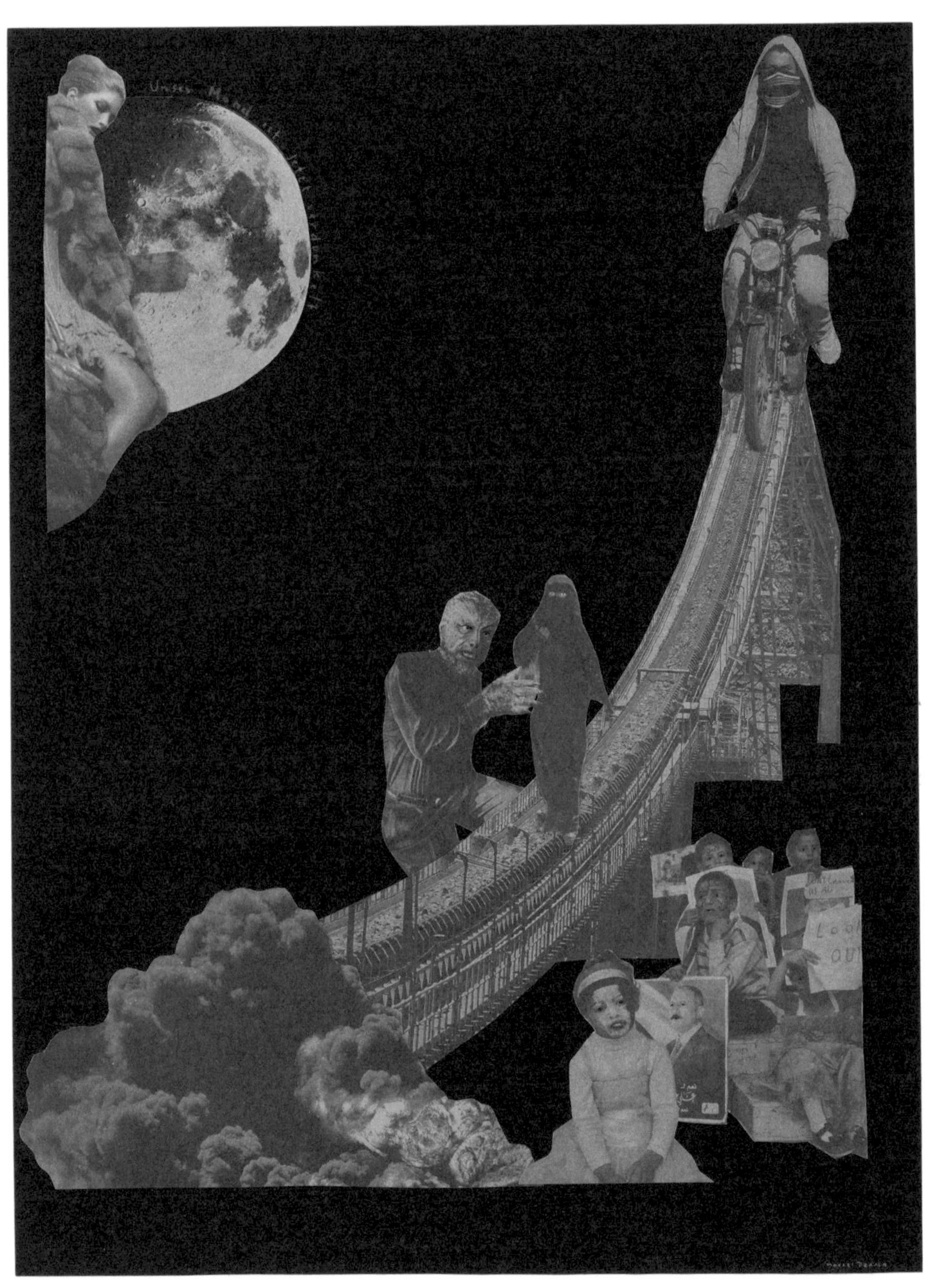

Our moon is now eclipsed, 2013

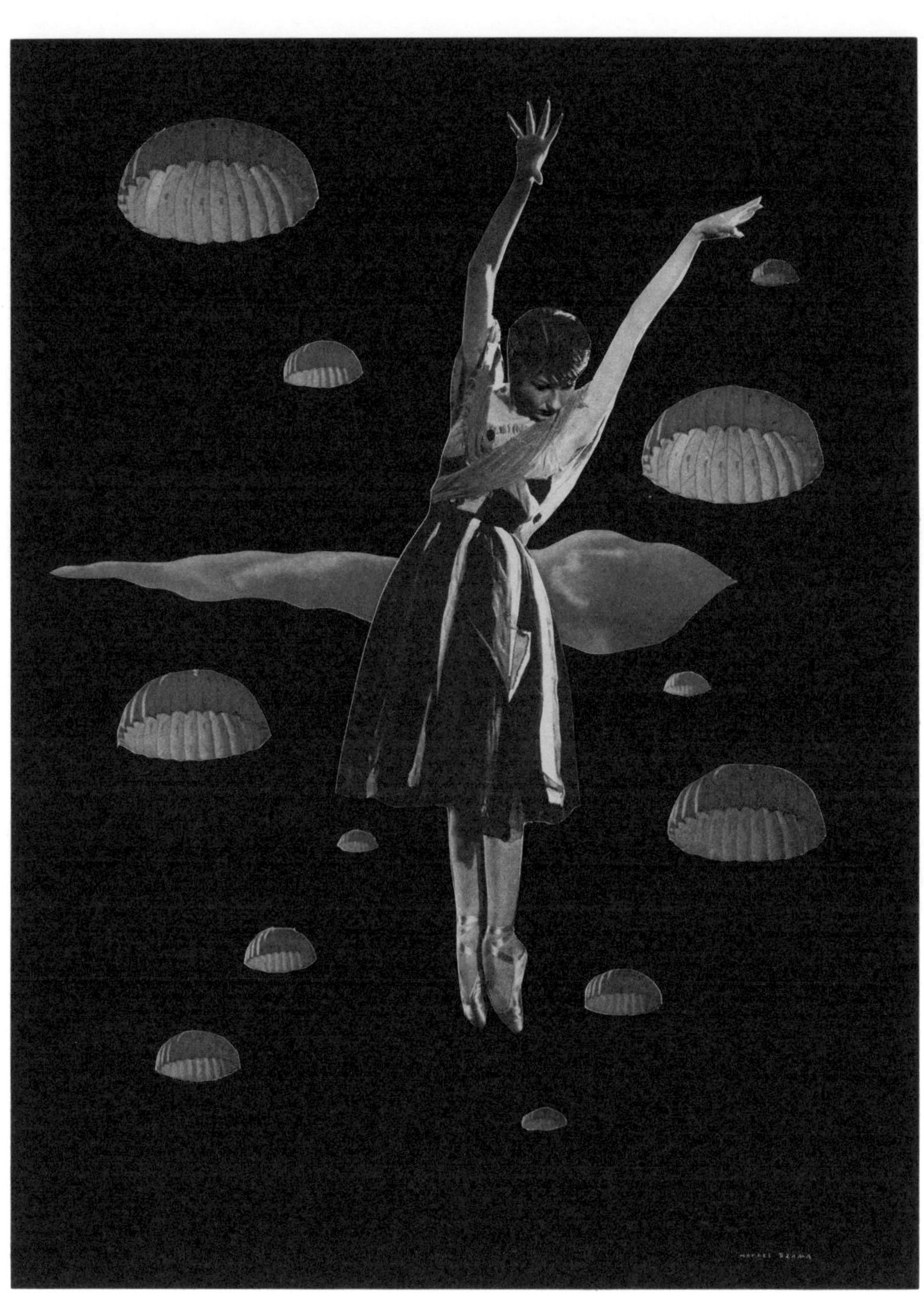

Some falls are a means to a happier rise, 2013

Films

Death Disco Dance, 2011

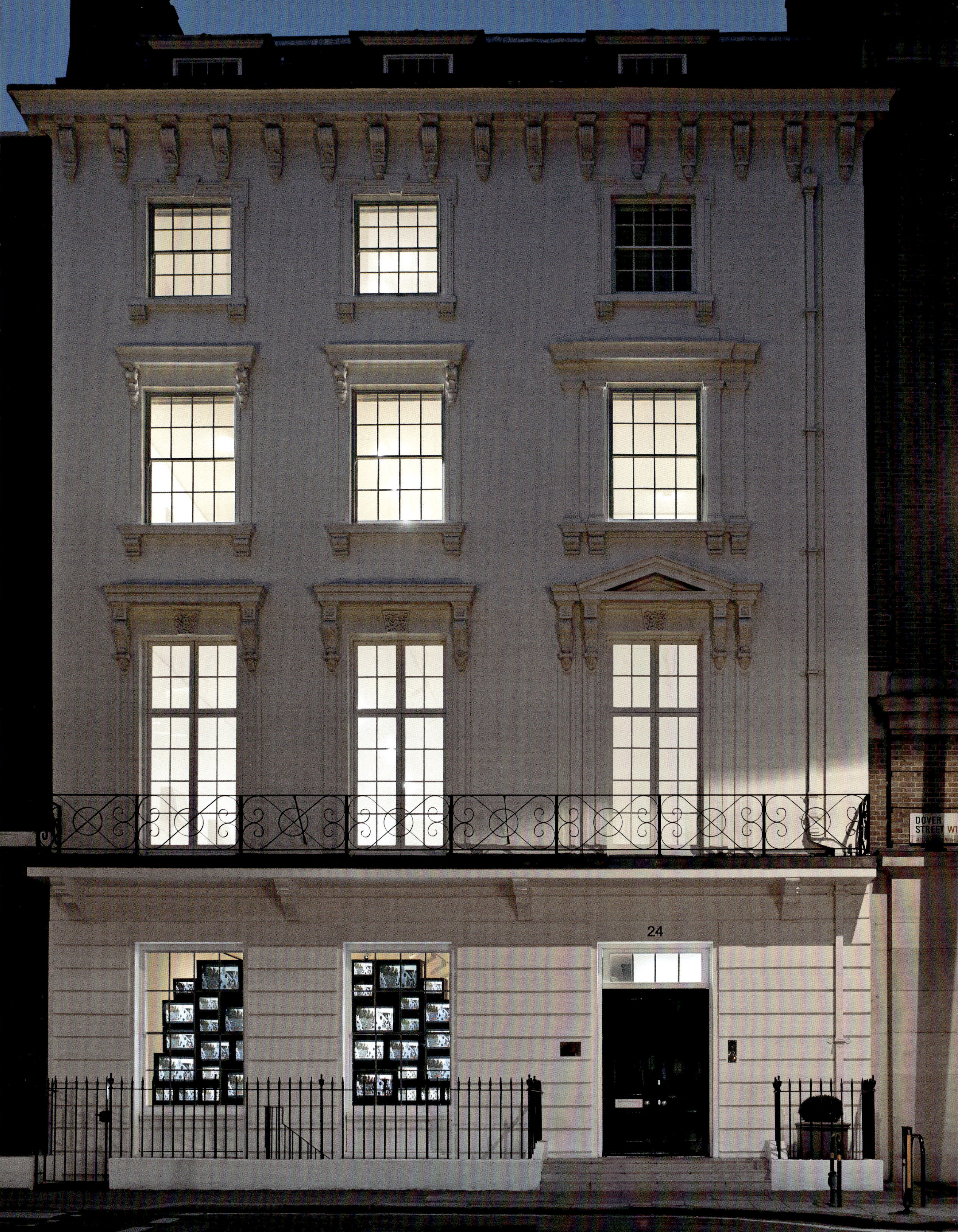
24
DOVER
STREET W1

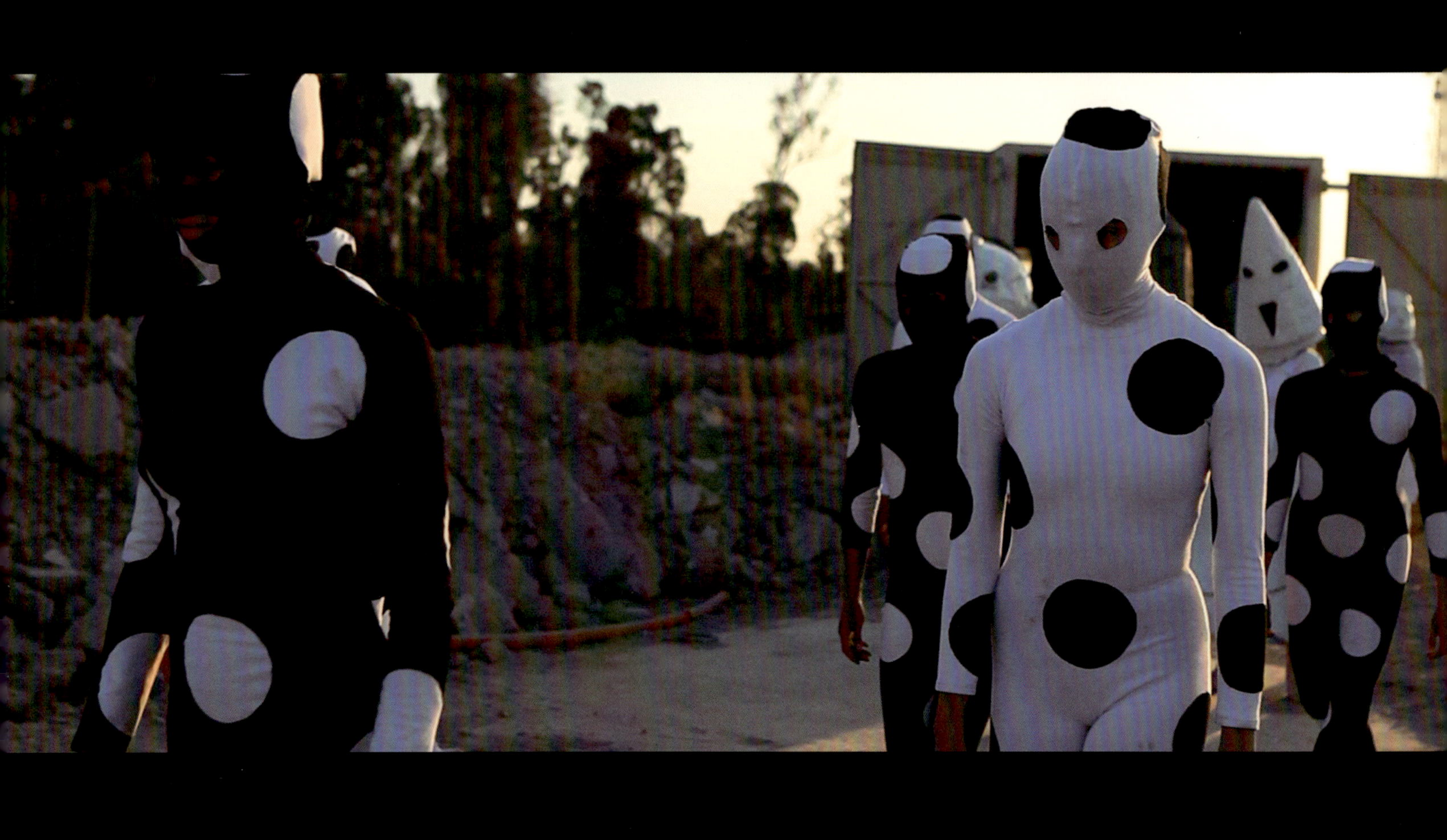

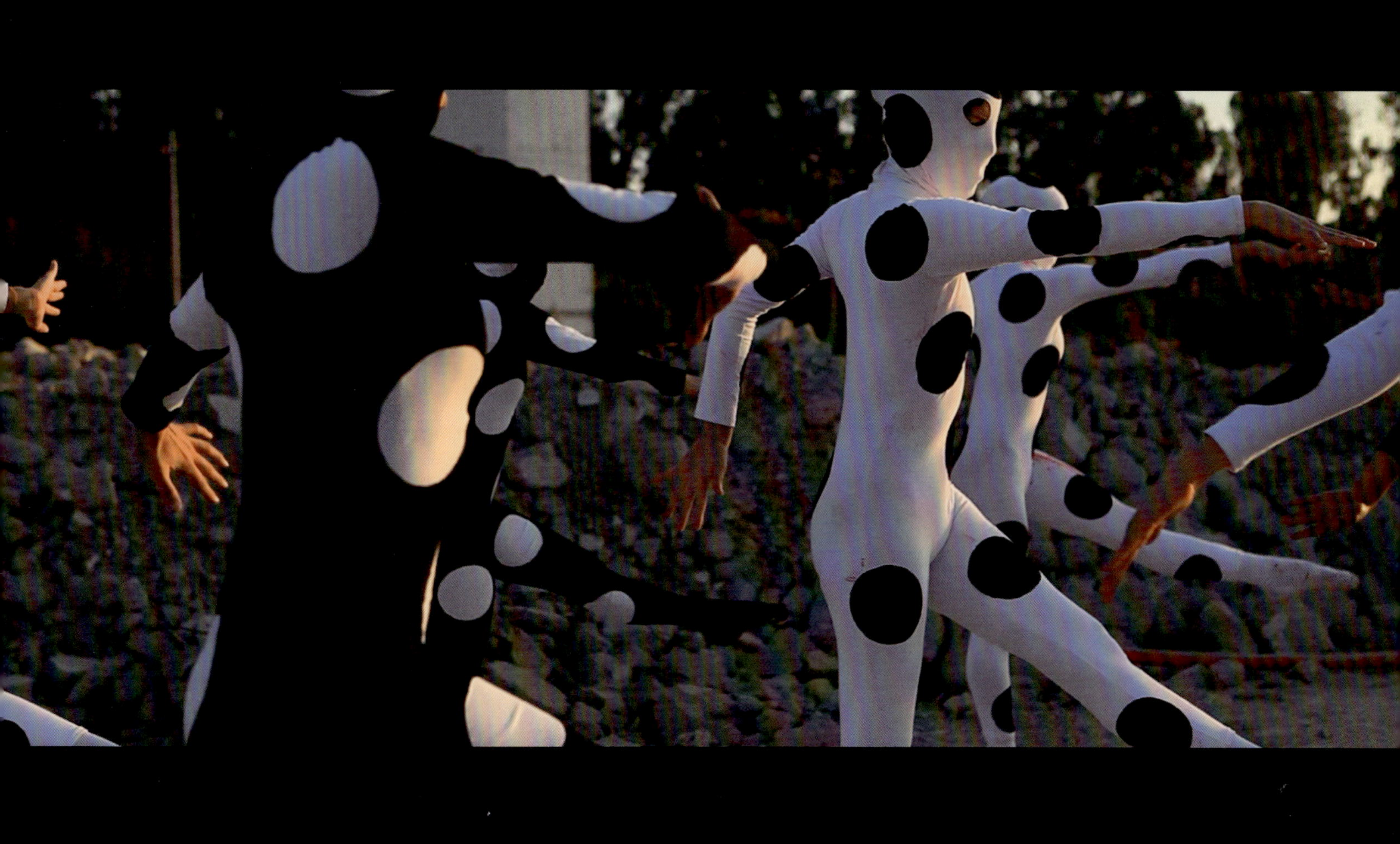

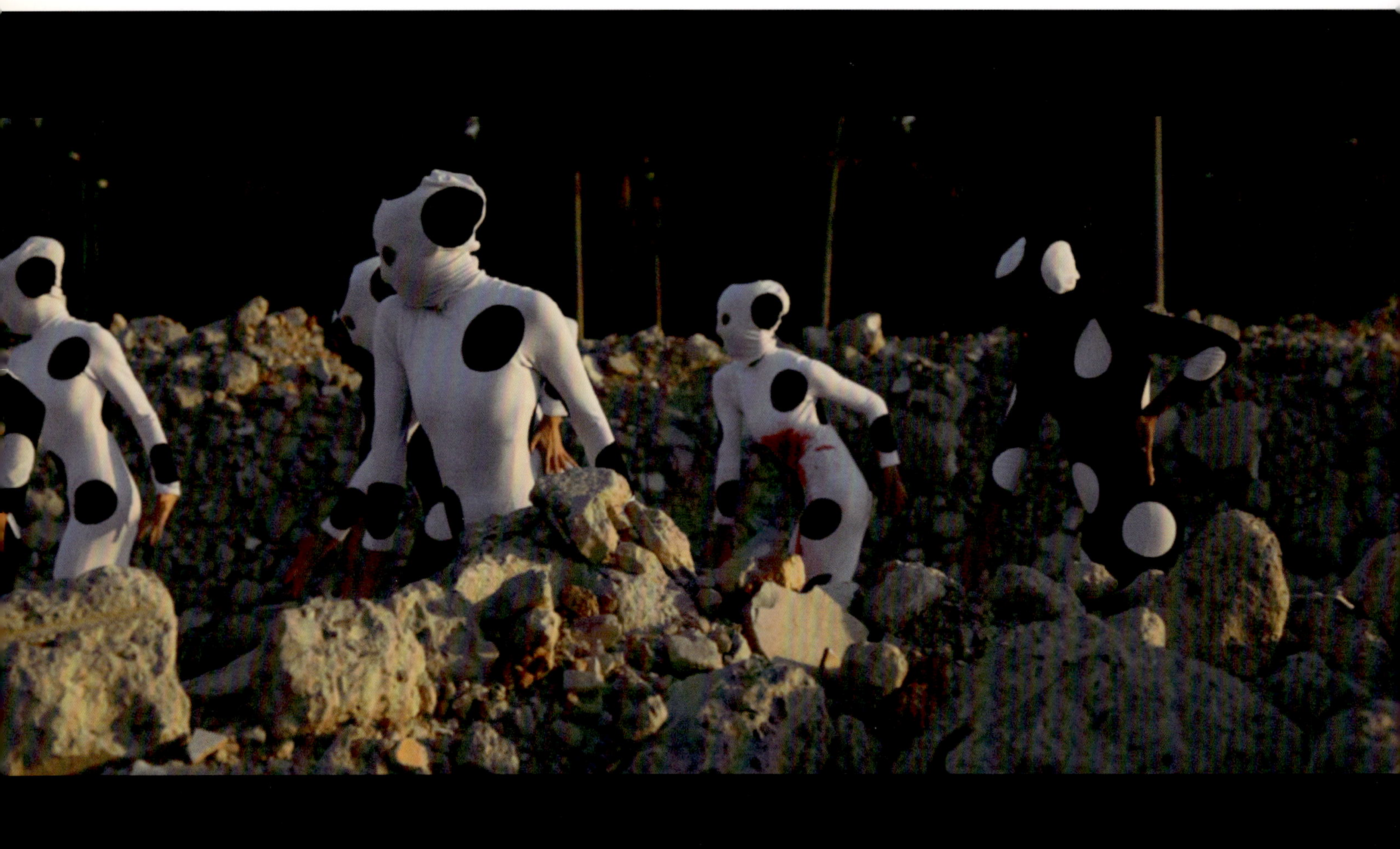

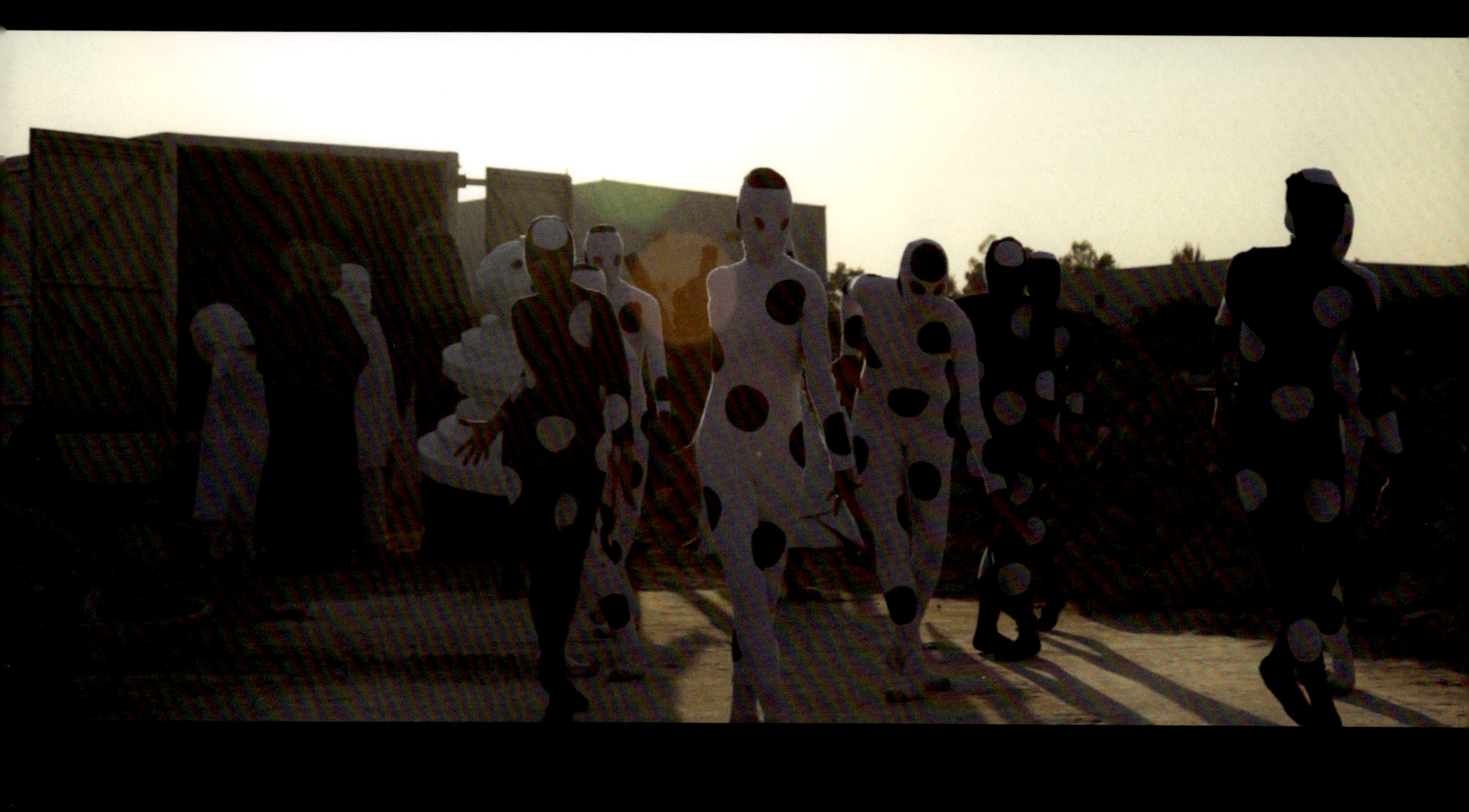

Sister Squares, 2012

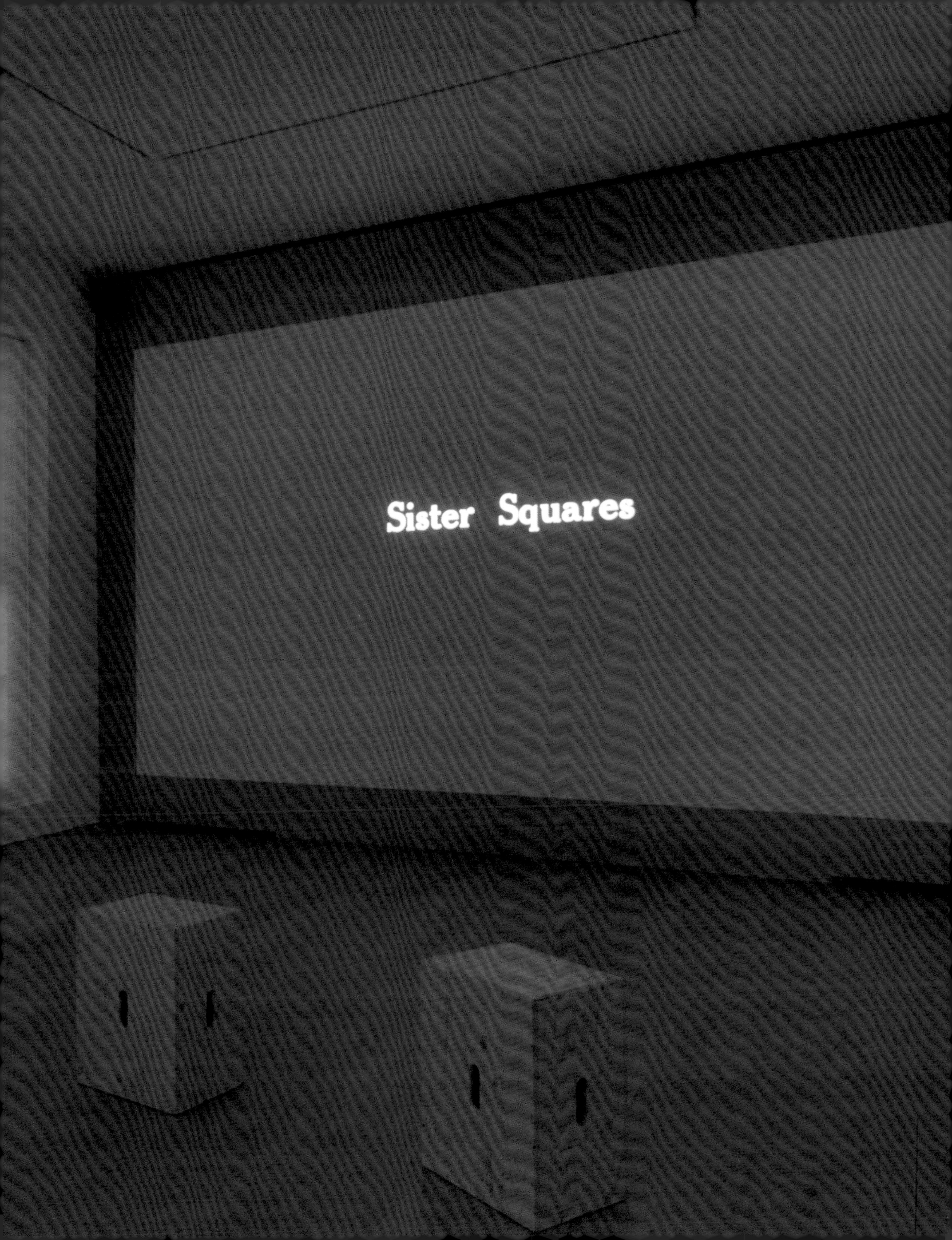
Sister Squares

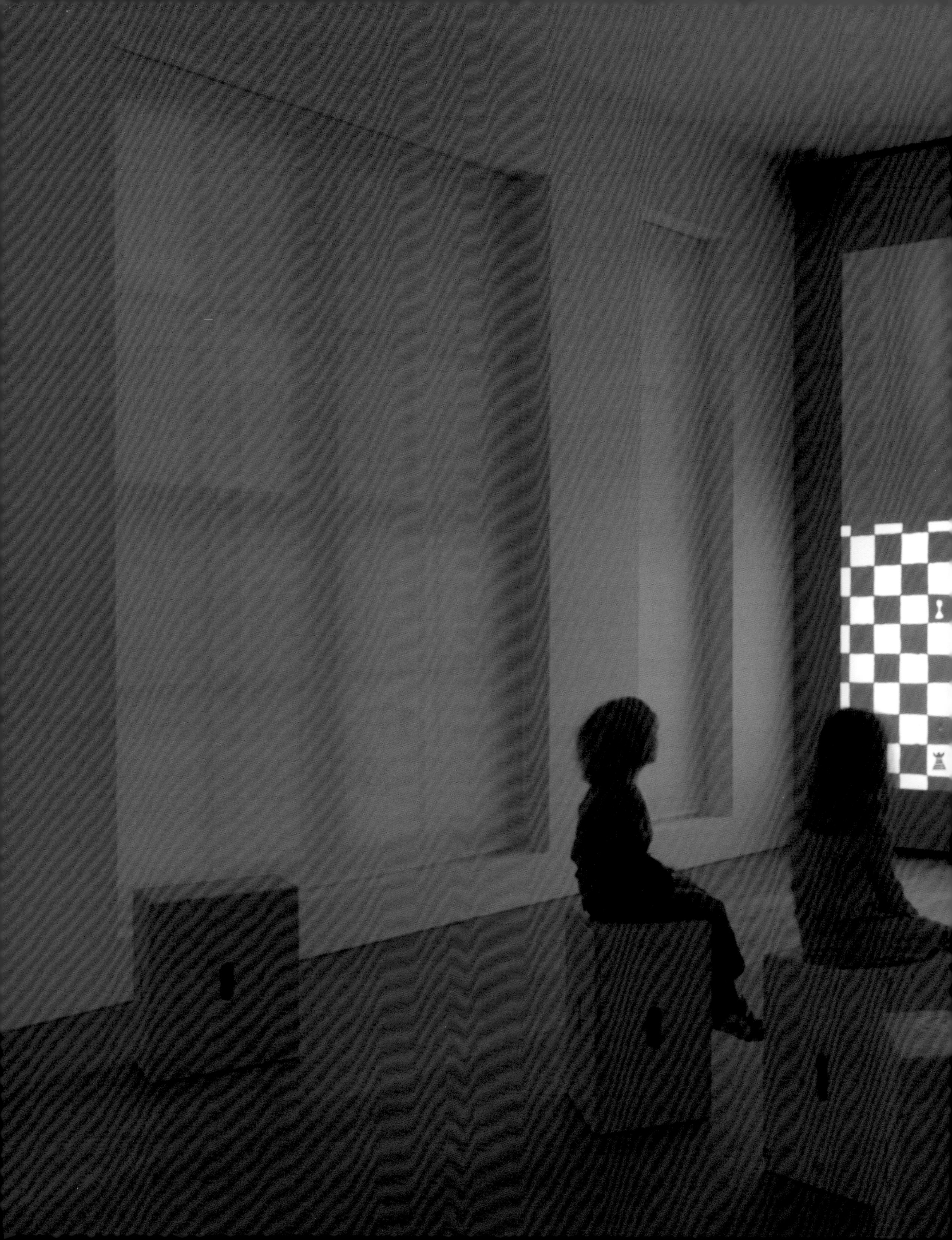

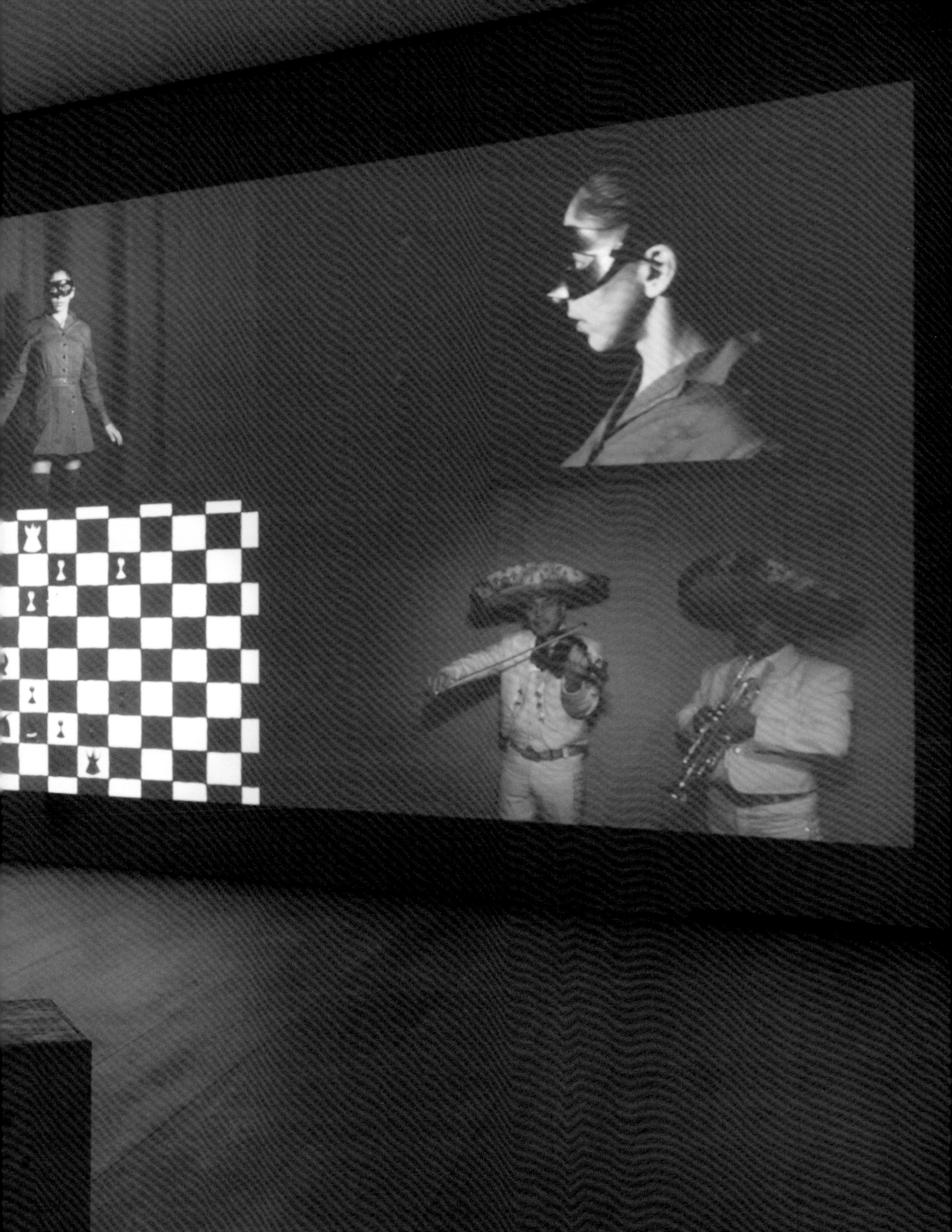

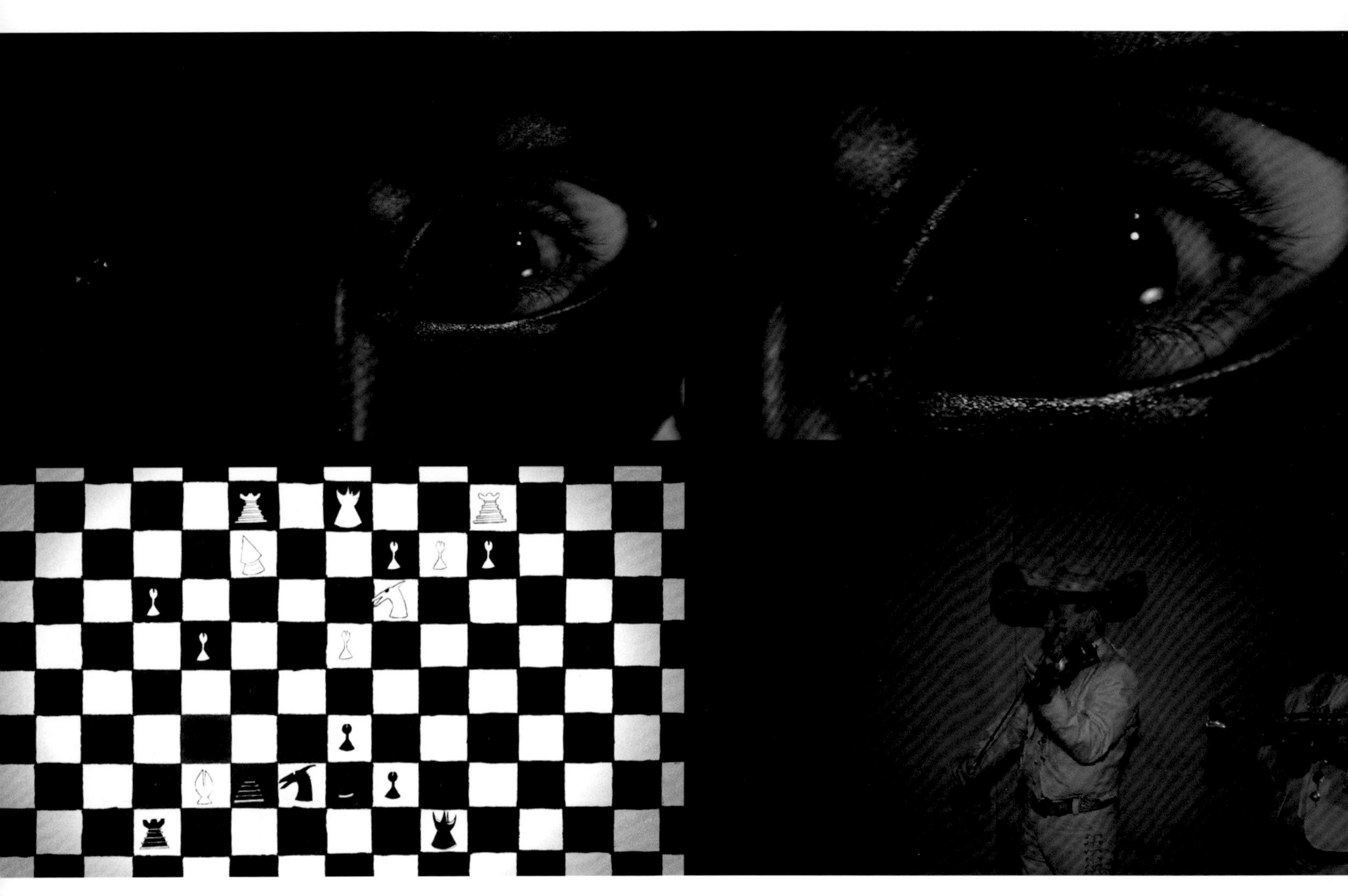

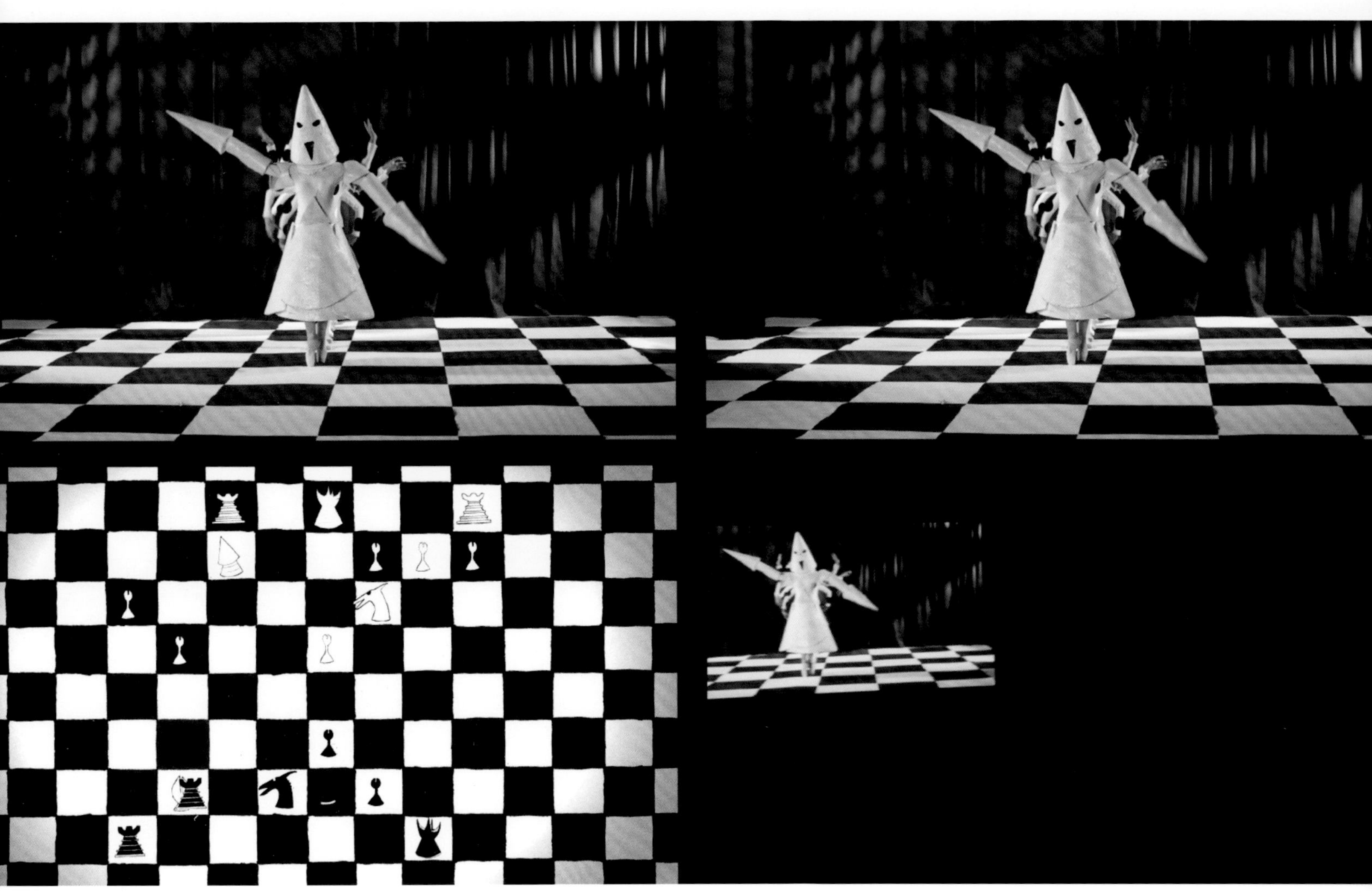

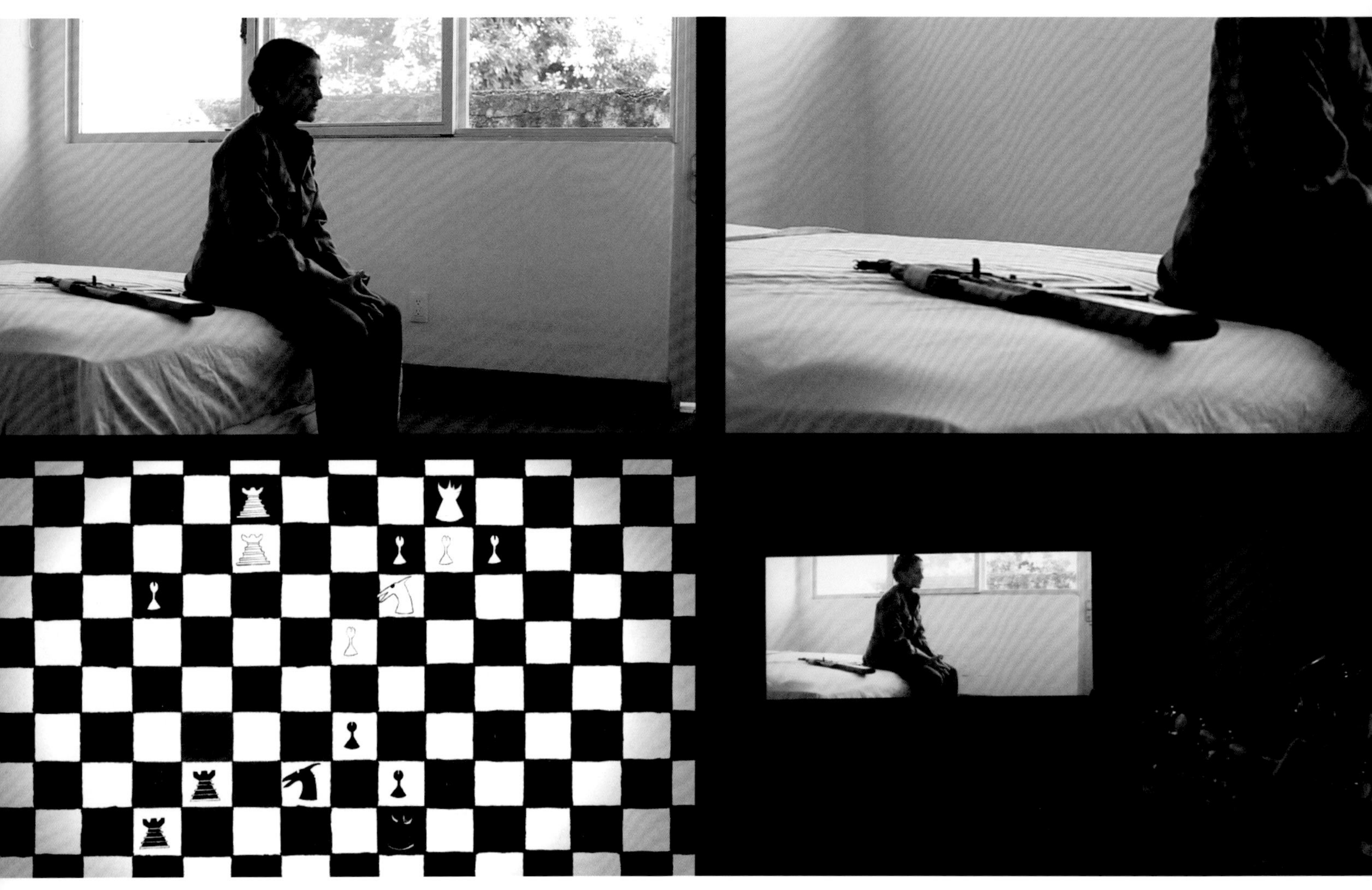

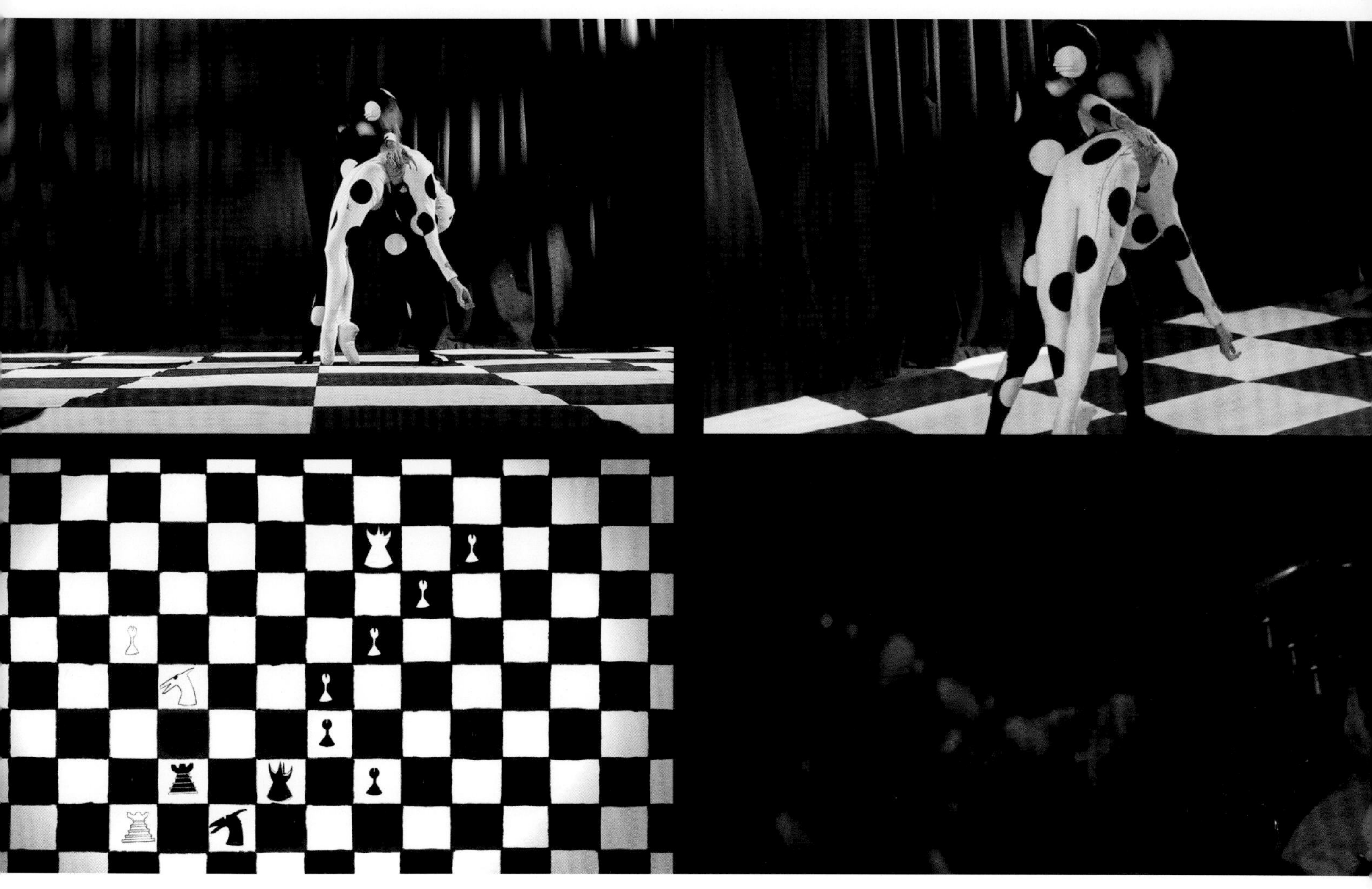

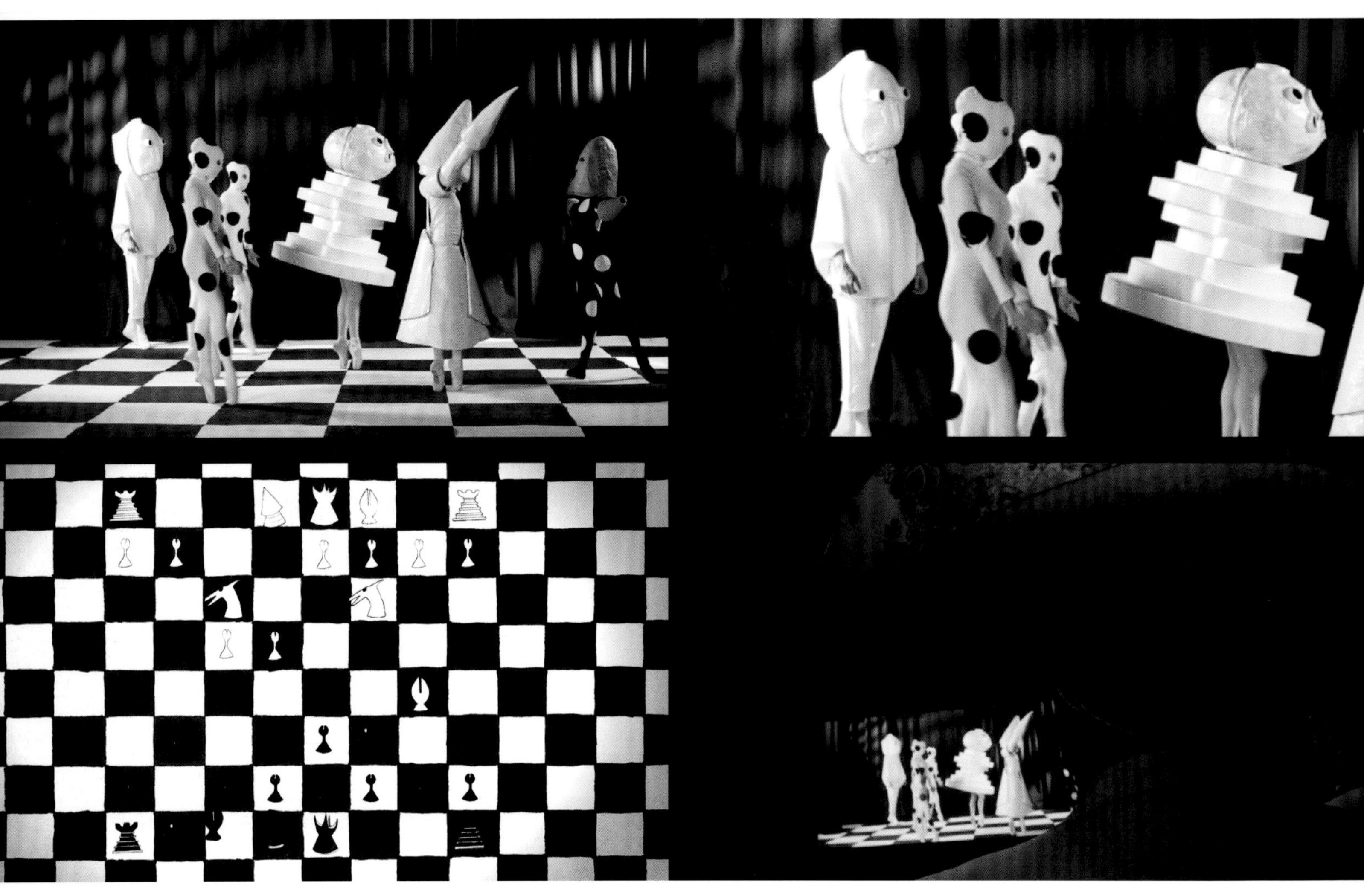

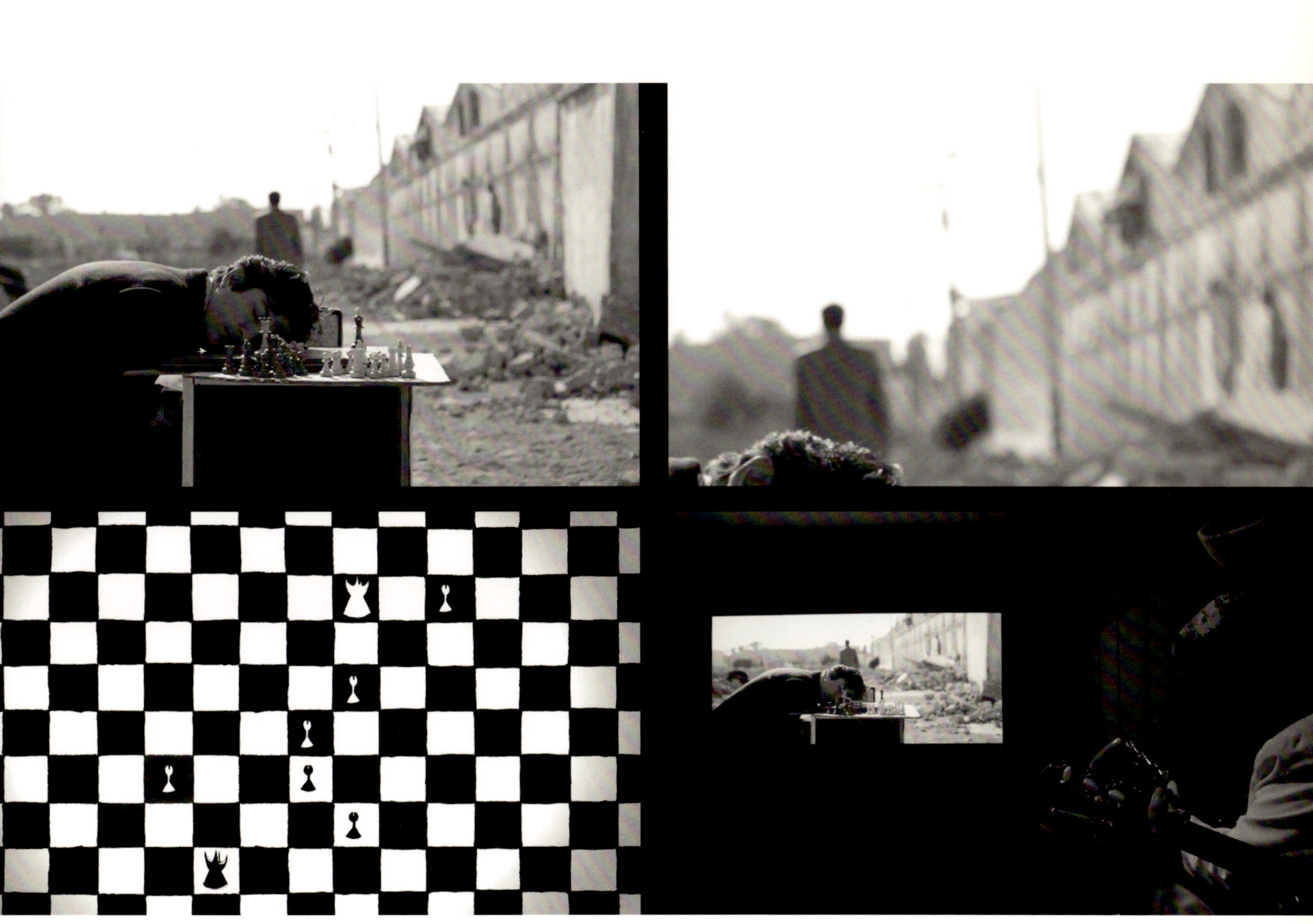

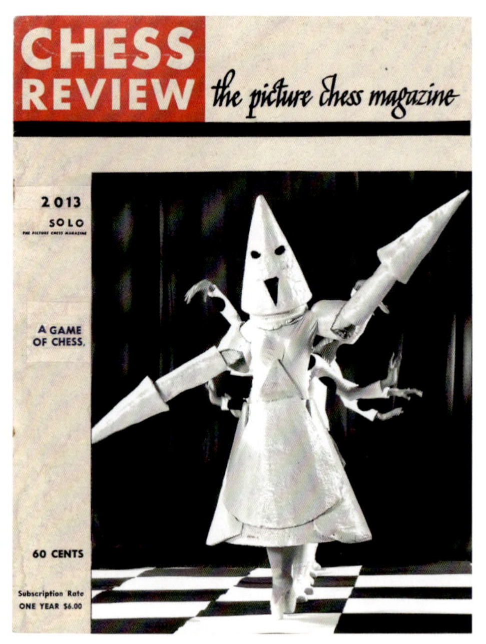

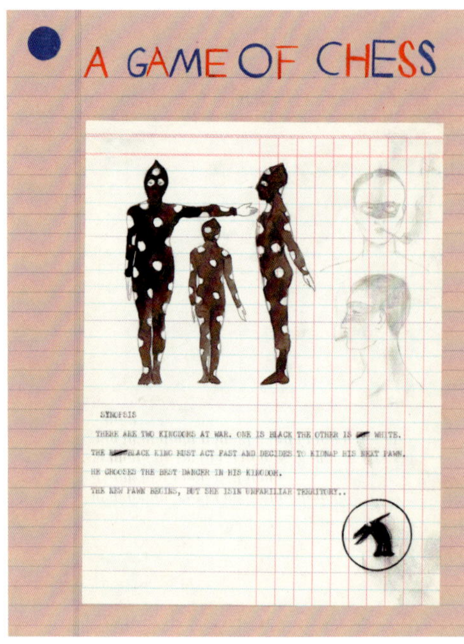

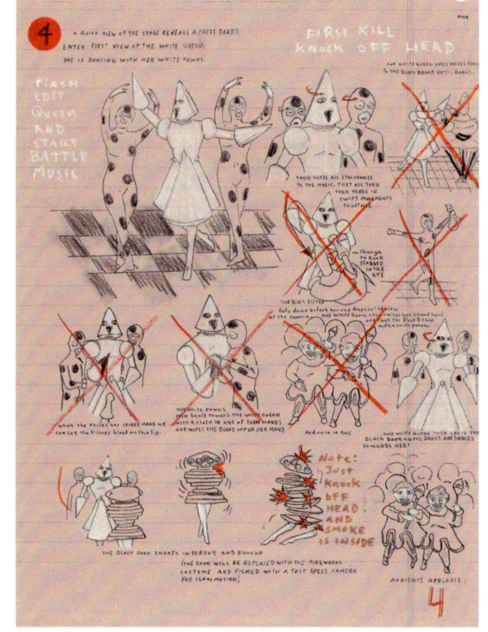

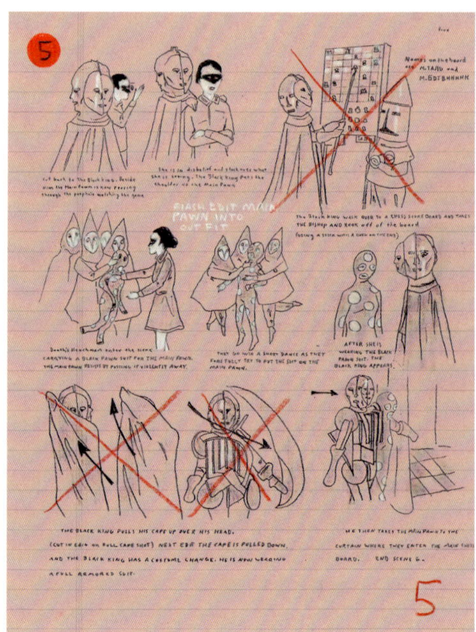

Chess Review storyboard, 2012–2013

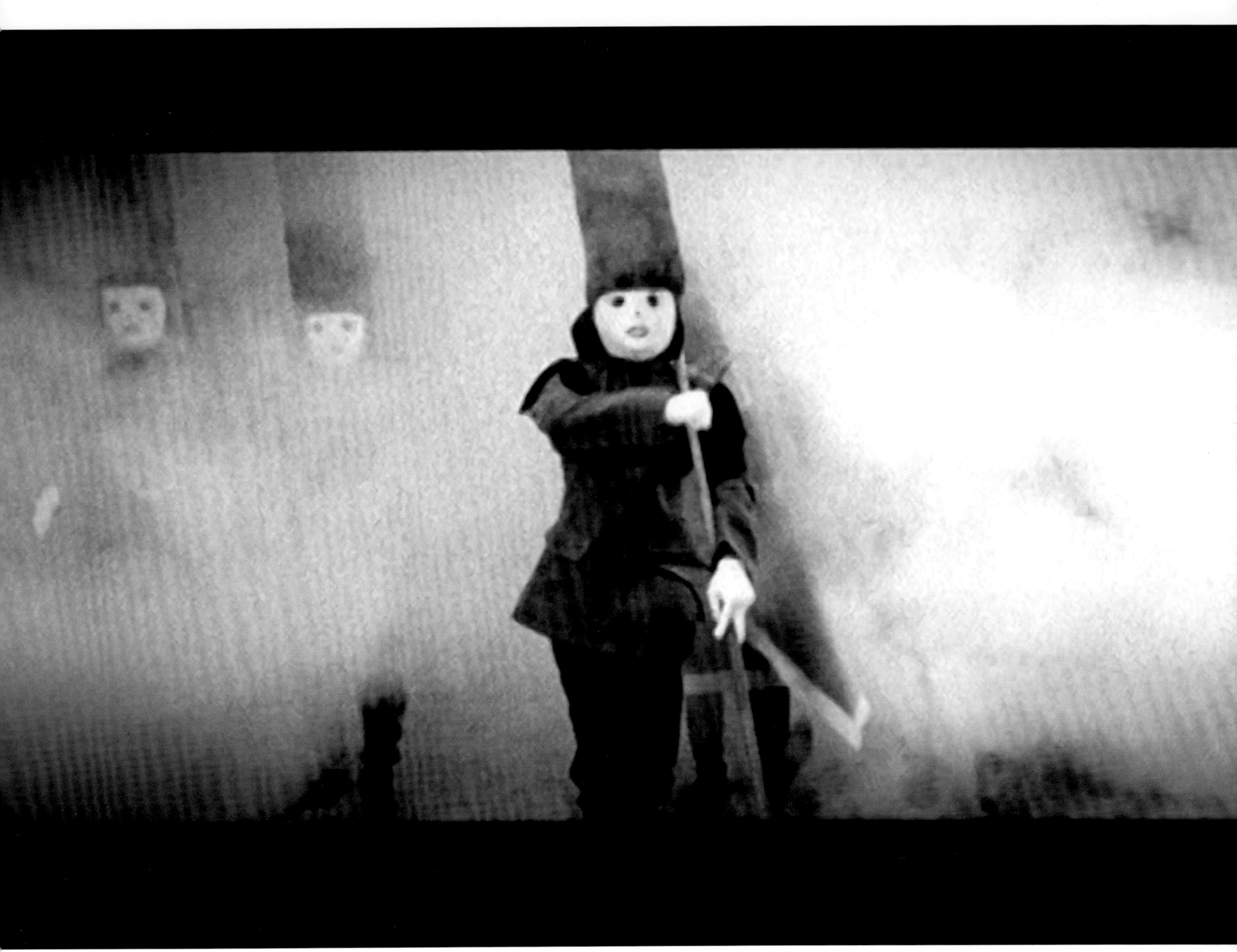

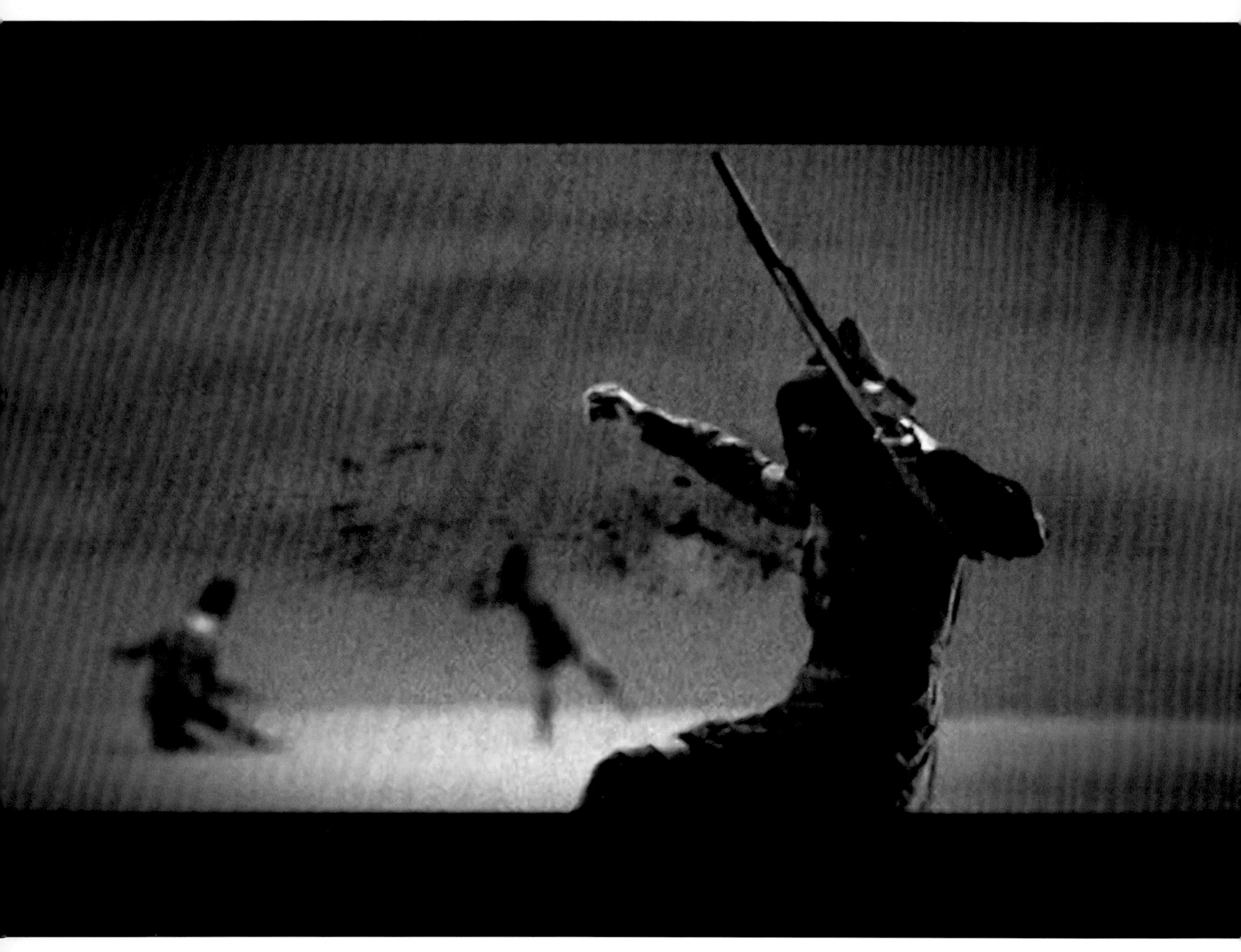

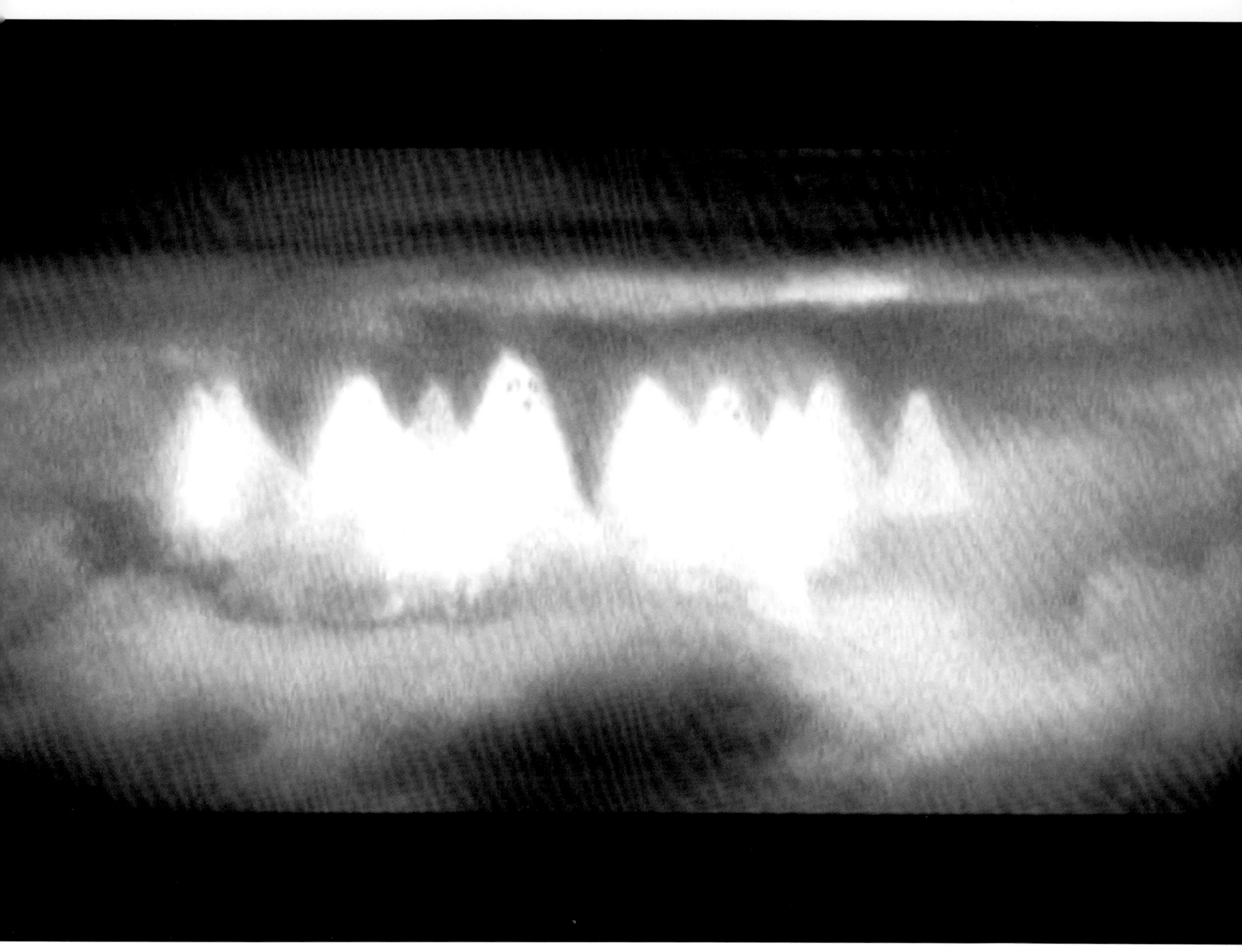

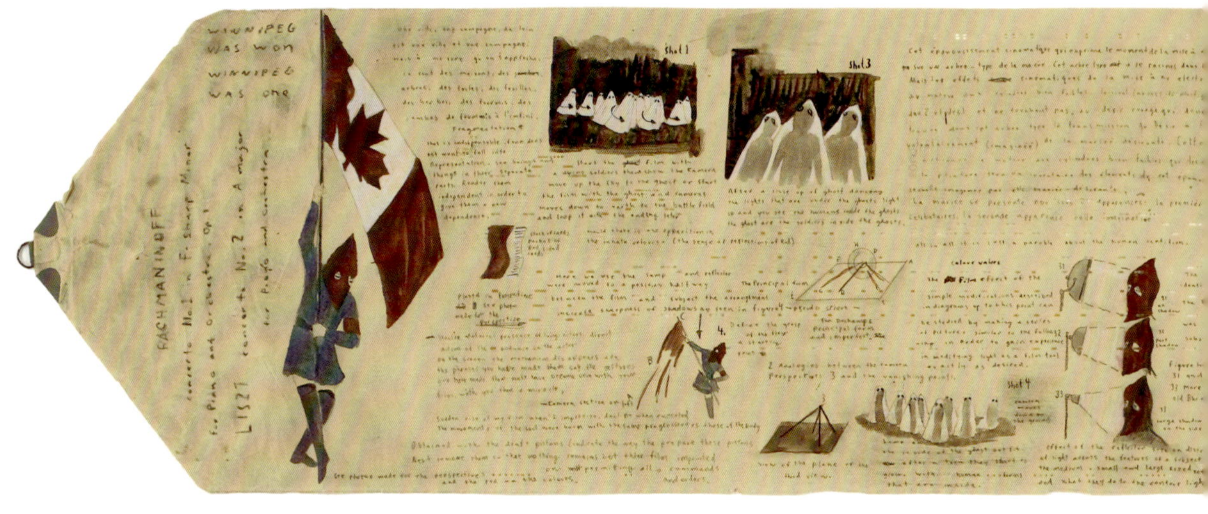

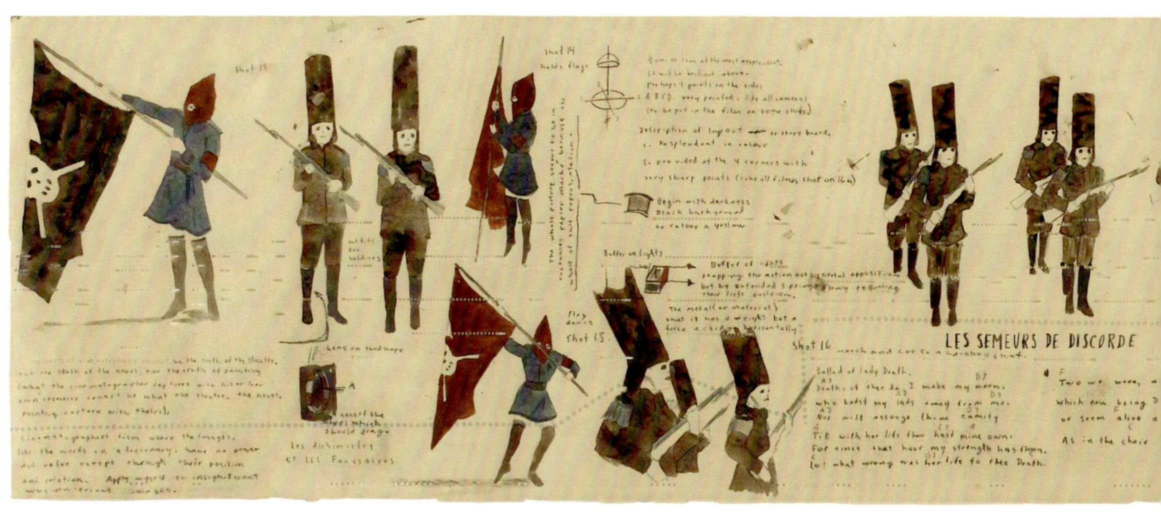

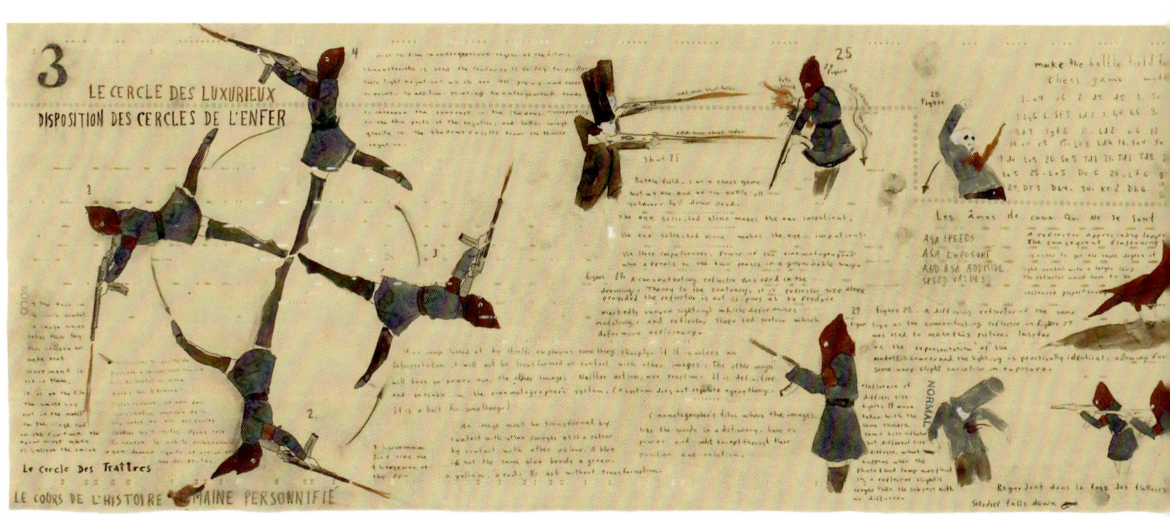

Winnipeg was won, Winnipeg was one, 2009

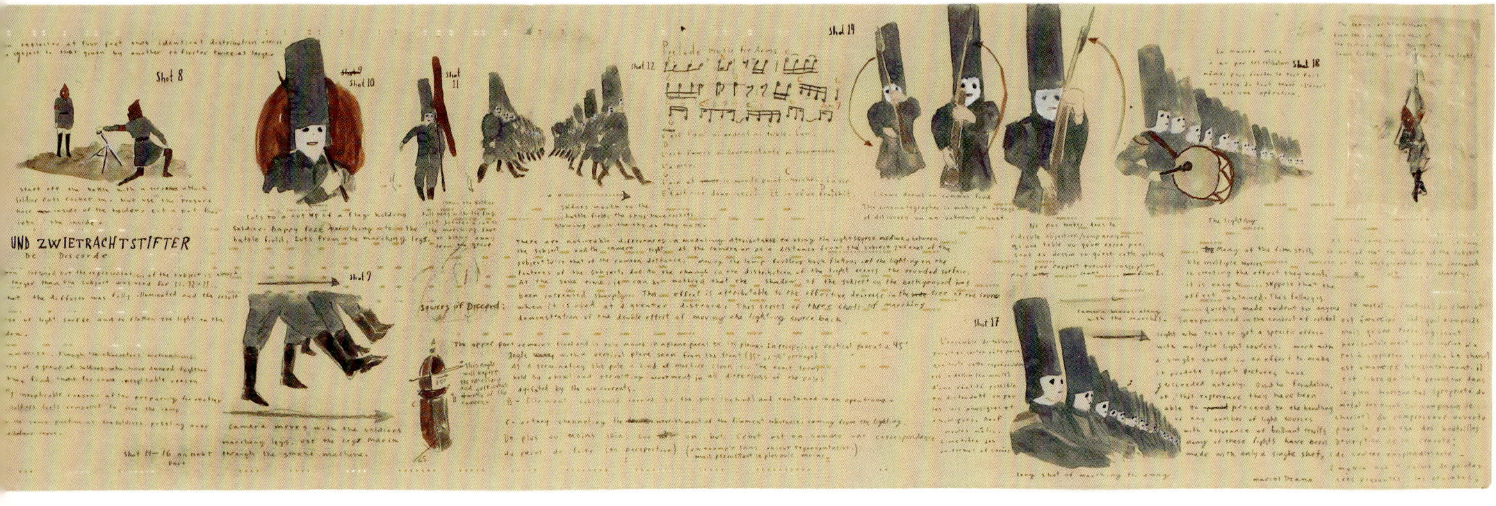

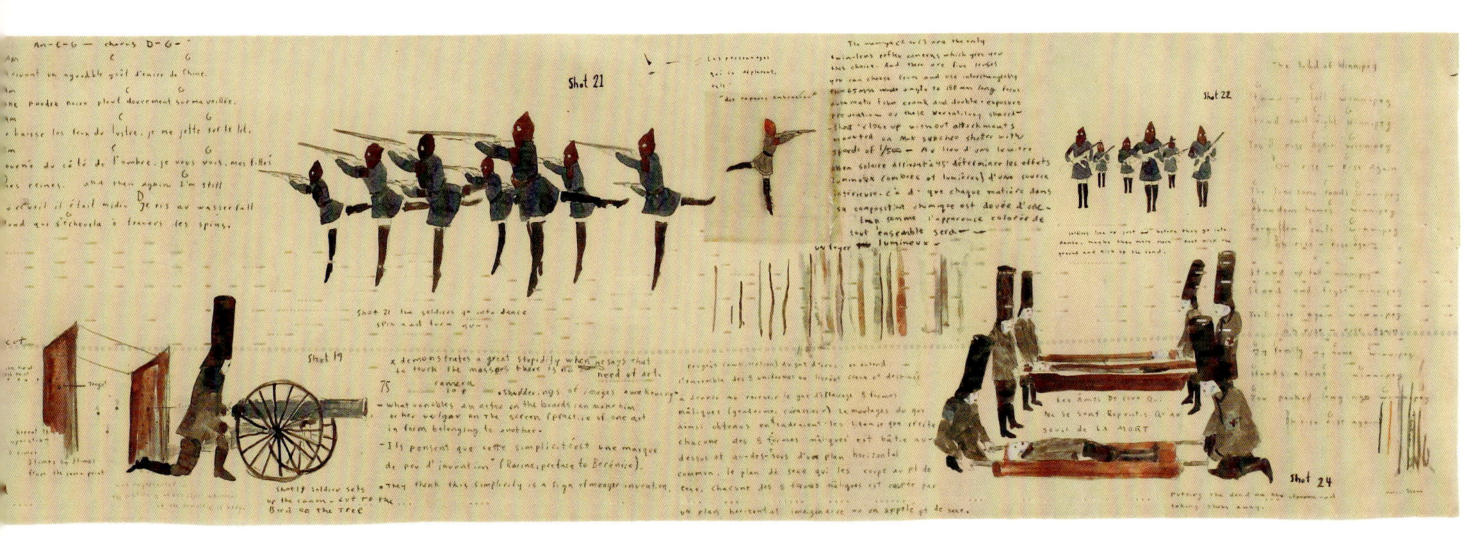

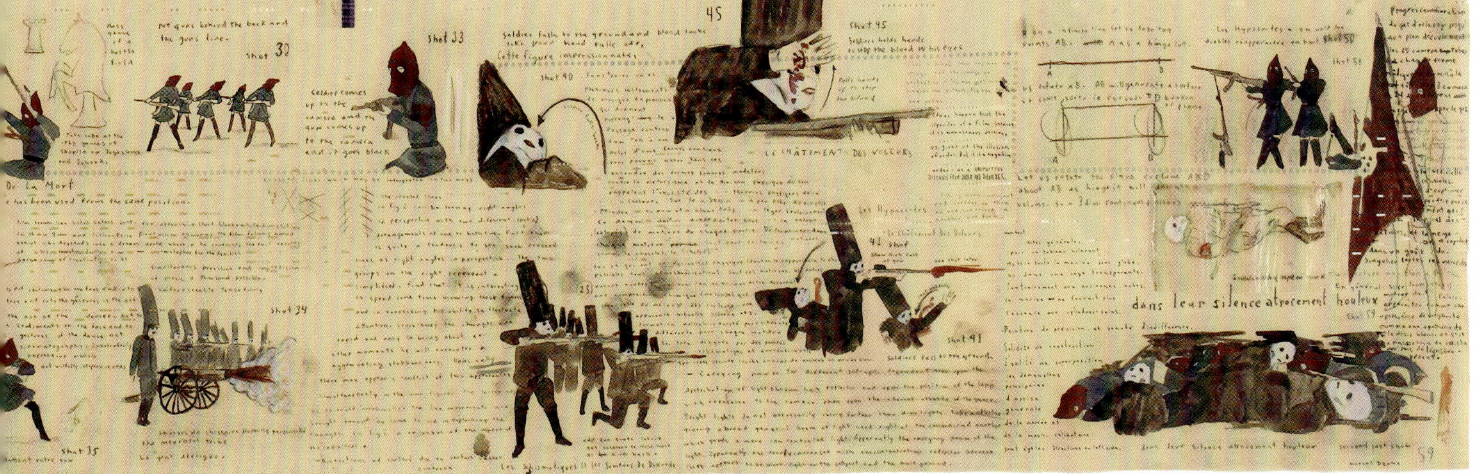

The following works were presented in the exhibition *Marcel Dzama: Puppets, Pawns, and Prophets* held at David Zwirner's 24 Grafton Street space in London from April to May 2013. Those entries without a page number indicate works included in the exhibition but not illustrated in the catalogue. Entries with an asterisk after the page number indicate works illustrated in the catalogue but not included in the exhibition.

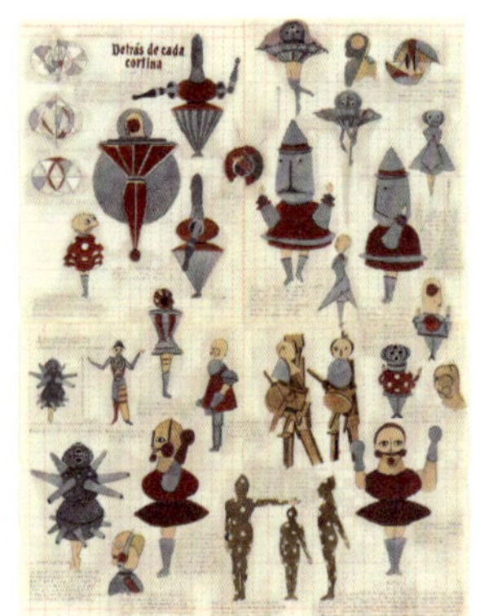

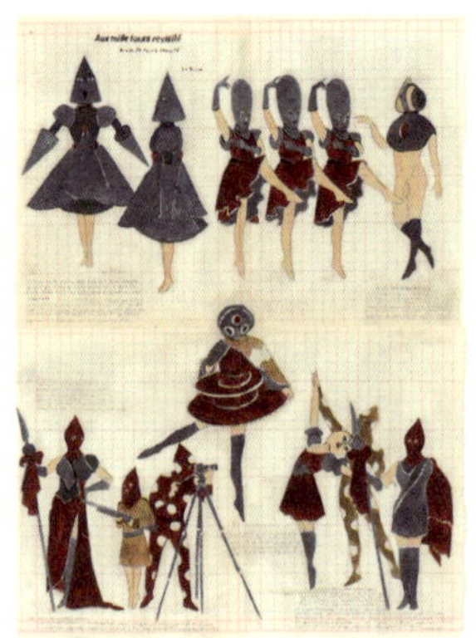

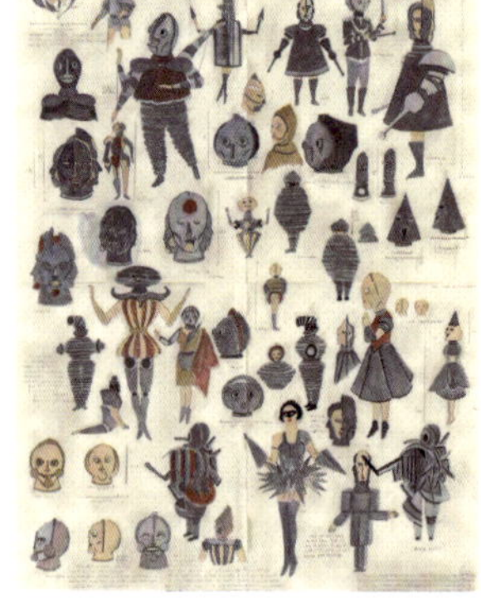

Detrás de cada cortina
or Metete un palo en el culo

2010

Ink, watercolor, and
graphite on paper

4-part work

Overall: 19¼ x 14¼ inches
(48.9 x 36.2 cm)

Each: 9⅝ x 7⅛ inches
(24.4 x 18.1 cm)

The queen's profile
or Aux mille tours revisité

2010

Ink, watercolor, and
graphite on paper

4-part work

Overall: 19¼ x 14¼ inches
(48.9 x 36.2 cm)

Each: 9⅝ x 7⅛ inches
(24.4 x 18.1 cm)

The chessmen

2010

Ink, watercolor, and
graphite on paper

4-part work

Overall: 20 x 15 inches
(50.8 x 38.1 cm)

Each: 10 x 7½ inches
(25.4 x 19.1 cm)

Page 69

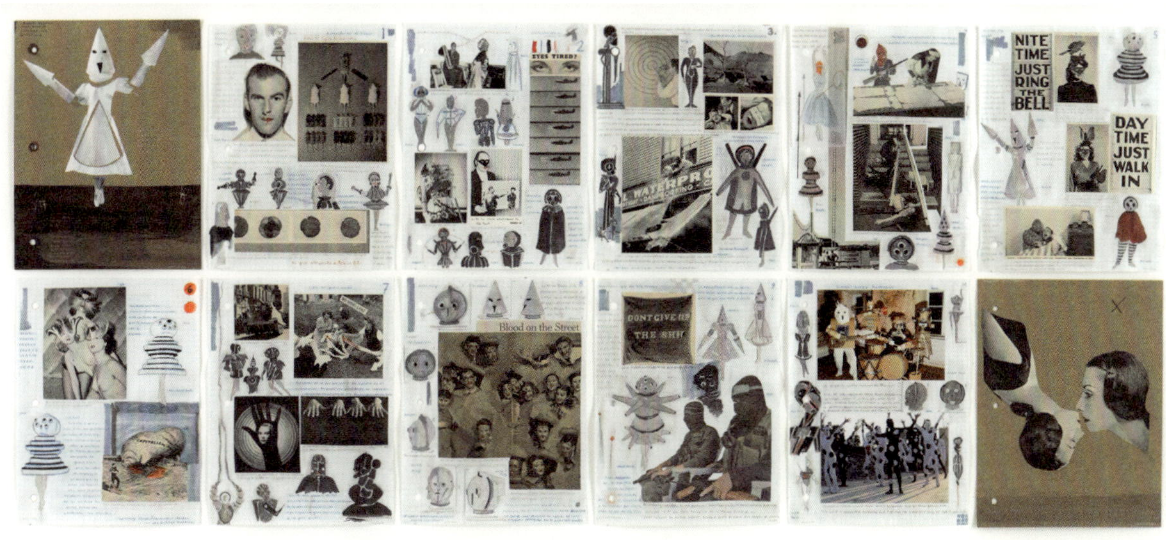

The strategy of a pure symbolic order

2011

Ink, watercolor, graphite, and
collage on paper

12-part work

Framed: 26 3/8 x 56 3/4 inches
(67 x 144.1 cm)

Each: 10 3/4 x 8 1/4 inches
(27.3 x 21 cm)

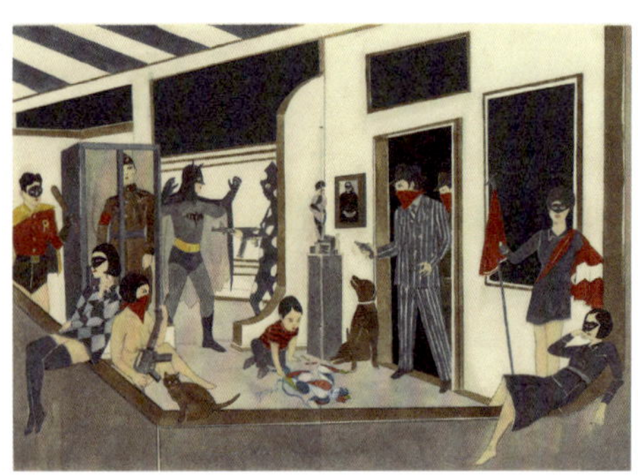

If you can't bring good news,
then don't bring me any

2012

Ink, gouache, graphite, and
collage on paper

2-part work

Overall: 16½ x 23⅝ inches
(41.9 x 60 cm)

Each: 16½ x 11¾ inches
(41.9 x 29.8 cm)

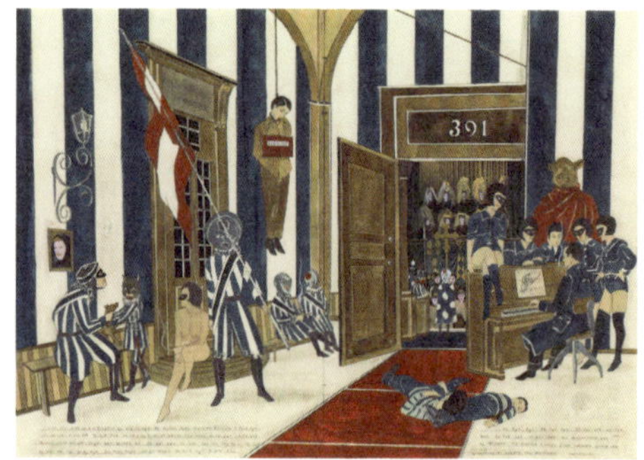

Opportunists mingling with combatants

2012

Ink, gouache, and
graphite on paper

2-part work

Overall: 16½ x 23⅝ inches
(41.9 x 60 cm)

Each: 16½ x 11¾ inches
(41.9 x 29.8 cm)

Pages 52–53

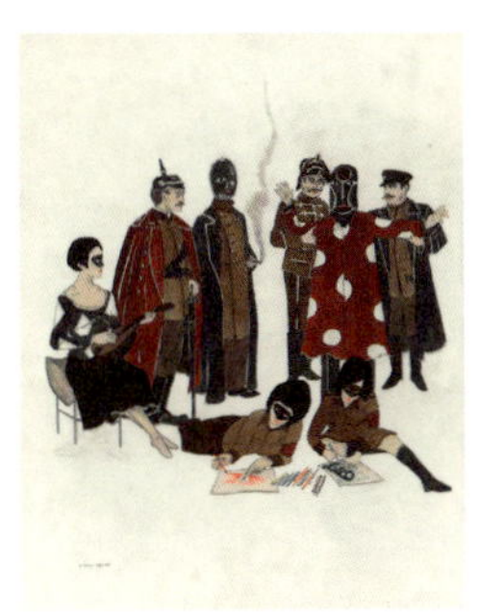

Kings have been his fellows

2012

Ink and gouache on paper

14 x 11 inches
(35.6 x 27.9 cm)

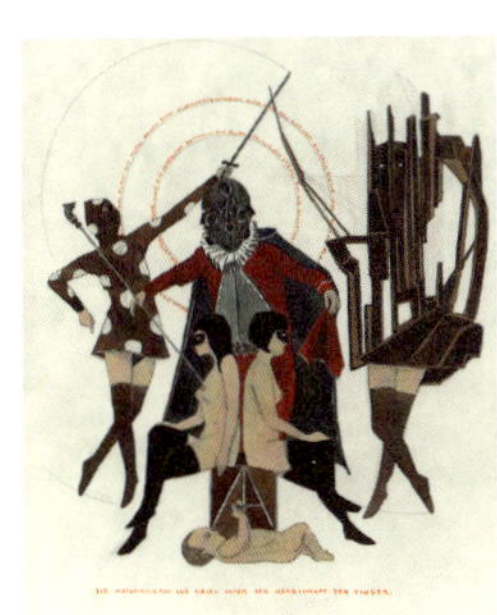

I fear I am attended by spies

2012

Ink and gouache on paper

14 x 11 inches
(35.6 x 27.9 cm)

Page 58

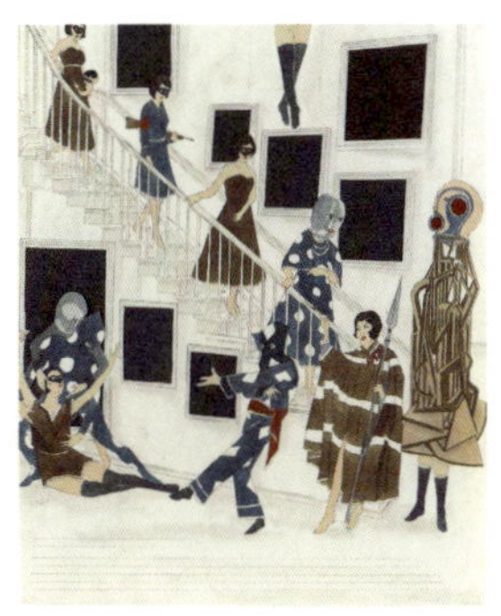

Shall we venture outside

2013

Ink, gouache, and
graphite on paper

17 x 14 inches
(43.2 x 35.6 cm)

Page 25

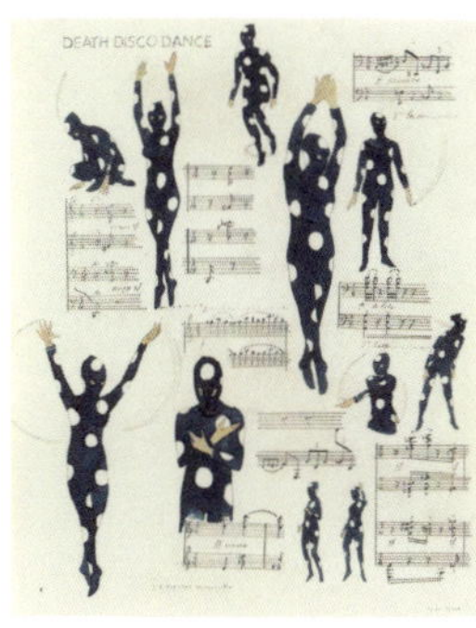

The Death Disco Dance steps

2013

Ink, gouache, and
graphite on paper

17 x 14 inches
(43.2 x 35.6 cm)

Page 31

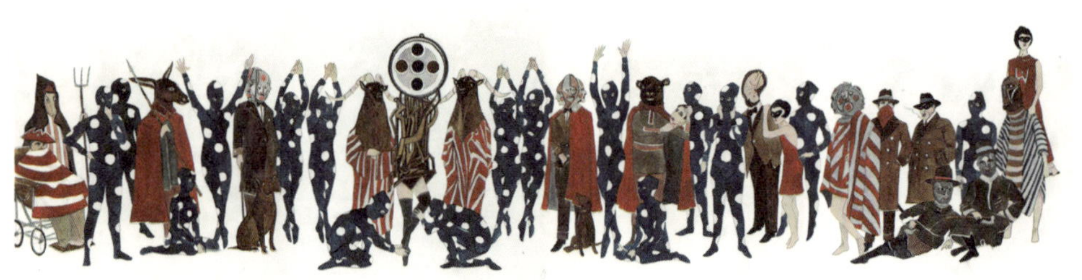

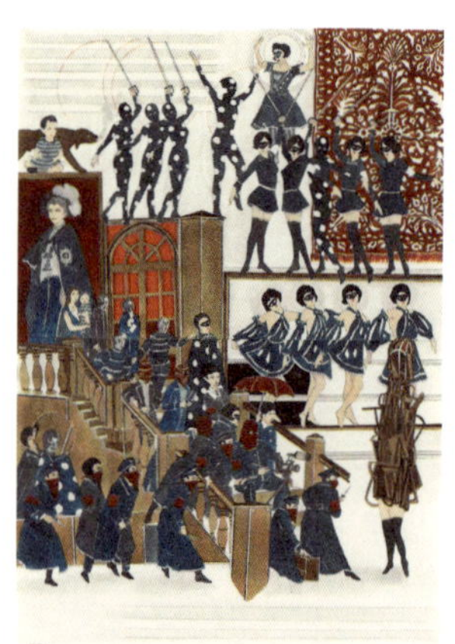

Myth, manifestos, and monsters

2013

Ink, gouache, and
graphite on paper

4-part work

Overall: 14 x 44 inches
(35.6 x 111.8 cm)

Each: 14 x 11 inches
(35.6 x 27.9 cm)

Pages 26–29

The tension around which
history is built

2013

Ink, gouache, and
graphite on paper

2-part work

Overall: 23⅛ x 16⅜ inches
(58.7 x 41.6 cm)

Each: 11⅝ x 16⅜ inches
(29.5 x 41.6 cm)

Page 35

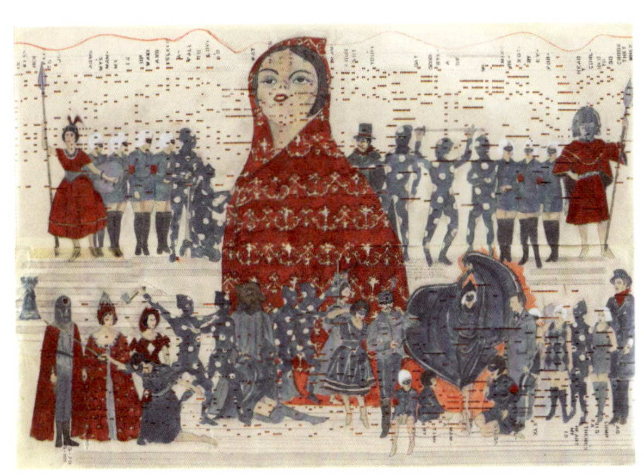

Malala will have her revenge

2013

Ink, gouache, and
graphite on piano scroll

2-part work

Overall: 22½ x 32 inches
(57.2 x 81.3 cm)

Each: 11⅛ x 32 inches
(28.3 x 81.3 cm)

Pages 36–39

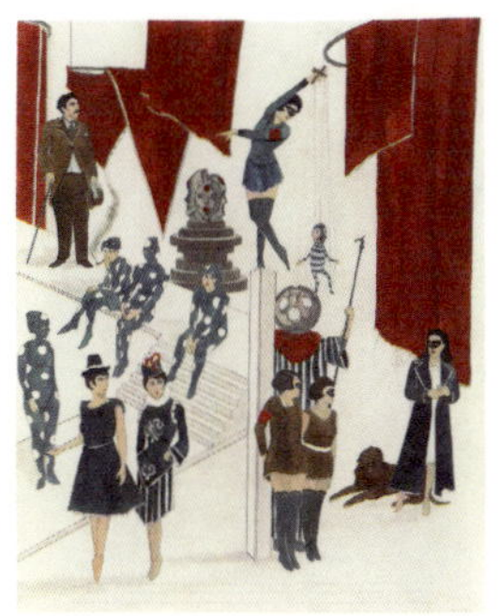

A play for puppets and people

2013

Ink, gouache, and
graphite on paper

17 x 14 inches
(43.2 x 35.6 cm)

Page 32

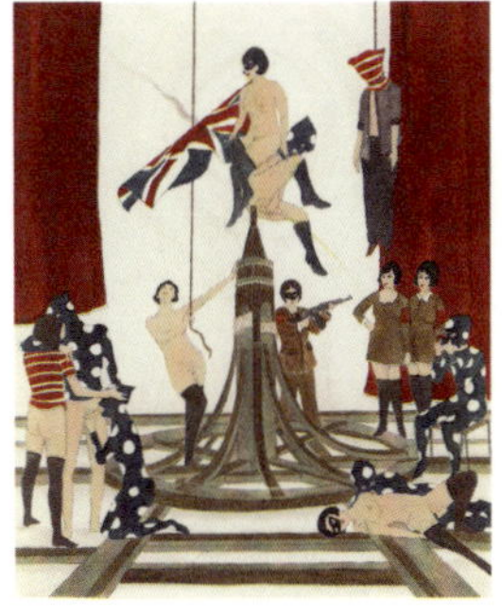

The renowned Union Jack off

2013

Ink, gouache, and
graphite on paper

17 x 14 inches
(43.2 x 35.6 cm)

Page 33

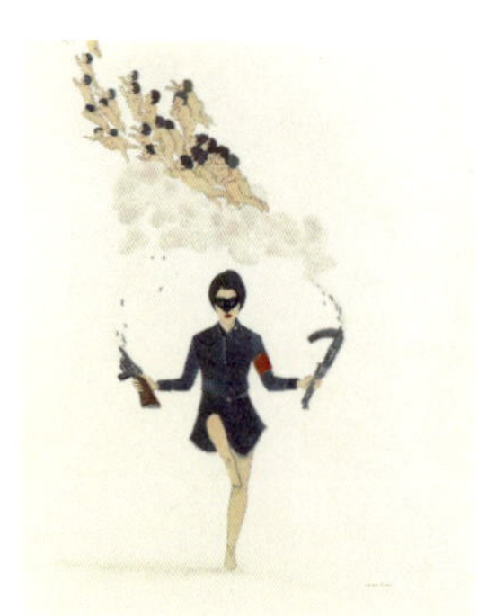

As innocent as grace itself

2012

Ink, gouache, and
graphite on paper

17 x 14 inches
(43.2 x 35.6 cm)

Page 41

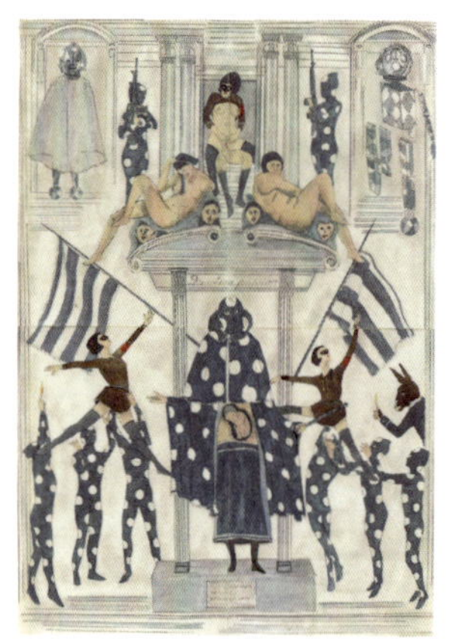

Was he not born of woman

2013

Ink, gouache, graphite, and
collage on paper

4-part work

Overall: 23⅛ x 16¼ inches
(58.7 x 41.3 cm)

Each: 11½ x 8⅛ inches
(29.2 x 20.6 cm)

Page 43

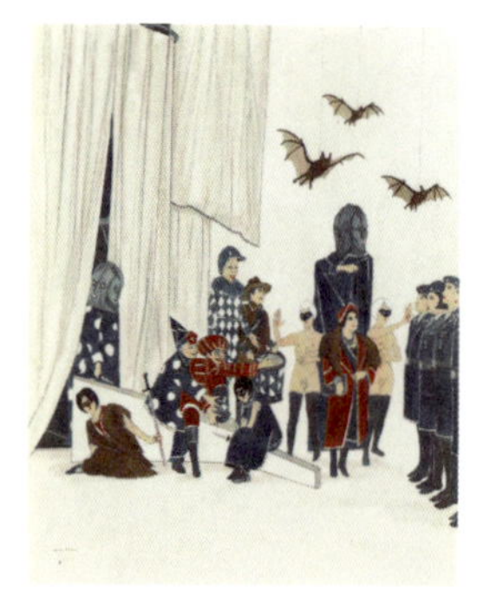

I am queen in title and in style

2013

Ink, gouache, and
graphite on paper

17 x 14 inches
(43.2 x 35.6 cm)

Page 44

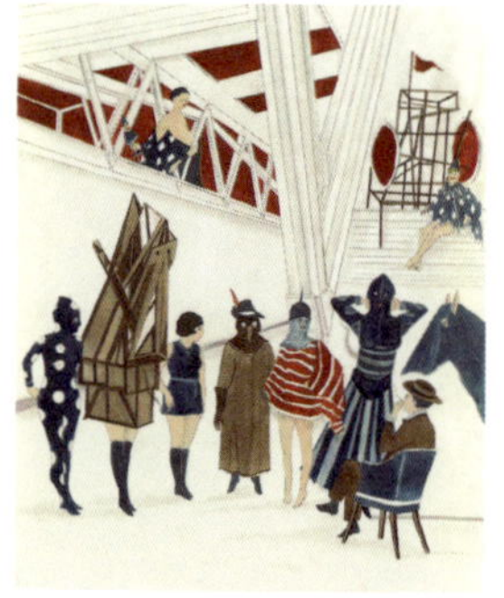

Waiting to be anointed

2013

Ink, gouache, and
graphite on paper

17 x 14 inches
(43.2 x 35.6 cm)

Page 45

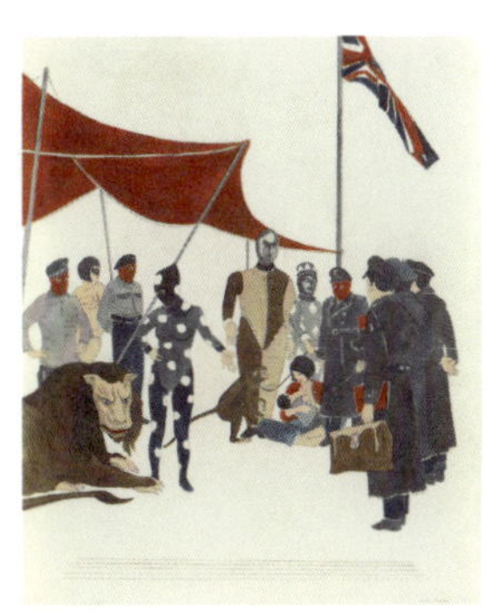

A creature, that did bear
the shape of man

2013

Ink, gouache, and
graphite on paper

17 x 14 inches
(43.2 x 35.6 cm)

Pages 47–49

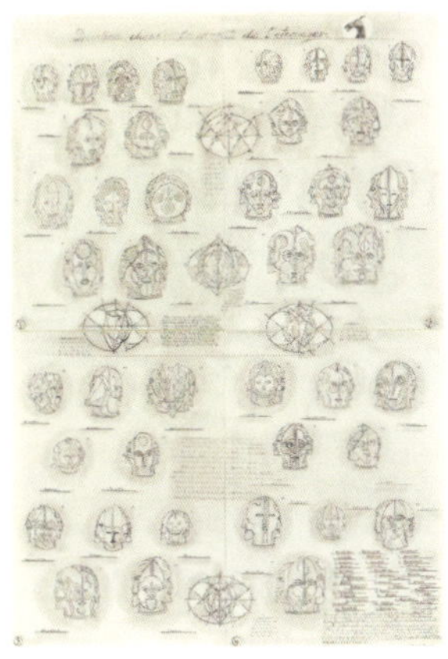

Perhaps they are gods

2013

Graphite and collage on paper

4-part work

Overall: 23 ¼ x 16 ¼ inches
(59.1 x 41.3 cm)

Each: 11 ½ x 8 ⅛ inches
(29.2 x 20.6 cm)

Page 51

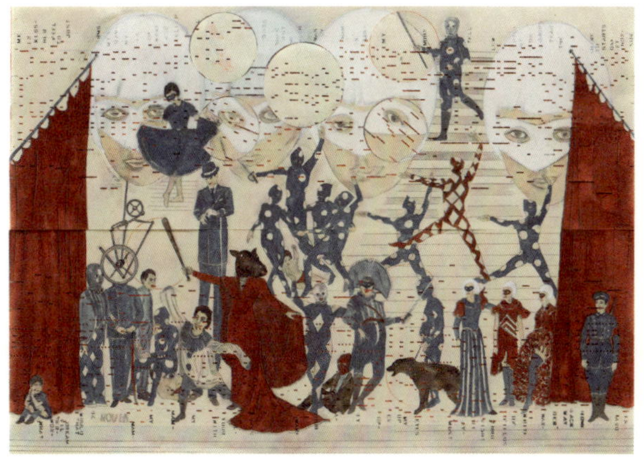

The queen's ghost vanish'd from our sight

2013

Ink, gouache, and
graphite on piano scroll

2-part work

Overall: 22 ½ x 32 ⅜ inches
(57.2 x 82.2 cm)

Each: 11 ⅛ x 32 inches
(28.3 x 81.3 cm)

Pages 54–55

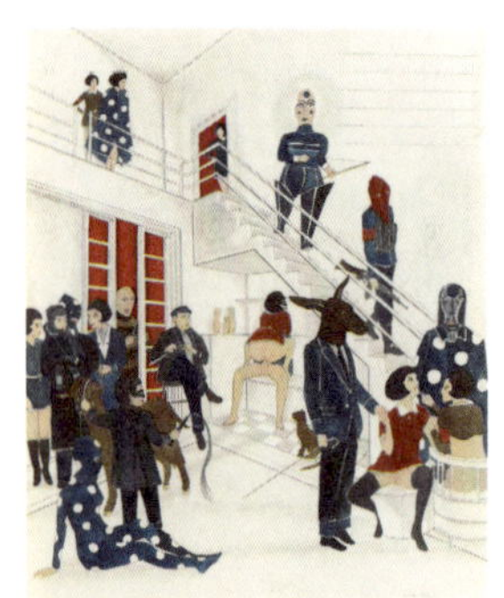

The factious feast

2013

Ink, gouache, and
graphite on paper

17 x 14 inches
(43.2 x 35.6 cm)

Page 57

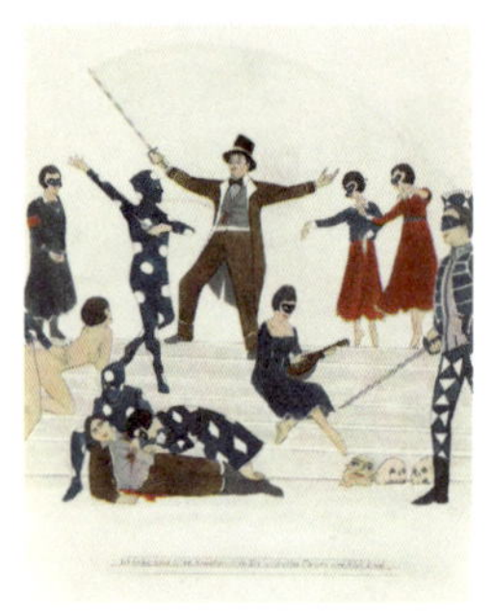

I have been a wicked creature,
as you and all flesh and blood are

2013

Ink, gouache, and
graphite on paper

14 x 11 inches
(35.6 x 27.9 cm)

Page 59

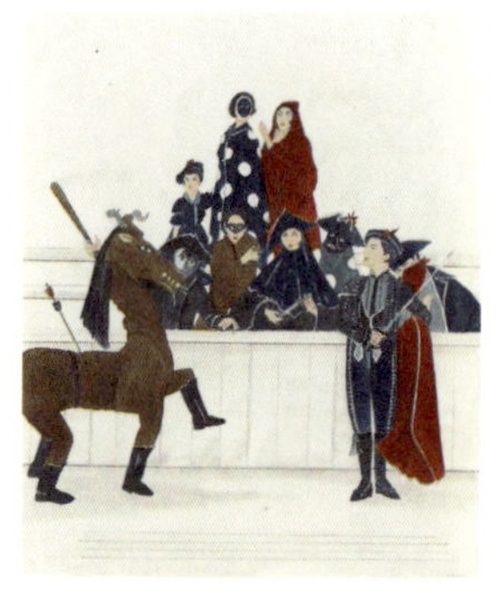

Picasso's cock fight

2013

Ink, gouache, and
graphite on paper

17 x 14 inches
(43.2 x 35.6 cm)

Page 61

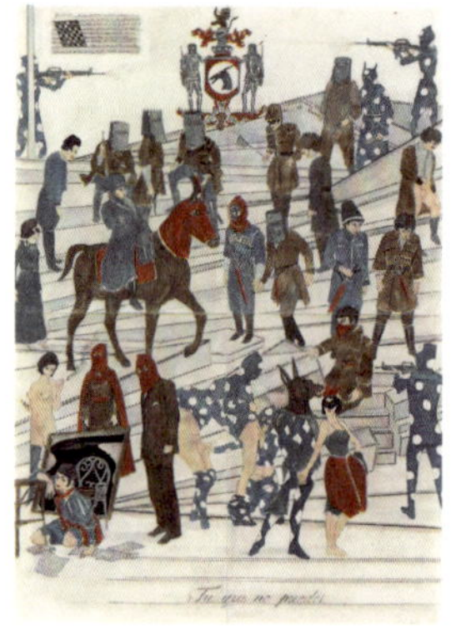

The Ned Kelly armour defense

2013

Ink, gouache, graphite, and
collage on paper

4-part work

Overall: 23⅛ x 16¼ inches
(58.7 x 41.3 cm)

Each: 11½ x 8⅛ inches
(29.2 x 20.6 cm)

Pages 63–65

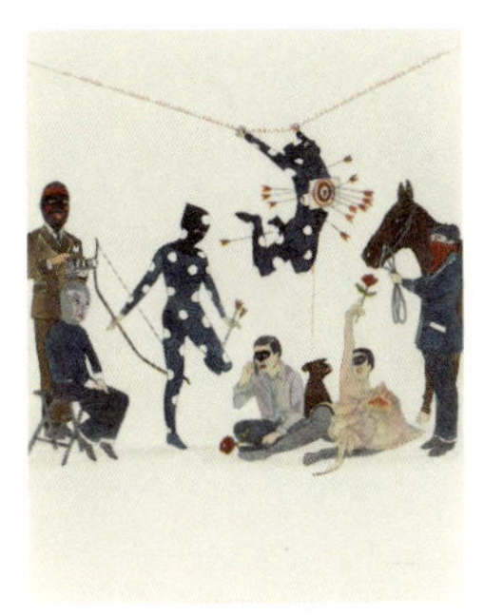

The photo shoot or
(Blood has fingers)

2013

Ink, gouache, and
graphite on paper

14 x 11 inches
(35.6 x 27.9 cm)

Page 67

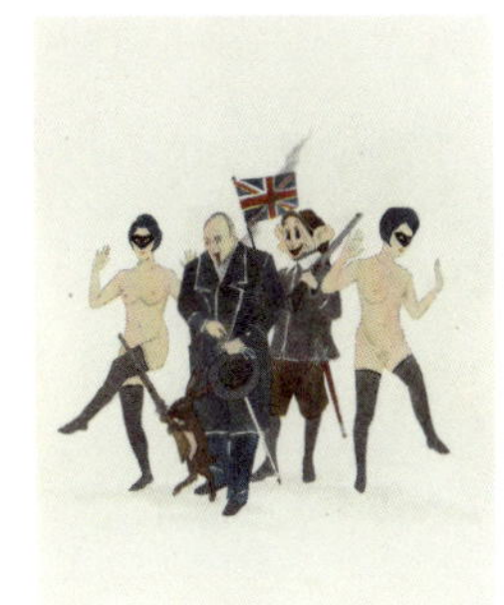

After we won the war

2013

Ink, gouache, and
graphite on paper

14 x 11 inches
(35.6 x 27.9 cm)

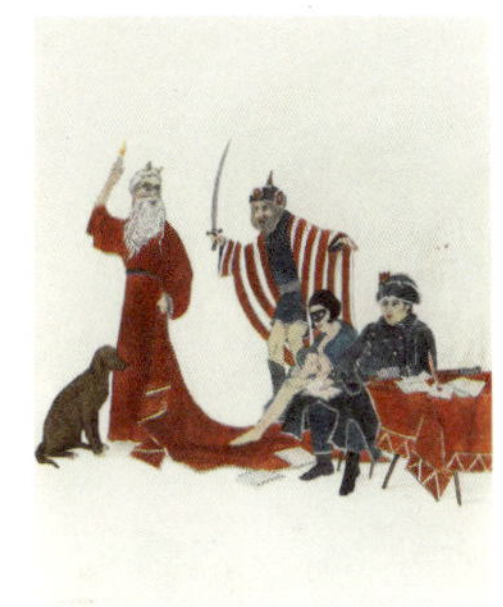

Who will lead forth

2013

Ink, gouache, and
graphite on paper

14 x 11 inches
(35.6 x 27.9 cm)

Page 70

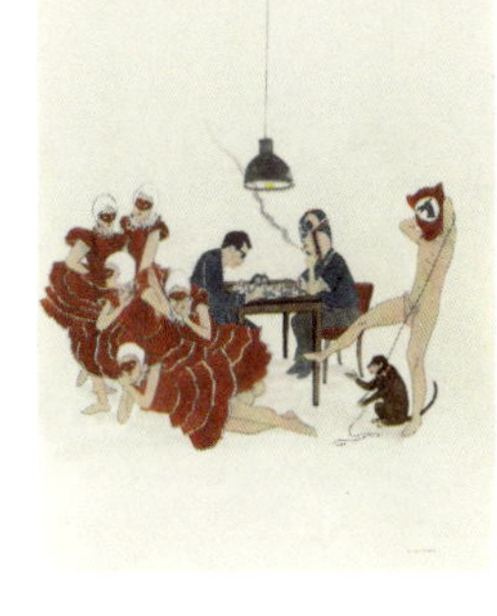

Let me be cruel, not unnatural

2013

Ink, gouache, and
graphite on paper

14 x 11 inches
(35.6 x 27.9 cm)

Page 71

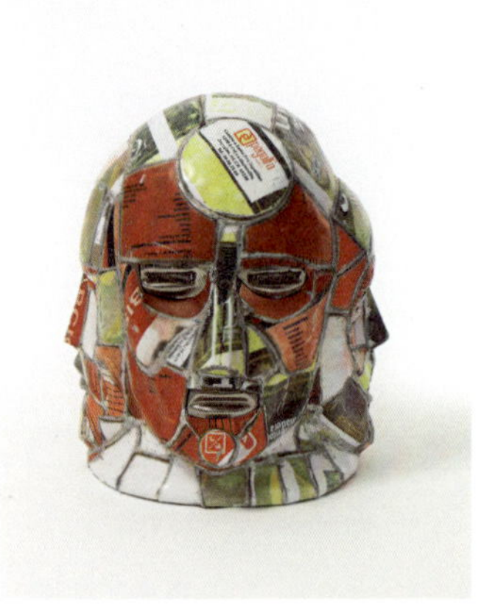 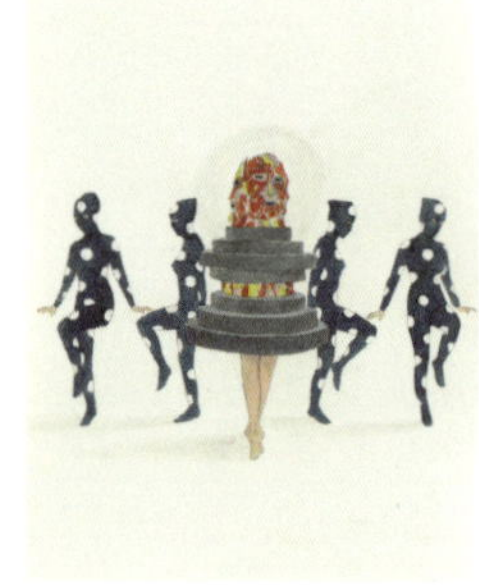

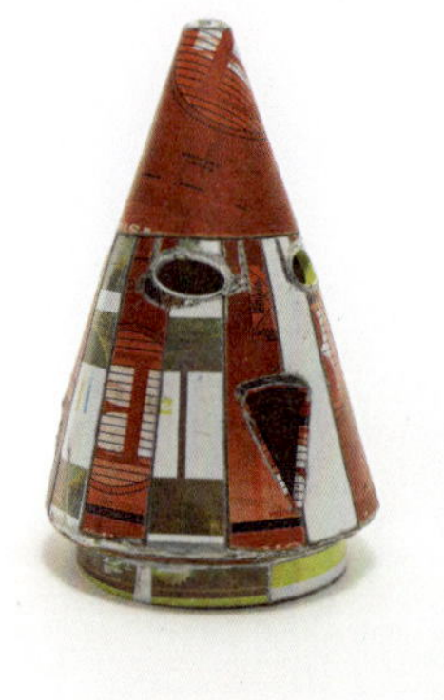 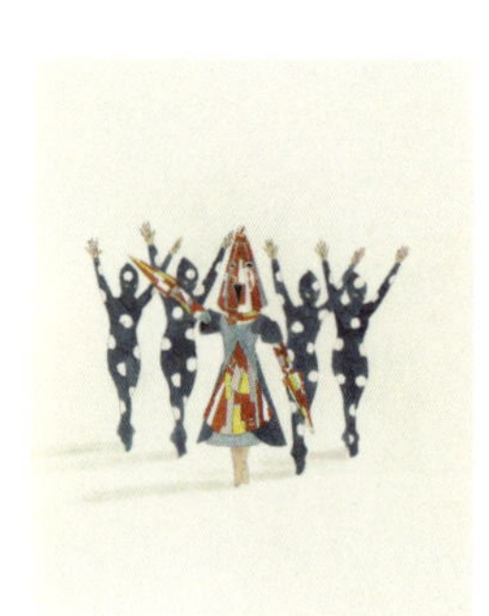

The king's Janus times two

2012

Ceramic and tin; ink, gouache,
and graphite on paper

Sculpture:
height, 17 inches (43.2 cm)
diameter, 13 inches (33 cm)

Drawing:
14 x 11 inches
(35.6 x 27.9 cm)

Pages 76–77

The queen's head

2012

Ceramic and tin; ink, gouache,
and graphite on paper

Sculpture:
height, 23 inches (58.4 cm)
diameter, 14 inches (35.6 cm)

Drawing:
14 x 11 inches
(35.6 x 27.9 cm)

Pages 78–79

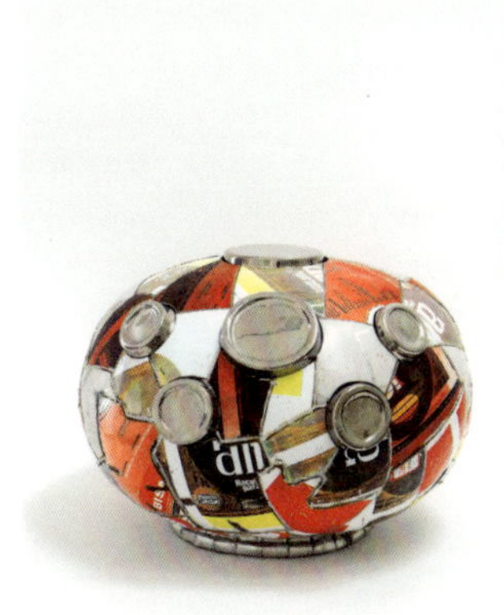 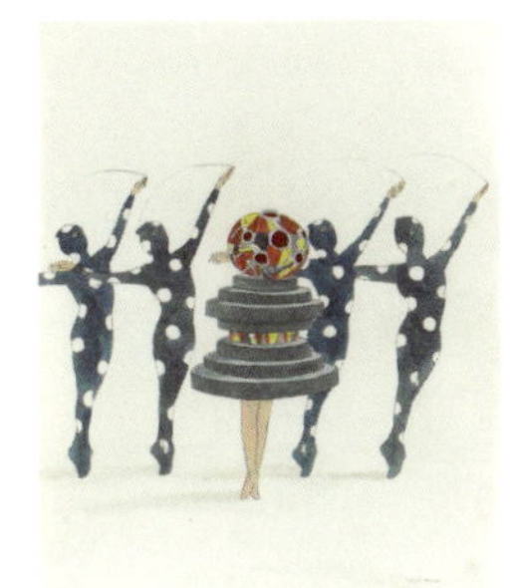

The rook's head

2012

Ceramic and tin; ink, gouache,
and graphite on paper

Sculpture:
height, 15½ inches (39.4 cm)
diameter, 21 inches (53.3 cm)

Drawing:
14 x 11 inches
(35.6 x 27.9 cm)

Pages 80–81

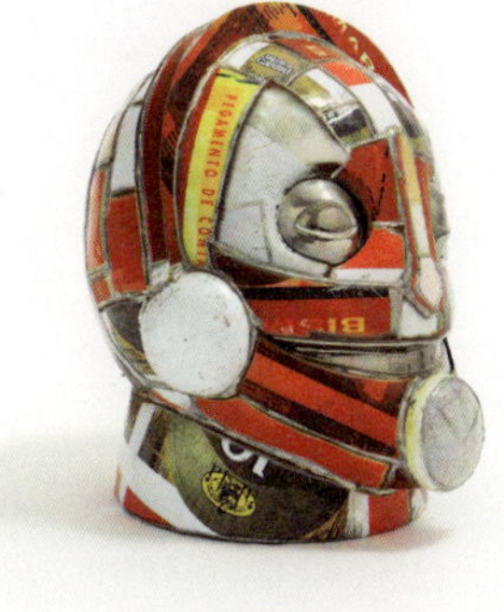 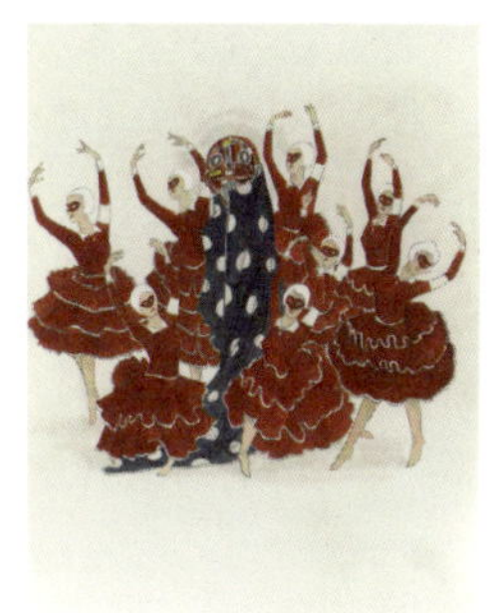

The jester's head

2012

Ceramic and tin; ink, gouache,
and graphite on paper

Sculpture:
17½ x 13½ x 14½ inches
(44.5 x 34.3 x 36.8 cm)

Drawing:
14 x 11 inches
(35.6 x 27.9 cm)

Pages 82–83

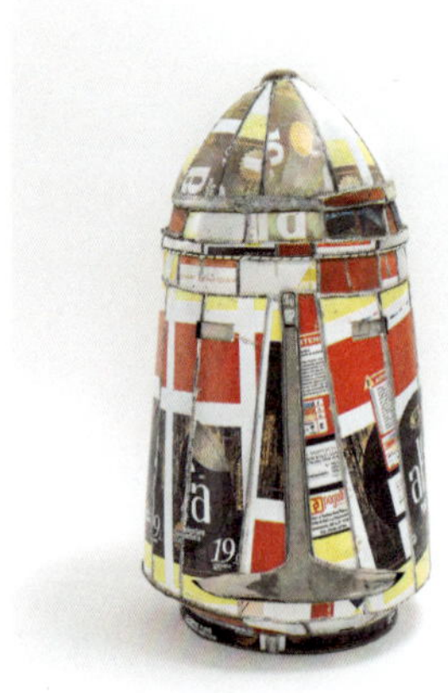 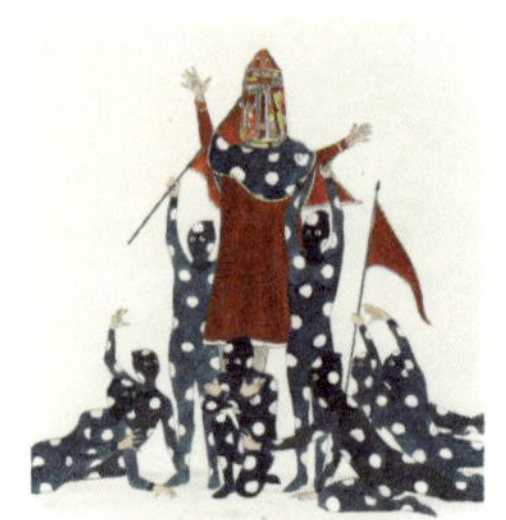

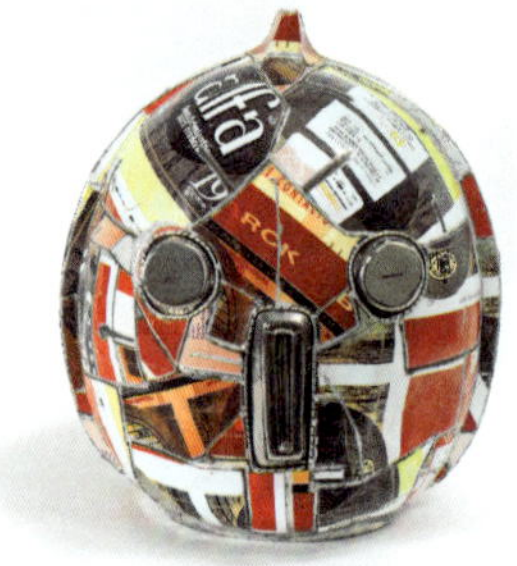 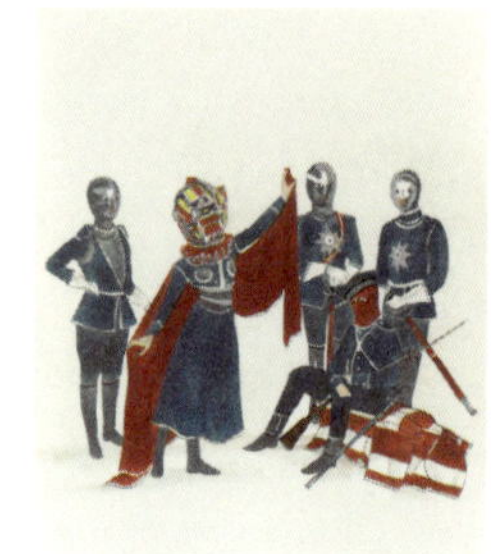

The bishop's head

2012

Ceramic and tin; ink, gouache,
and graphite on paper

Sculpture:
height, 28½ inches (72.4 cm)
diameter, 16½ inches (41.9 cm)

Drawing:
14 x 11 inches
(35.6 x 27.9 cm)

Pages 84–85

The king's head

2012

Ceramic and tin; ink, gouache,
and graphite on paper

Sculpture:
21 x 16½ x 19 inches
(53.3 x 41.9 x 48.3 cm)

Drawing:
14 x 11 inches
(35.6 x 27.9 cm)

Pages 86–87

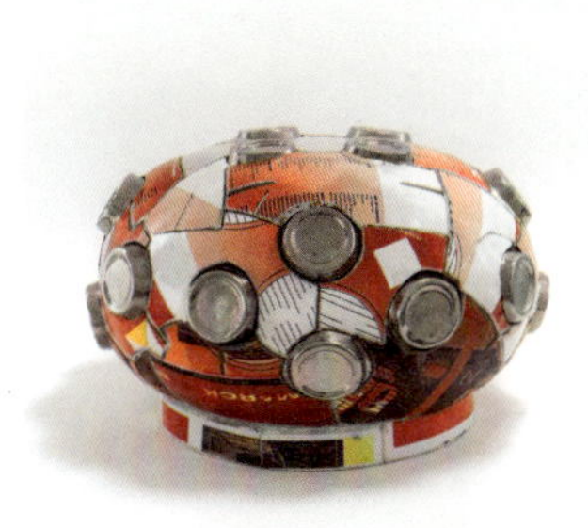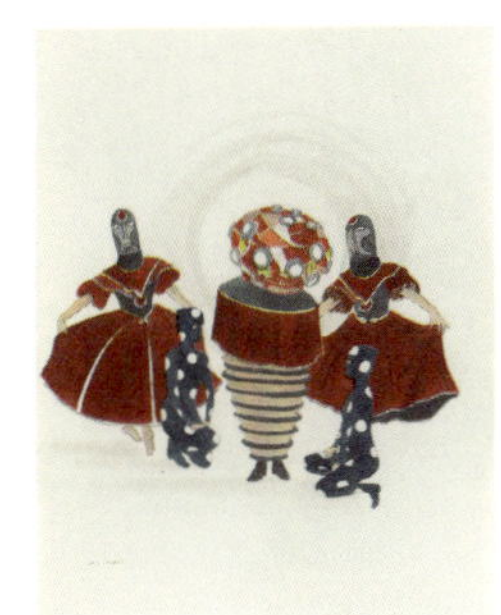

The rook's head

2012

Ceramic and tin; ink, gouache,
and graphite on paper

Sculpture:
height, 16 inches (40.6 cm)
diameter, 24 inches (61 cm)

Drawing:
14 x 11 inches
(35.6 x 27.9 cm)

Pages 88–89

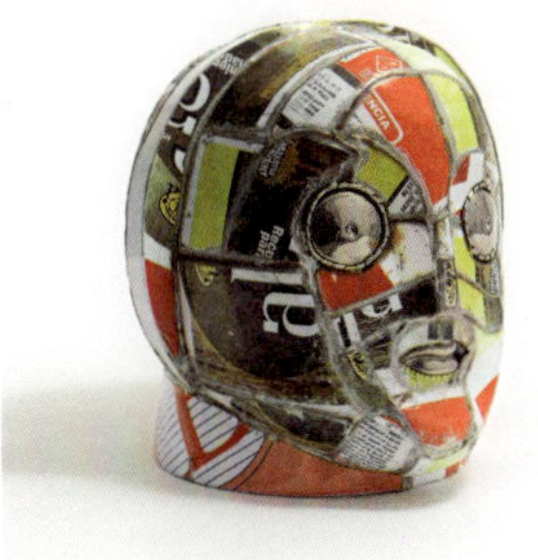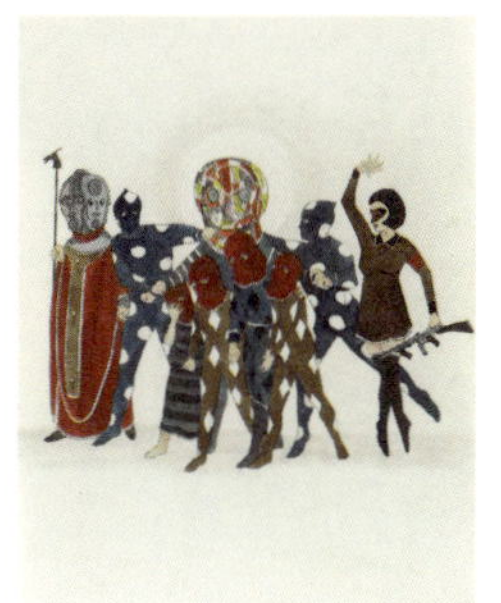

The pawn's head

2012

Ceramic and tin; ink, gouache,
and graphite on paper

Sculpture:
14½ x 13½ x 15½ inches
(36.8 x 34.3 x 39.4 cm)

Drawing:
14 x 11 inches
(35.6 x 27.9 cm)

Pages 90–91

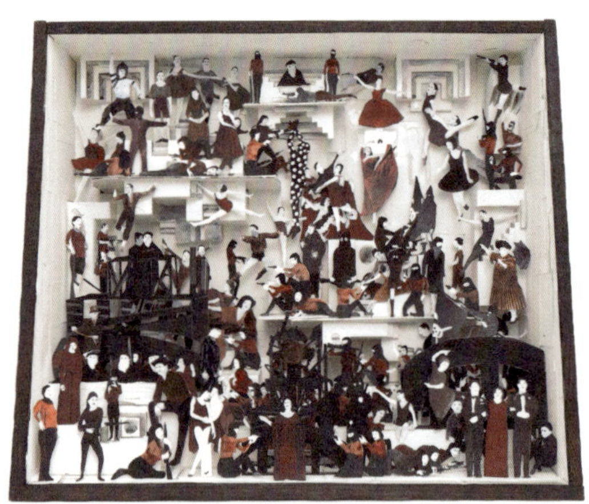

An age of discord and continual strife

2011

Wood, glass, cardboard, paper collage,
watercolor, and ink

21½ x 25¼ x 12 inches
(54.6 x 64.1 x 30.5 cm)

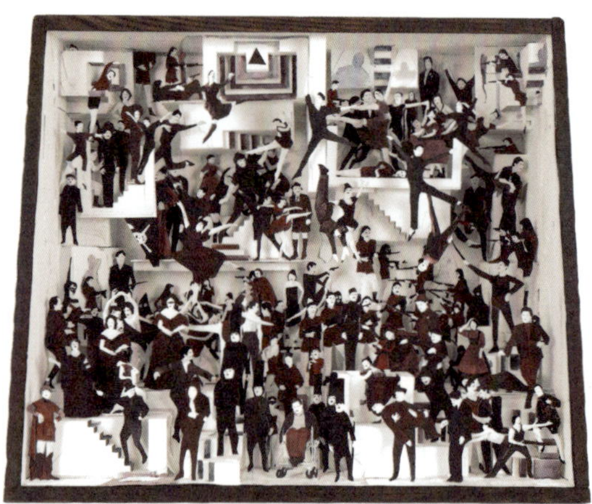

Feeding squirrels to the nuts

2011

Wood, glass, cardboard, paper collage,
watercolor, and ink

21½ x 25¼ x 12 inches
(54.6 x 64.1 x 30.5 cm)

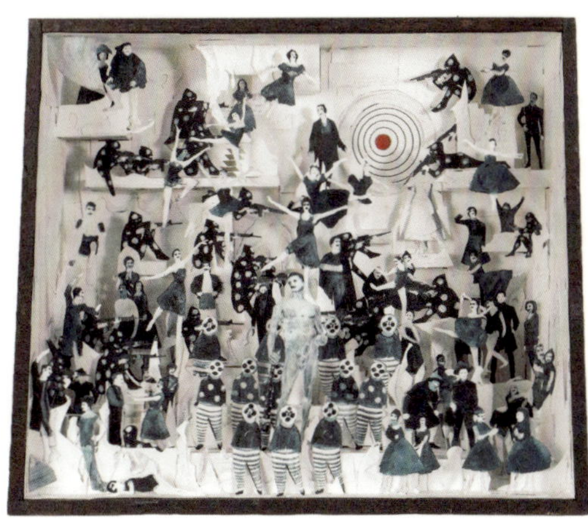

If you think this is just a game, you're wrong

2013

Wood, glass, cardboard, paper collage,
watercolor, and ink

21½ x 25⅛ x 12 inches
(54.6 x 63.8 x 30.5 cm)

Pages 101–103

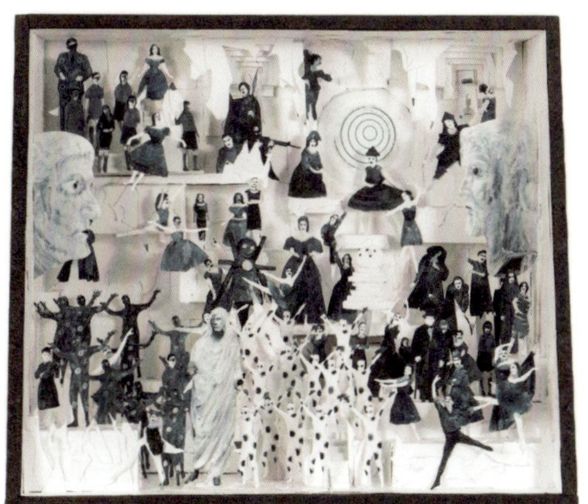

Hastily grabbing those innocent pawns

2013

Wood, glass, cardboard, paper collage,
watercolor, and ink

21½ x 25⅛ x 12 inches
(54.6 x 63.8 x 30.5 cm)

Pages 105–107

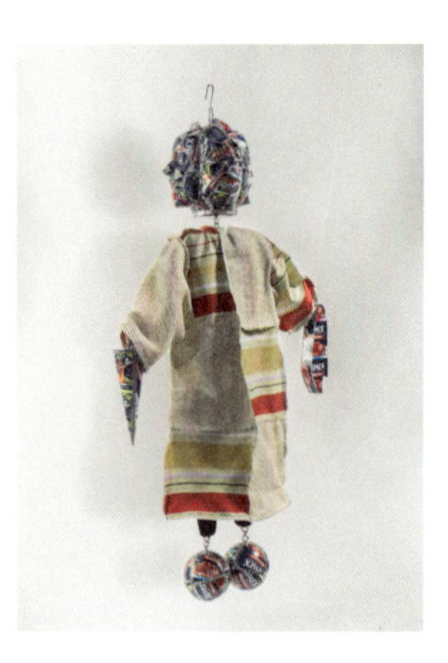

The king's Janus
times two puppet
for all the Sister Squares

2013

Printed steel, leather, and cloth

35 x 20 x 6 inches
(88.9 x 50.8 x 15.2 cm)

Edition of 8 + 1 AP

Page 93

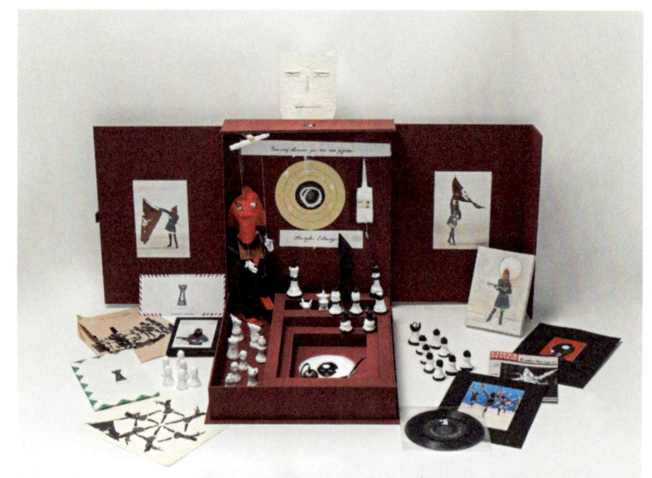

A red box for Marcel

2013

Fabric, acrylic, wood, plaster, metal,
paper, photographs, Polaroid, vinyl,
record, collage, and string

Closed: 5⅛ x 19¾ x 17¾ inches
(13 x 50.2 x 45 cm)

Open: 27 x 57⅞ x 30 inches
(68.6 x 147 x 76.2 cm)

Edition of 15 + 1 AP

Pages 95–97

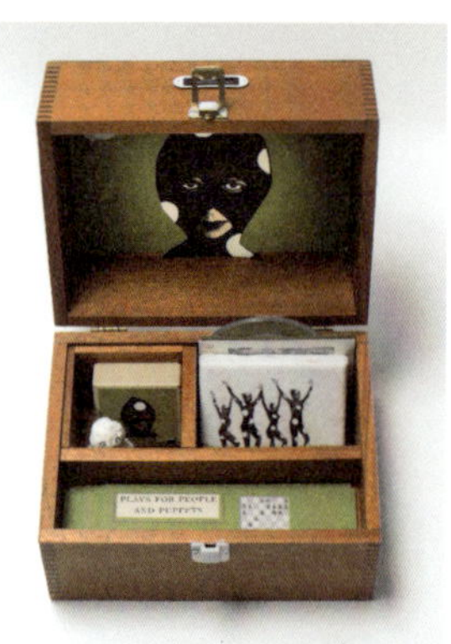

Wooden box (Death Disco Dance)

2013

Wood, acrylic, collage, plastic,
and plaster

Closed: 8⅛ x 11 x 8⅛ inches
(20.6 x 27.9 x 20.6 cm)

Open: 13 x 11 x 11 inches
(33 x 27.9 x 27.9 cm)

Edition of 4 + 1 AP

Page 99

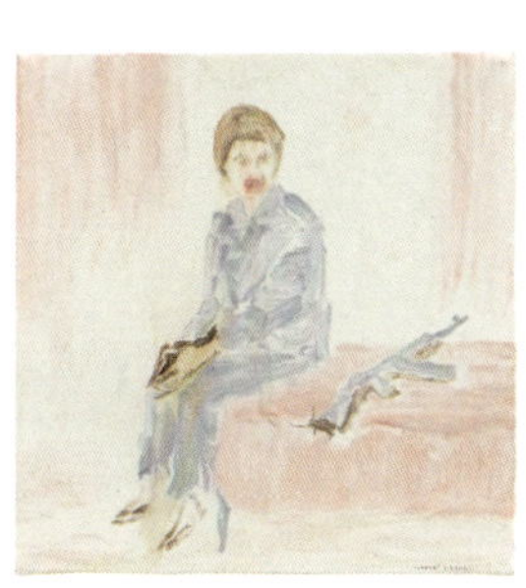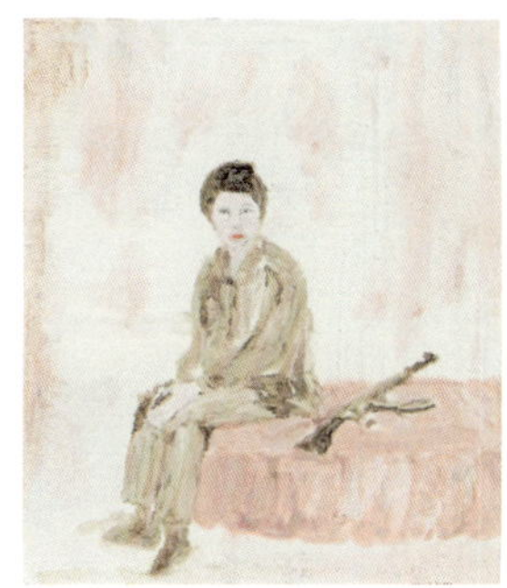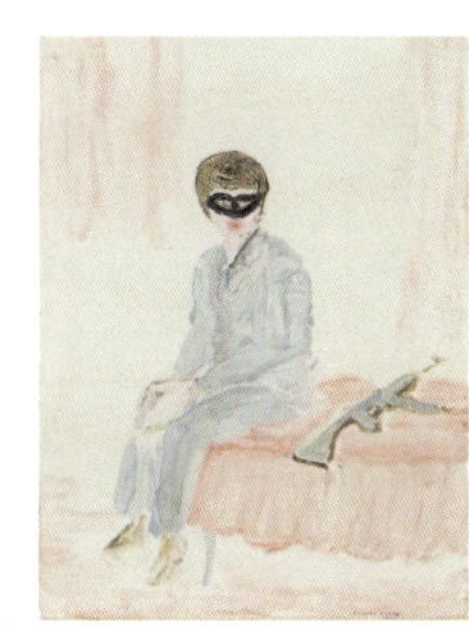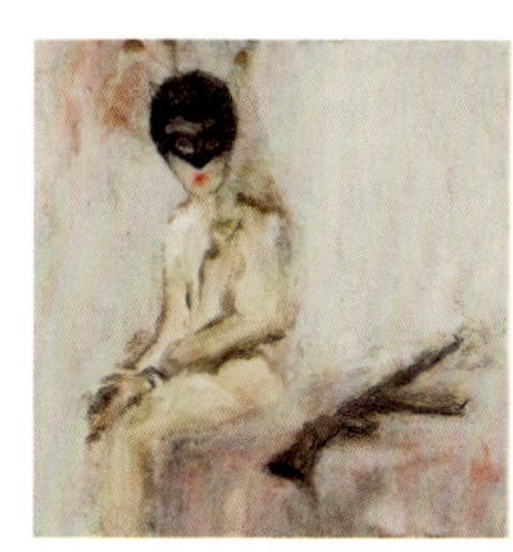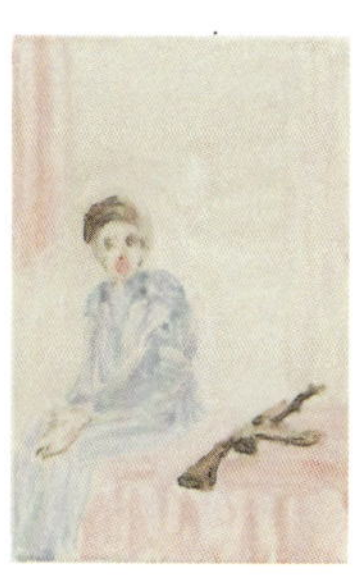

Forgotten terrorists (Unknown 1–5)

2011

Acrylic on canvas; acrylic on board

5-part work

Part 1: 6 x 6 inches
(15.2 x 15.2 cm)

Part 2: 9 x 7 ¾ inches
(22.9 x 19.7 cm)

Part 3: 8 x 6 inches
(20.3 x 15.2 cm)

Part 4: 5 ⅞ x 6 inches
(14.9 x 15.2 cm)

Part 5: 6 x 4 inches
(15.2 x 10.2 cm)

Pages 111–115 *

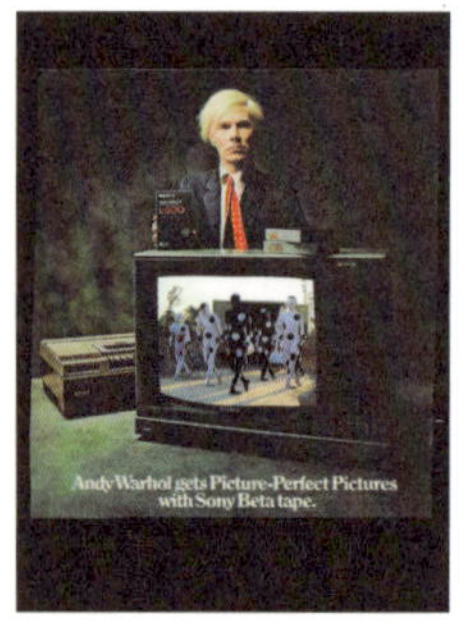

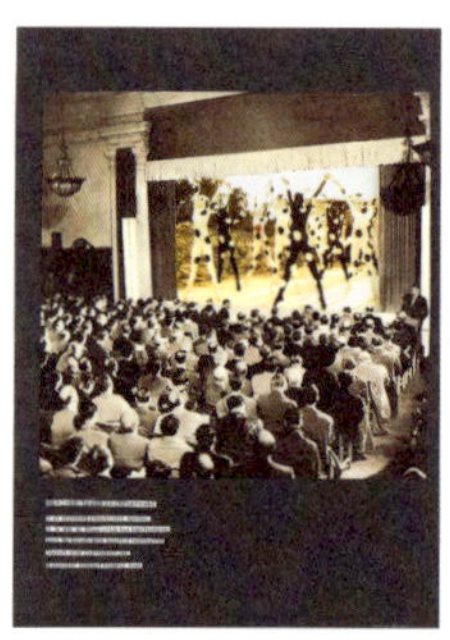

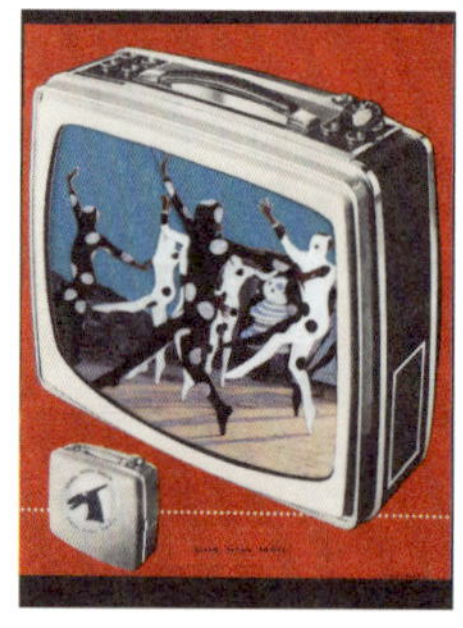

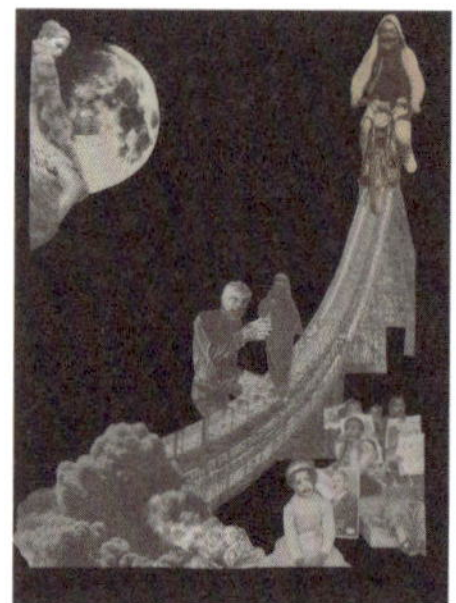

Andy's Death Disco

2012

Collage on paper

11¾ x 8¾ inches
(29.8 x 22.2 cm)

Page 119

Death Disco Dance defense

2013

Collage on paper

12 x 9 inches
(30.5 x 22.9 cm)

Page 120 *

The portable Death Disco Dance

2013

Collage on paper

12 x 9 inches
(30.5 x 22.9 cm)

Page 121

Our moon is now eclipsed

2013

Collage on paper

12 x 9 inches
(30.5 x 22.9 cm)

Page 122 *

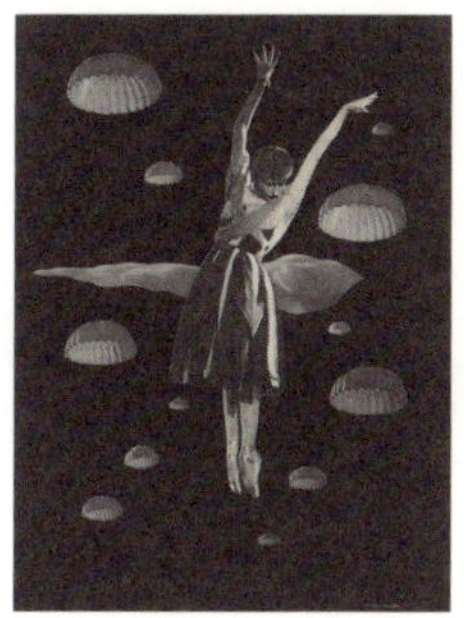

Some falls are a means
to a happier rise

2013

Collage on paper

12 x 9 inches
(30.5 x 22.9 cm)

Page 123 *

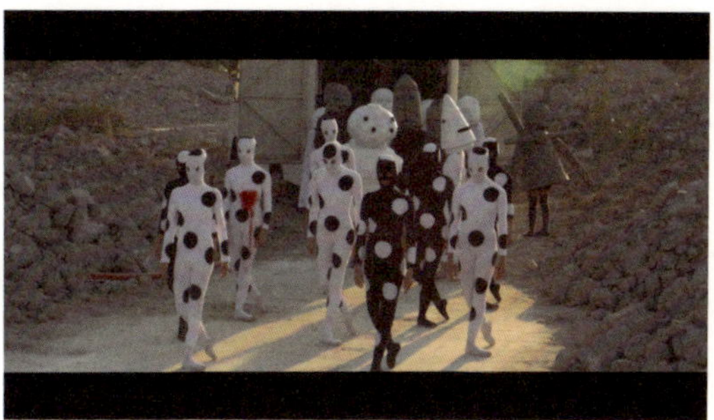

Death Disco Dance

2011

Video on monitors
4 min (loop), color, sound

Overall dimensions
vary with installation

Edition of 4 + 2 APs

Pages 127–131

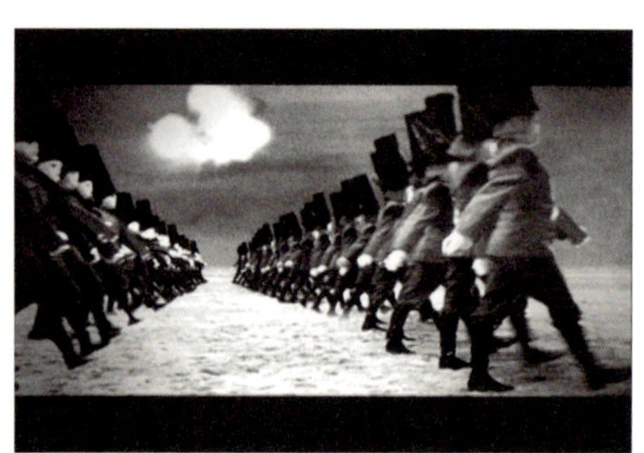

The Infidels

2009

35 mm film transferred to DVD
2:01 min, black and white, sound

Overall dimensions
vary with installation

Edition of 15 + 1 AP

Pages 145–149

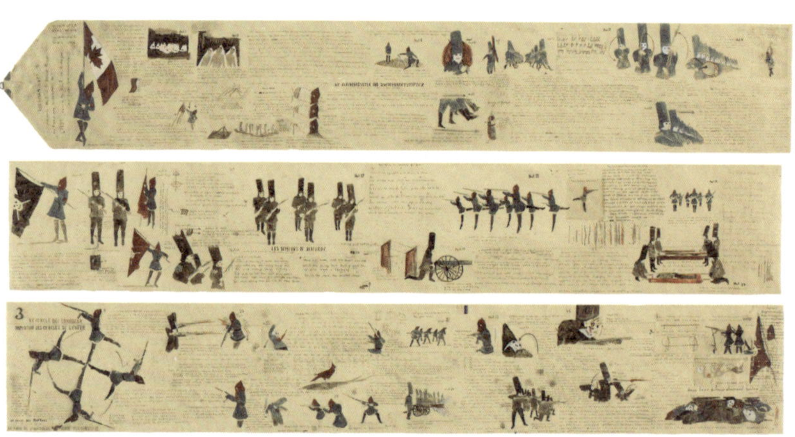

Winnipeg was won, Winnipeg was one

2009

Ink, watercolor, graphite, and
tracing paper on piano scroll

3-part work

Framed: 40½ x 75¾ inches
(102.9 x 192.4 cm)

Part 1, top: 11¼ x 71 inches
(28.6 x 180.3 cm)

Part 2, center: 11¼ x 69⅛ inches
(28.6 x 175.6 cm)

Part 3, bottom: 11¼ x 69¾ inches
(28.6 x 177.2 cm)

Pages 150–151

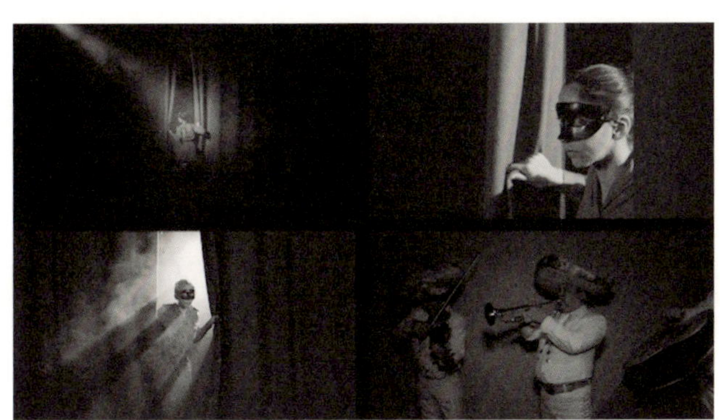

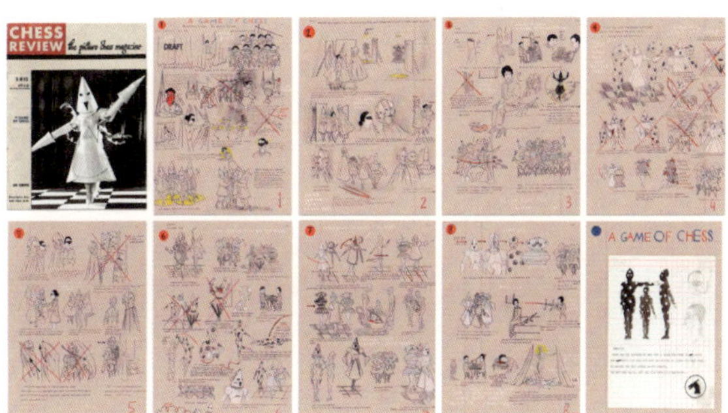

Sister Squares

2012

Video projection
13:55 min, black and white, sound

Overall dimensions
vary with installation

Edition of 8 + 1 AP

Pages 133–141

Chess Review storyboard

2012–2013

Collage on magazine; ink, graphite,
and colored pencil on paper

10-part work

Overall: 22 ⅛ x 43 inches
(56.2 x 109.2 cm)

Collage: 10¾ x 8 ⅛ inches
(27.3 x 21.3 cm)

Drawings, each: 11½ x 8 ⅛ inches
(29.2 x 21.3 cm)

Pages 142–143

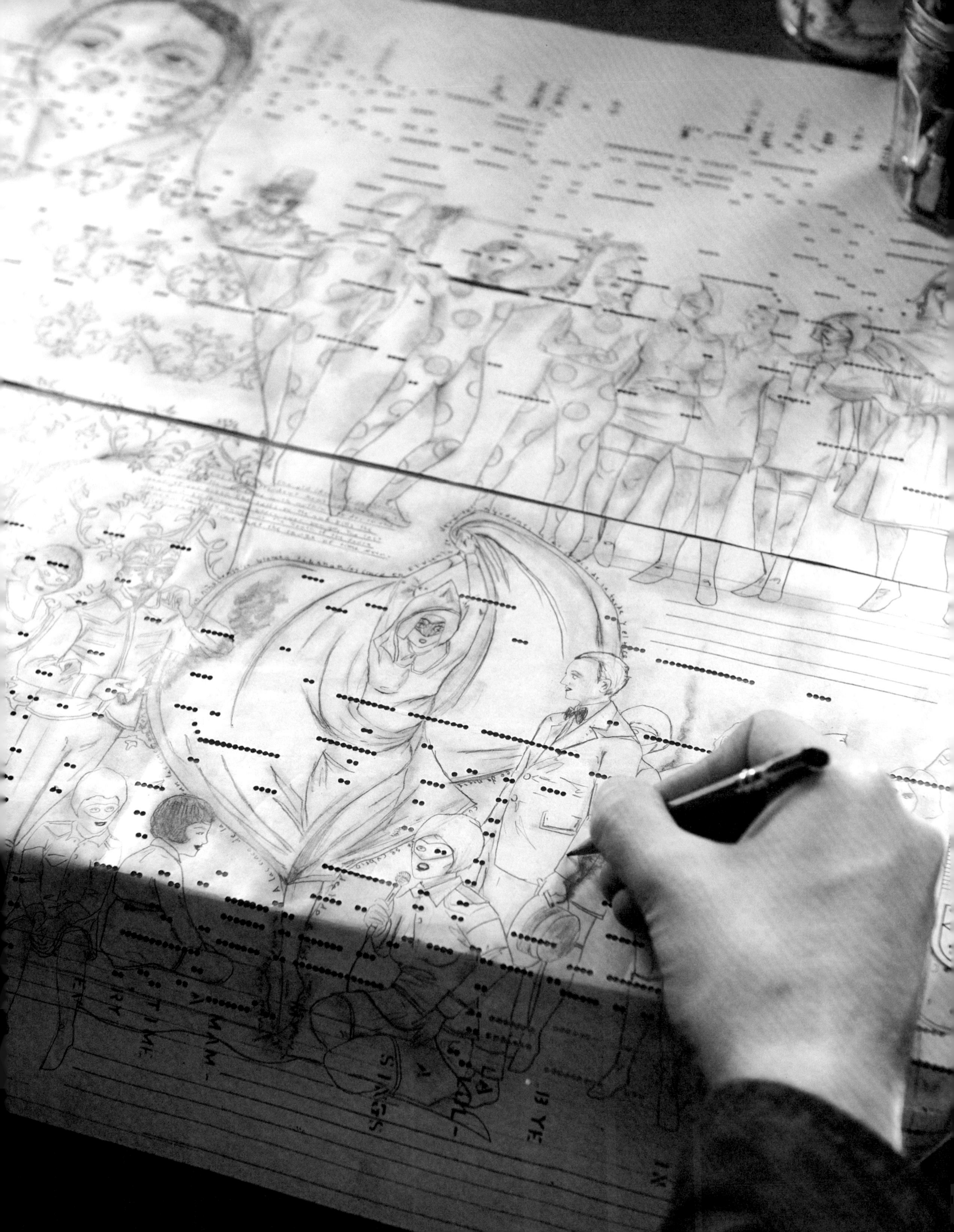

Born 1974 in Winnipeg, Canada. Lives and works in Brooklyn.

EDUCATION

B.F.A., University of Manitoba, Winnipeg, Canada

SELECTED SOLO EXHIBITIONS

2013   *Puppets, Pawns, and Prophets*, David Zwirner, London [catalogue]

2012   *Con razón o sin ella/With or Without Reason*, Centro de Arte
        Contemporáneo de Málaga, Spain [catalogue]
        The End Game, World Chess Hall of Fame, St. Louis, Missouri
        A Game of Chess, Sies + Höke, Düsseldorf [catalogue]
        A Touch of Evil/Un toque de maldad, Museo de Arte de Zapopan
        (MAZ), Zapopan, Mexico

2011   *Behind Every Curtain*, David Zwirner, New York [catalogue]
        A Game of Chess, Gemeentemuseum, The Hague
        Jockum Nordström and Marcel Dzama, Galleri Magnus Karlsson, Stockholm
        [two-person exhibition]
        The Never Known into the Forgotten, Kunstverein Braunschweig, Germany
        [catalogue published in 2012]

2010   *Aux mille tours/Of Many Turns*, Musée d'art contemporain de Montréal
        [catalogue]
        Delila's Dance, Galería Helga de Alvear, Madrid

2009   *The Infidels*, Sies + Höke, Düsseldorf [catalogue]

2008   *Edition 46 – Marcel Dzama*, Pinakothek der Moderne, Munich
        [special publication by Süddeutsche Zeitung Magazin]
        Even the Ghost of the Past, David Zwirner, New York [catalogue]

2007   *Celluloid Ceremony*, Galleri Magnus Karlsson, Stockholm
        Marcel Dzama, Oficina para Proyectos de Arte, Guadalajara, Mexico
        Moving Picture, Timothy Taylor Gallery, London [catalogue]

2006   *Marcel Dzama*, The Richard L. Nelson Gallery & Fine Art Collection,
            University of California, Davis, California
        Marcel Dzama, Sies + Höke, Düsseldorf [catalogue published in 2007]
        Tree with Roots, Ikon Gallery, Birmingham, England [itinerary: Centre
            for Contemporary Arts, Glasgow] [catalogue]
        Works on Paper, Greg Kucera Gallery, Seattle

2005   *The Course of Human History Personified*, David Zwirner, New York
            [catalogue]
        The Lotus Eaters, Centre d'Art Santa Mònica, Barcelona [itinerary:
            Le Magasin – Centre National d'Art Contemporain de Grenoble, France]

2004   *The Albatross Note*, Galleri Magnus Karlsson, Stockholm
        The Last Winter, Timothy Taylor Gallery, London [catalogue]
        Marcel Dzama, Olga Korper Gallery, Toronto
        Marcel Dzama, Sies + Höke, Düsseldorf [catalogue]
        Marcel Dzama, Susan Inglett Gallery, New York

2003   *Drawings by Marcel Dzama: From the Bernardi Collection*, Art Gallery of
            Windsor, Canada [catalogue]
        Marcel Dzama & Jockum Nordström, David Zwirner, New York
            [two-person exhibition]
        New Work, Richard Heller Gallery, Santa Monica, California
        Welcome to Winnipeg, Rizziero Arte, Pescara, Italy [catalogue published in 2004]

2002   *Drawings for Dante*, Timothy Taylor Gallery, London [catalogue]
        Marcel Dzama, Sies + Höke, Düsseldorf [catalogue]

2001   *Marcel Dzama*, Greg Kucera Gallery, Seattle
        Marcel Dzama, Monica De Cardenas Galleria, Milan
        Marcel Dzama, Richard Heller Gallery, Santa Monica, California
        New Drawings, Galleri Magnus Karlsson, Stockholm

2000   *Marcel Dzama,* David Zwirner, New York
        Marcel Dzama, Sies + Höke, Düsseldorf

More Famous Drawings, Plug In Institute of Contemporary Art, Winnipeg,
Canada [itinerary: Morris and Helen Belkin Art Gallery, University of British
Columbia, Vancouver; Mendel Art Gallery, Saskatoon, Canada; Olga Korper
Gallery, Toronto; Saidye Bronfman Centre for the Arts, Montreal; Agnes
Etherington Art Centre, Queen's University, Kingston, Canada; Art Gallery
of Calgary, Canada; Susan Whitney Gallery, Regina, Canada; Laforet
Harajuku Museum, Tokyo] [catalogue published in 1999]

1999 *Marcel Dzama*, Casa Triângulo, São Paulo
Marcel Dzama, Espaço Produções, Rio de Janeiro
Marcel Dzama, Richard Heller Gallery, Santa Monica, California

1998 *Marcel Dzama*, Artpace, San Antonio, Texas
Marcel Dzama, Casa Triângulo, São Paulo
Marcel Dzama, David Zwirner, New York
Marcel Dzama, Espaço Purplex, Capacete Entretenimentos, Rio de Janeiro
Marcel Dzama, Richard Heller Gallery, Santa Monica, California

1997 *Marcel Dzama*, Richard Heller Gallery, Santa Monica, California

SELECTED MONOGRAPHS, SOLO EXHIBITION CATALOGUES
& SPECIAL PUBLICATIONS

2013 *Marcel Dzama: Sower of Discord*. Texts by Bradley Bailey, Dave Eggers,
and Raymond Pettibon. Interview with the artist by Spike Jonze. Abrams,
New York

2012 *Marcel Dzama: Con razón o sin ella/With or Without Reason.*
Text by Juan Francisco Rueda. Centro de Arte Contemporáneo de Málaga,
Spain (exh. cat.)
Marcel Dzama: A Game of Chess. Text by Katrin Meder. Verlag Kettler, Bönen,
Germany (exh. cat.)
Marcel Dzama: The Never Known into the Forgotten. Texts by Katrin Meder
and Hilke Wagner. Verlag Kettler, Bönen, Germany (exh. cat.)

2011 *Marcel Dzama: Behind Every Curtain.* David Zwirner, New York (exh. cat.)
Marcel Dzama presents Opposition and Sister Squares Reconciled.
Edited by Gerhard Theewen. Edition Ex Libris Nr. 20, Salon Verlag,
Cologne [limited edition artist book]

2010   *Marcel Dzama: Aux mille tours/Of Many Turns*. Text by Mark Lanctôt.
        Musée d'art contemporain de Montréal (exh. cat.)

2009   *Marcel Dzama: The Infidels*. Sies + Höke, Düsseldorf and Verlag Kettler,
        Bönen, Germany (exh. cat.)

2008   *Edition 46 – Marcel Dzama*. Text by Cameron Shaw. Interview with the artist
        by Julia Decker and Holger Liebs. Süddeutsche Zeitung Magazin
        (November 14, 2008) [special publication]
        Marcel Dzama: The Berliner Ensemble Thanks You All. McSweeney's Books,
        San Francisco
        Marcel Dzama: Even the Ghost of the Past. Text by Cameron Shaw.
        Interview with the artist by Spike Jonze. David Zwirner, New York and
        Steidl, Göttingen, Germany (exh. cat.)

2007   *333: Marcel Dzama*. Nieves, Zürich [limited edition zine]
        Marcel Dzama. Interview with the artist by Lars Bang Larsen. Sies + Höke,
        Düsseldorf (exh. cat.)
        Marcel Dzama: Moving Picture. Interview with the artist by Julien Bismuth.
        Timothy Taylor Gallery, London (exh. cat.)

2006   *Marcel Dzama: Tree with Roots*. Interview with the artist by Carter Foster.
        Ikon Gallery, Birmingham, England (exh. cat.)

2005   *The Course of Human History Personified: Marcel Dzama*. Texts by
        Jason Rosenfeld and Jason Tougaw. David Zwirner, New York (exh. cat.)

2004   *Marcel Dzama: The Last Winter*. Text by Marcel Dzama. Timothy Taylor Gallery,
        London (exh. cat.)
        Marcel Dzama: Paintings and Drawings. Text by Catrin Lorch.
        Verlag der Buchhandlung Walther König, Cologne and Sies + Höke,
        Düsseldorf (exh. cat.)
        Marcel Dzama: Welcome to Winnipeg. Text by Marcel Dzama. Rizziero Arte,
        Pescara, Italy (exh. cat.)

2003   *Drawings by Marcel Dzama: From the Bernardi Collection*. Texts by Wayne
        Baerwaldt and James Patten. Art Gallery of Windsor, Canada (exh. cat.)
        Marcel Dzama: The Berlin Years. Texts by Viggo Mortensen and Sarah Vowell.
        McSweeney's Books, San Francisco

2002   *Marcel Dzama.* Sies + Höke, Düsseldorf (exh. cat.)
         Marcel Dzama: Drawings for Dante. Text by Marcel Dzama. Timothy Taylor
            Gallery, London (exh. cat.)

1999   *Marcel Dzama: More Famous Drawings.* Text by Wayne Baerwaldt.
            Plug In Editions, Winnipeg, Canada (exh. cat.)

1998   *Famous Drawings Presents Marcel Dzama.* Text by Wayne Baerwaldt.
            Smart Art Press, Santa Monica, California

SELECTED PUBLIC COLLECTIONS

Bass Museum of Art, Miami, Florida
Corcoran Gallery of Art, Washington, D.C.
Dallas Museum of Art, Texas
Kresge Art Museum, Michigan State University, East Lansing, Michigan
Musée d'art contemporain de Montréal
Musée national d'art moderne/Centre de création industrielle, Paris
Museo de Arte Contemporáneo de Castilla y León, León, Spain
Museum of Contemporary Art, Los Angeles
Museum of Contemporary Art, North Miami, Florida
The Museum of Modern Art, New York
National Gallery of Canada, Ottawa
The Rhode Island School of Design Museum, Providence, Rhode Island
Solomon R. Guggenheim Museum, New York
Tate Gallery, London
Vancouver Art Gallery

In memory of Noe Suro

Acknowledgments

The artist would like to thank Shelley Dick, David Zwirner, Angela Choon, Bellatrix Hubert, and Branwen Jones for their close collaboration and generous support of this exhibition and catalogue.

A special thanks goes to Deborah Solomon for her essay.

The artist also wishes to thank David Chickey, Andrew Crichton, Elizabeth De Mase, Anna Drozda, Tim Edeker, Young Sun Han, Markus Hartmann, Julia Joern, Harriet Miller, Sidonie Motion, Tom Pilgrim, Louise Sørensen, Electra Soutzoglou, Jose Noe Suro, Jules Thomson, and Jade Yang for their contributions.

This catalogue has been produced with David Zwirner
on the occasion of the exhibition held at the gallery's 24 Grafton Street space in London.

Marcel Dzama: Puppets, Pawns, and Prophets
April 6 – May 11, 2013

Graphic design and typesetting: David Chickey
Copyediting: Anna Drozda [David Zwirner]
Proofreading: Leina González
Production: Nadine Schmidt [Hatje Cantz]; Jules Thomson [David Zwirner]
Photography Coordination: Elizabeth De Mase [David Zwirner]
Typefaces: Avenir and Perpetua
Paper: Hello Fat matt, 170 g/m^2; Munken Lynx, 150 g/m^2
Printing: Offsetdruckerei Karl Grammlich GmbH, Pliezhausen
Binding: Lachenmaier GmbH, Reutlingen

All artwork © 2013 Marcel Dzama
Essay © 2013 Deborah Solomon

Publication © 2013 HATJE CANTZ VERLAG, Ostfildern; **David Zwirner**, New York/London

Published by

HATJE CANTZ VERLAG

Zeppelinstrasse 32, 73760 Ostfildern, Germany
Tel. +49 711 4405-200 Fax +49 711 4405-220
hatjecantz.com
A Ganske Publishing Group company

David Zwirner

525 West 19th Street, New York, New York 10011
Tel. +1 212 727 2070 Fax +1 212 727 2072
davidzwirner.com

Hatje Cantz books are available internationally at selected bookstores. For more information about our
distribution partners, please visit our website at www.hatjecantz.com.

ISBN 978-3-7757-3732-6
Printed in Germany

Photography Credits:

Ron Amstutz: pp. 25 (detail on p. 16), 31, 32, 33, 35, 36–39, 41, 43, 44, 45, 47–49, 51, 54–55, 57, 59, 61, 63–65, 67, 69, 70, 71, 76–77, 78–79, 80, 82–83, 84, 86, 88, 90–91, 113, 115, 120, 121, 122, 123, 150–151

Alex Delfanne: pp. 2–3, 4–5, 6–7, 8, 9, 10–11, 74–75, 93, 96–97, 111, 127 (back cover), 133, 134–135, 145

EPW Studio/Maris Hutchinson, 2013: pp. 81, 85, 87, 89, 95, 99, 101–103 (cover), 105–107

Ian Mazursky: pp. 26–29, 58, 119, 142–143

Adam Reich: pp. 52–53

Jason Schmidt: pp. 14, 176, endpapers

Cover: Detail of *If you think this is just a game, you're wrong*, 2013

Back cover: Exterior view of David Zwirner, London, featuring *Death Disco Dance*, 2011, as a multi-monitor window installation

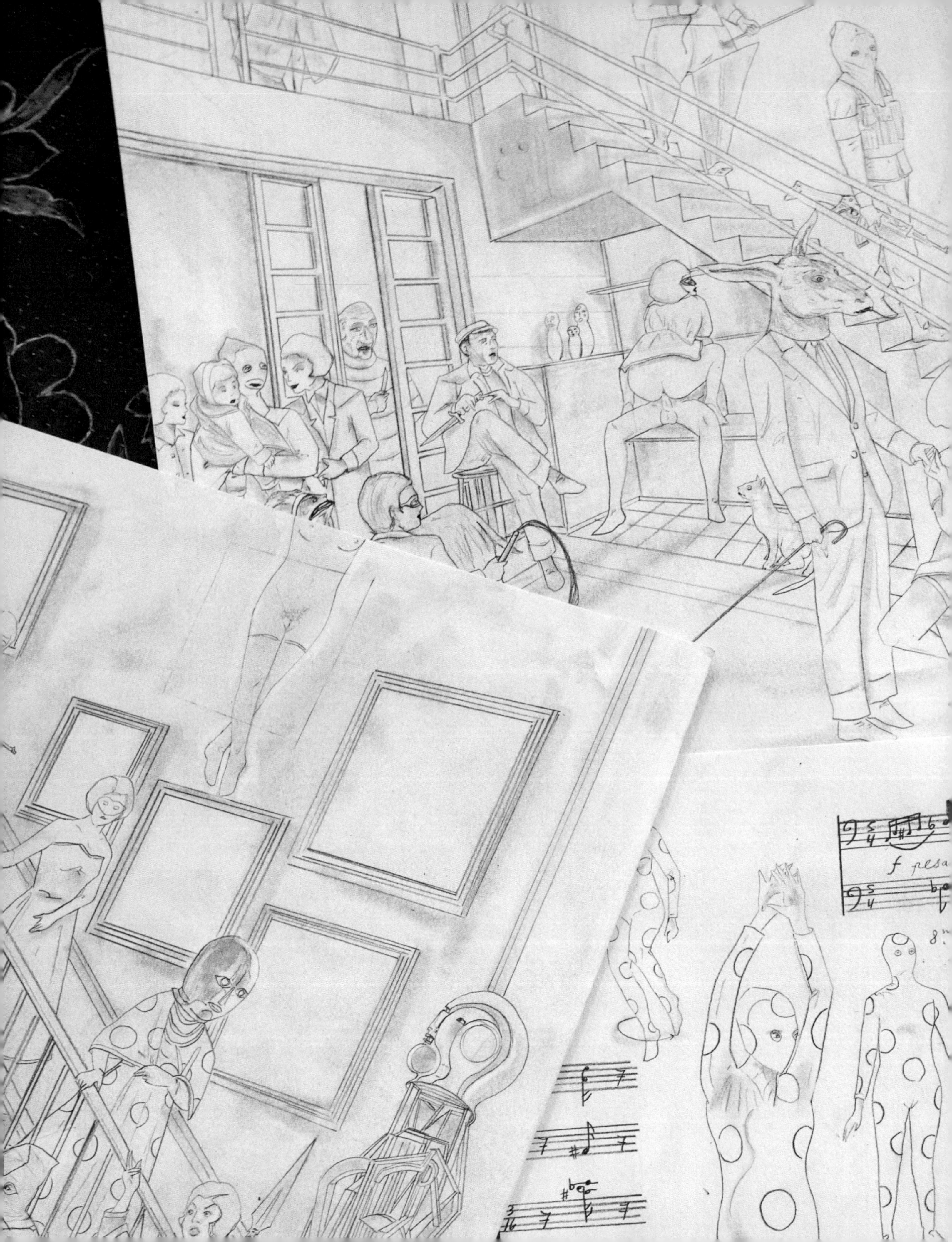